SUCCESSFUL LEGAL WRITING

SUCCESSFUL LEGAL WRITING
3rd edition

EDWINA HIGGINS
Manchester Law School

LAURA TATHAM
The Open University Law School

SWEET & MAXWELL

 THOMSON REUTERS

Published in 2015 by Thomson Reuters (Professional) UK Limited,
Trading as Sweet & Maxwell, Friars House, 160 Blackfriars Road, London SE1 8EZ,
(Registered in England & Wales, Company No 1679046.
Registered Office and address for service: 2nd floor, 1 Mark Square, Leonard Street,
London EC2A 4EG)

For further information on our products and services,
visit *www.sweetandmaxwell.co.uk*

Typeset by Servis Filmsetting Ltd, Stockport, Cheshire
Printed in Great Britain by Ashford Colour Printers

No natural forests were destroyed to make this product; only farmed timber was used and re-planted.

A CIP catalogue record for this book is available from the British Library

ISBN 978 0 414 03704 5

Thomson Reuters and the Thomson Reuters logo are trademarks of Thomson Reuters.
Sweet & Maxwell ® is a registered trademark of Thomson Reuters (Professional) UK Limited.

For Dave Higson and Mary Higgins

Contents

COMPLETING YOUR ASSIGNMENT

OTHER LEGAL WRITING

APPENDICES

INDEX

Acknowledgements

In producing this edition of this book, we remain grateful to everyone who helped us with the previous editions.

The idea for this book grew from our participation in a seminar on Legal Writing organised by the UK Centre for Legal Education and the Society of Legal Scholars at Bournemouth University in March 2005, where we gave a brief presentation about the classes we run at MMU to encourage students to engage with our assessment criteria. It became apparent during the course of a very lively day that legal academics have strong feelings about the importance of good writing, and therefore how much students have to gain by working on their skills. We'd like to thank everyone at our session for their contributions.

We are still as grateful as we were in previous editions for all the help given to us by colleagues, friends and family, in particular Joanne Urmston and Nick Longworth at MMU. As always, we are most grateful to students at our respective institutions.

How to use this book

Our aim is to help you become successful legal writers. We've designed this book to be flexible so you can use it in different ways according to your own particular needs. This means taking a moment to think about your purpose in selecting this book. Whatever your motivation, the advice within it will be of most value if you take some time to identify exactly what you need to get out of it.

The book is arranged into four parts. The first part will take you through what writing at university level in law requires. The second part takes you through the steps needed to research and plan your assignment. The third part takes you through completing your assignment and developing your writing from feedback. Finally, in the fourth part we look at other types of legal writing including the particular demands of writing an undergraduate dissertation.

Although we provide lots of advice, we can't give you a blueprint which will automatically work for you; what you must do is reflect on what you need to do to improve so you can target the parts of the book which will help you to write more successfully. For example, perhaps:

- you are beginning your studies and want to develop a good technique from the start. Start with Chapter 1 where we explore the qualities that your tutors will be looking for in a good piece of writing and some of the common weaknesses we've seen in student work, and then work through our suggested cycle for successful writing which we explain in Chapter 2. This should help you reflect on the areas you need to focus on, and therefore which further chapters to work through, or you may prefer to read all the remaining chapters in order to maximise the benefits;
- you already know a particular weakness in your work, perhaps from feedback, and want to tackle that. We've used an FAQ format throughout the book, so use the contents page to find the relevant section you need;
- you don't have a specific issue already but know you need to make some general improvements somewhere. Again, start with Chapter 1 to gain a better understanding of the qualities good writing has, identify your strengths and weaknesses and move to the right parts of the book to help you.

COMPLETING THE ACTIVITIES

You will be invited to work through several activities as you read, so it will be useful to have a pen and pad of paper ready. Many of the activities do not have a correct answer but instead will invite you to compare your thoughts with ours to encourage reflection. We know it is tempting to skip straight on to the "answers" without completing self-study activities in a textbook, but we have designed them to help you develop your own writing skills so if you don't work through them, you won't get as much value from the book. If you have a tendency towards a "just give me the answer" mentality, work on overcoming that if you are serious about becoming a successful legal writer.

AND FINALLY

We can't offer a shortcut to getting better marks with less effort. There is no substitute for working hard on the activites you are asked to do, whether in the classroom or in your own time. What we can do is help you to make the most of the time you spend carrying out this work, by showing you how to convert all your efforts into successful legal writing. We wish you well with it.

PART 1

Writing at university

▶ 1
Introduction

WHAT IS THE PURPOSE OF THIS CHAPTER?

In this chapter we will encourage you to think about the qualities which make successful writing, with particular reference to the sort of writing you will be asked to do as part of your legal studies. This will provide a basis for you to work on improving your own writing. By the end of this chapter you will:

▶ 1.1

- understand what we mean by successful legal writing;
- have thought about the purpose of writing in different situations in the context of your studies;
- have learned more about common mistakes made in legal writing and how to avoid them;
- have had an opportunity to reflect on your own writing skills.

WHAT IS "SUCCESSFUL" LEGAL WRITING?

The ability to communicate is probably the most important skill that marks out a good lawyer (whether a practising lawyer or an academic lawyer like you, now you're a law student). The most brilliant academic will be a terrible lecturer if he or she cannot get a message across in class—and similarly a barrister in court might be wonderfully well-prepared but will need to argue clearly and effectively in order to have the best chance of winning the case.

▶ 1.2

When we say someone is a "good communicator", we often mean that they speak and argue well, just as in the example given above. But written communication is just as important. A practising solicitor needs to be able to write appropriately to clients and other solicitors in order to advise and negotiate; a barrister must write effective advice notes and briefs. In fact, any graduate job will require good written communication.

Therefore the ability to communicate effectively in writing is vital for law students. You demonstrate that you understand the aspects of law you will be studying through the work you produce—much of which will be written—for your assessments such as essays, reports, exams and projects or dissertations. For your legal writing to be *successful*, it must be an effective communication of your understanding of the law.

Here are some activities about legal writing. There are not necessarily any right and wrong answers to this, but try to think about them yourself before looking at our comments.

ACTIVITY 1.1

1.3 ▶ The following activity contains a number of statements about studying law successfully and producing legal writing. To what extent do you agree or disagree with these?

	Strongly agree	Agree	Neither agree nor disagree	Disagree	Strongly disagree
The students who put the most work in get the best results.					
The cleverest students get the best results.					
If you've done well in writing-based subjects at A level, you will do well in the degree.					
Being able to write is something you are either good at or you are not.					
The key to successful writing is effective communication.					

Activity feedback—here are our thoughts:

1. The students who put the most work in get the best results.

We would agree that the amount of work you do is certainly important: if you want to do well, then you will have to put the work in. But clocking up so many hours in the law library is no guarantee of success in itself; you need to reflect on whether you are working *effectively*, and whether or not you have developed the skills to translate that effort into good marks through effective communication. You will also need to have a clear idea of the *purpose* of any particular assessment in order to complete it successfully, and we consider this further later in this chapter.

2. The cleverest students get the best results.

Well, again we would agree that cleverness is a factor, but you may be surprised to learn that it is not necessarily the most important. The most intelligent student will lose marks if he or she has failed to put in the necessary work, or communicates poorly. That is why it is important to understand what you are being asked to do, and why, so that you can plan accordingly. (We might also argue that a student who fails to put in the necessary work without good reason is not really showing much sign of this supposed cleverness!) Students who work effectively and make the most of their skills will do better.

3. If you've done well in writing-based subjects at A level, you will do well in the degree.
Certainly if you have done well in essay writing at A level this will be a promising basis for your writing at university. However, it is important to think about these skills as just a starting point because at university not only will you be expected to improve on what you have done at A level but you will also be expected to improve year by year. Additionally there are particular conventions in legal writing which you will need to familiarise yourself with.

4. Being able to write is something you are either good at or you are not.
It can seem like this. Certainly some people find it easier to write effectively than others—which is great if you happen to be one of those people, and frustrating if you aren't—but we would disagree with this statement because most of the techniques of good legal writing can be acquired through practice. There is more detailed information on how to improve your writing throughout this book, so it is worth spending some time thinking which aspects of your work you wish to improve upon. If your perception is that you are "not good" at writing, aim to do more reading. You'll be learning by example.

5. The key to successful writing is effective communication.
We hope that you will have realised from the introduction that we strongly agree with this statement. Merely learning all those rules and cases isn't enough in itself. Working to improve your writing skills now will not only help you achieve better marks during your studies, but will also help you in your future career. You may already have come across the term "employability"— developing your communication skills is an important aspect of that.

By now, you might be starting to think that the amount of work you do makes no difference. This isn't what we're saying! Of course you will still need to put in the work to understand the substantive law, but all those long hours in the law library will be more effective if you also work on your writing skills. There is nothing more disheartening for us, as law tutors, than a student who comes to us with a disappointing mark for a piece of work and says "but I worked so hard on it—I don't understand how I could have done so badly". (And if it's disheartening for us, imagine what it's like for the student in question.) Basically that student has failed to translate all that work into an effective piece of communication.

You won't be expected to be brilliant at this straight away. There are national standards for higher education (the Framework for Higher Educational Qualifications: *www.qaa.ac.uk/ academicinfrastructure/fheq/default.asp*), which set expectations for students at each level of the degree. For full-time students on a three-year programme, your first year will be Level 4, your second year Level 5 and your final year Level 6. For degree studies exceeding three years (for example part-time degrees) the levels are likely to be split across different years. Your institution will explain this to you (probably in a programme, course handbook, or regulations). Students studying for the Common Professional Examination (graduate conversion course) will normally find they are being assessed at Level 6, in other words, at the same standard as the final year of your degree.

Without worrying too much about the detail of these different levels, the point is that your work is expected to develop to the standard expected of a law graduate by the end of your course. This standard is not expected from the outset.

ACTIVITY 1.2

1.4 ▶ In order to communicate effectively you need to have a clear idea of the *purpose* of your communication, in other words, why you are doing it. It can be tempting to think merely "because I've been told to" here, but thinking more clearly about why you have been set a particular assignment and what you think the tutor wants you to demonstrate by doing that assignment will help you remain focused on your task.

We're going to think about the sort of writing you might be asked to do during your legal studies (and what your tutors are looking for when they read it) later in this chapter, but for now, we want you to think about the purpose of various types of everyday written communication.

In this activity consider the following list. For each item (a) identify the purpose of the reader in reading it, and (b) consider what the writer would have to do to communicate successfully in meeting that purpose.

- A detective novel
- A TV listings guide
- BBC News website
- Flat pack instructions

Type of communication	(a) The purpose of the reader in reading this would be . . .	(b) So to communicate successfully, the writer would have to make the writing . . .
A detective novel		
A TV listings guide		
BBC News website		
Flat pack instructions		

Activity feedback—here are our thoughts:

A *detective novel*—(a) you might read this for entertainment, suspense, relaxation; therefore (b) in order to communicate successfully, the writer needs to make the novel exciting, interesting, a "page-turner". If the novel is too stodgy or difficult to read, or dull, then someone reading purely for entertainment is unlikely to persevere with it.

A *TV listings guide*—(a) you might read this either for quick information on what's on or perhaps for reviews/recommendations as to which of the forthcoming programmes are the ones to watch; (b) consequently, to be successful, the listings need to be clear and easy to read and the reviews need to be accurate and appropriate.

The *BBC News website*—(a) fairly obviously, people read a news website in order to get news and views (and of course the choice of website will be influenced by the type of news and views they want to read); (b) clearly therefore a news website must be up to date, and accurate in order to satisfy its readership.

Flat pack instructions—(a) these are intended to give the reader the instructions needed to build, for example, a piece of furniture. The reader reads them to learn that process, so (b) the instructions need to be clear and simple (preferably with diagrams) and well-ordered. They also need to be accurate!

Don't worry if your ideas are not exactly the same as these—the aim is to encourage you to think about the purpose of writing, so there are no right or wrong answers.

WHAT WILL I BE ASKED TO WRITE ?

Now let's focus more on the type of writing you'll be doing on your course. During your studies   ▶ 1.5
you will be asked to write some or all of the following:

- Critical essays
- Answers to "problem" questions
- A dissertation or project
- Critical reviews
- Literature reviews, research proposals
- Case-notes
- Reports
- Judgments
- Memoranda, briefs, opinions, letters
- Posters, leaflets
- Journals, logs, blogs, diaries, discussion forums
- Lecture notes, research notes

Critical essays and problem answers remain the most common type of legal assessment for undergraduates. We're going to consider these in more detail in relation to improving your writing throughout the text (we also give further advice about dissertations in Chapter 10).

Essay questions
Essay questions are common to many disciplines, and you are bound to have tackled an essay   ▶ 1.6
question in some sort of assessment before, although not necessarily in law. The different types of essay question you are likely to be asked to tackle during your legal studies are as follows:

1. A *question* type essay is asking you provide an answer (obviously!) with reference to evidence:

   > Does the Practice Statement 1966 pose a threat to the stability of the doctrine of precedent?

2. An *instruction* question is similar in type to the question essay but turns it round into an "order" which you have to carry out:

> Critically assess whether the Practice Statement 1966 poses a threat to the stability of the doctrine of precedent.

3. A *statement* type question will usually adopt a particular position on an issue, or pose a hypothesis (a hypothesis is simply a position statement the truth of which can be tested), which you are then asked to 'discuss' or 'critically evaluate'.

> "The Practice Statement 1966, whilst representing an erosion of the doctrine of precedent, is a necessary development in order to allow modernisation of the law". Discuss.

Variations might include a more particular instruction, for example "Discuss with reference to the case of X" or "Discuss, illustrating your answer with recently decided cases."

Problem questions

1.7 ▶ These consist of a paragraph or so setting out a set of *facts*—in other words, a scenario where various circumstances have affected various people—and you are asked to "advise" one or more of them about particular legal issues arising out of the facts given.

An example of a problem question is as follows (we return to this one in more detail in Chapter 3):

> Zebedee has been suffering from persistent headaches about which he has consulted his doctor. One morning he is driving to university when he suffers a sudden seizure and collapses at the wheel. His car veers towards Abdul who is standing on some scaffolding and jumps off it to avoid the impact of the car, suffering a broken wrist and ankle when he hits the ground. Zebedee's car ploughs into the scaffolding and on into the path of an oncoming bus. Brenda and Carl are both passengers on the bus and are standing next to each other. Carl is carrying a firework which the crash impact causes to explode, injuring Brenda. Brenda suffers severe burns. The police arrive at the scene and as the police officers are escorting people off the bus the scaffolding collapses altogether, injuring Dan, a spectator who was trying to take photographs of the incident on his mobile phone. Dan suffers injuries to his head. He has now suffered a personality change, and has attempted suicide, causing him further injury.
> Advise Zebedee about his potential liabilities.

This is a very common type of question in legal study, and you are likely to discuss a number of these scenarios in class as well as being asked to prepare them for assessments.

ACTIVITY 1.3

1.8 ▶ Now, putting yourself in your tutor's position, take a few moments to consider *why* a tutor would set:

1. An essay question.
2. A problem question.

What *skills* do you think a tutor is looking to test, in setting each of these? In other words, what is the purpose of each type of assignment?

Activity feedback—here are our thoughts:

1. What is the purpose of an essay?

Writing a critical essay will test whether you have a number of different skills, for example, the following:

- Can you work out the nuances of a particular question?
- Can you carry out research based on the particular subject matter of the essay?
- Can you construct a coherent argument?
- Can you compare and synthesise arguments by different writers on a particular subject?
- Can you pursue a particular issue in depth?
- Can you write in good English using appropriate legal terms?

Was one of your thoughts something like: "To see how much you know or can remember about the general topic of law mentioned in the question"? Probably not: yet this is one of the most common complaints from tutors marking assignments: that students write a general, rather than a specific, answer. Learning to be specific is therefore an important skill which we consider in Chapter 3.

2. What is the purpose of a problem question?

The skills that a problem question will test include the following:

- Can you apply your understanding of the law to particular facts and people?
- Can you work out the facts which are in dispute?
- Can you identify further facts which are needed to resolve areas of dispute?
- Can you identify the relevance of particular cases to a particular set of facts?
- Can you identify the legal issues that arise?
- Can you provide advice to the appropriate person in the scenario?
- Can you identify issues where there is conflicting authority?
- Can you give a balanced view which takes into account the strengths and weaknesses of a particular argument?
- Can you structure your advice appropriately?

You will see from this that the purpose of a problem question is never to check whether you can write generally on the topic or speculate about facts which don't exist. We return to this in Chapter 3.

HOW WILL MY WORK BE JUDGED?

1.9 ▶ It seems to be a common misconception that what is being tested in legal assignments is how much information you can include. *This is not the case. Accuracy*—in other words getting your law right—is an important skill in academic work of course. However, your tutors are looking for much more than evidence that you can repeat legal principles. In higher education, you are expected to make a progression from transmission of information to demonstrating that you can *use* it, *apply* it and *evaluate* it. This is sometimes described as "deep" rather than "surface" learning, or evidence of *understanding* rather than "rote learning" (which means simply memorising something and repeating it back parrot fashion).

It can be daunting as a student to understand this distinction: it is easier (and feels safer) to repeat things which you can be certain are "right" rather than grapple with the uncertainty of exploring the issues. If you can get to grips with the concept that your tutors are looking for *more* than description and repetition then there will be a huge improvement in the quality of your writing. You are missing the point if you ask "how many cases do I need to include ?" or "have I covered enough?" because this suggests you think there is a magic information "threshold" which will gain you a pass mark. There is not: your tutors are not looking simply for information but for what you *do* with the information. It would be like an art student saying "I want to paint a brilliant picture—how much paint should I use?" It is easier in this example to see that it is what the student *does* with the paint which is the vital part, but exactly the same is true of the information you are going to amass as a law student (your "paint") which you then need to transform into a successful piece of writing.

Use of assessment criteria

1.10 ▶ It is increasingly common for law schools to specify what they are looking for in relation to your written work with the use of *assessment criteria*. These will vary from institution to institution and they may well have been drawn up with reference to the nationally set standard for law degrees known as the benchmark statement for Law.[1]

Listed below are the kind of things that will, in some shape or form, be important in legal writing regardless of your institution's own criteria:

- Identification of issues/diagnosis of task/analysis of task—in other words, showing you understand what you have been asked to do.
- Knowledge/accuracy—in other words, that the information you rely on to build your arguments is factually correct.
- Understanding—that you can select relevant material and explain it in appropriate depth.
- Application—that you can take your knowledge and work out how it would be relevant to particular circumstances.
- Analysis or evaluation—that you can make critical judgments about your material; that your work is not just describing circumstances.
- Research—that you can find and use an appropriate range of quality materials as

---

[1] You can read more about this at *http://www.qaa.ac.uk/Publications/InformationandGuidance/Documents/Law07.pdf* [Accessed December 12, 2014].

evidence to support your arguments and reference these correctly.

- Organisational structure/argument—that you can put together your points into a logical sequence which builds towards an appropriate conclusion.
- Presentation—that your work is written using good English grammar and spelling and in an appropriate style, and that any requirements for submission are complied with (including a Bibliography if required).

> **TIPS** • *Make sure you find out whether criteria are used for your assignments and if so what they are and what they mean. It may help you to think of assessment criteria as being the "rules" of a game.*

HOW CAN I AVOID COMMON MISTAKES?

It might seem odd, in a book called *Successful Legal Writing*, to spend time thinking about common mistakes—in other words to focus on what is, essentially, *unsuccessful* legal writing. However, we believe it is vital that you understand the criticisms which tutors frequently make of written work, and even more importantly, what prompts these criticisms, so that you can take steps to avoid making these mistakes yourself. ▶ **1.11**

"Does not answer the question"

Other ways this might be phrased: "you haven't understood what was being asked of you"; "read the question more carefully next time"; "this is an answer but not the one we are looking for". ▶ **1.12**

This comment might indicate that you do not have the legal knowledge to answer the question, but it is much more likely that you have failed to show the tutor marking your work exactly what was being asked and have therefore put in irrelevant material and missed out material which was needed. Sometimes (especially in an exam situation) it may genuinely be that you didn't read the question properly, or wanted to include material it took hours to learn, just to show you learnt it, even though the question didn't ask for it. See further advice on these below.

"Discussion of irrelevant issues"

Other ways this might be phrased: "your answer goes off track"; "avoid a 'write all you know' approach"; "you weren't asked to discuss this". ▶ **1.13**

This kind of comment is made on work where the student has put down so much information that there is some relevant and correct material, but it is buried in a mass of other material which is only generally related to the topic. This is sometimes called the "scattergun" or "kitchen sink" approach. In other words you are putting in "everything but the kitchen sink" or randomly shooting out "bullets" of law with the hope that some of the shots will hit the target. This might be because you know an awful lot—great—but you are failing to show that you *understand* the material. As explained above being able to recite or regurgitate material does not, unfortunately, prove to the tutor marking your work that you understand it.

Perhaps the most crucial point in writing is to remember you cannot impress or gain marks by including irrelevant material you have not been asked for, no matter how complex the point or how laborious it was to find it and/or learn it. *You are wasting your own time and your tutor's* and you are failing to communicate your understanding. This understanding is shown as much by what you leave out as what you put in.

Think for a moment about watching politicians being interviewed on the news or answering questions on a programme like *Question Time*. It is common practice for them to deflect a tricky question about something they do not want to talk about by changing tack and answering a different question from the one asked. A good interviewer will point this out and repeat the original question. How do you rate the politician when this happens? Do you think to yourself "Wow, what a knowledgeable person, to be able to answer on something completely different from what was asked", or do you think "Shifty guy—can't even give a straight answer to a straight question"? Your tutors aren't necessarily going to think you are being shifty if you fail to answer the question as asked, but they are certainly not going to give you any bonus marks for being able to discuss something which is not relevant.

"Misses important points"

1.14 ▶ *Other ways this might be phrased:* "you should have discussed . . ."; "you have barely touched on. . ."; "you failed to consider the issue of . . .".

In other words, there was important material which was not discussed. This might be due to a number of different causes. Did you fail to understand the topic and to not realise that the missed issue was important? Did you waste too much time on irrelevant material and so did not have the time or words to include everything you wanted?

Did you run out of time in an exam?

Where you have a tight word limit, and in an exam where your time is limited, decisions will need to be made about the relative importance of points and what to include and not to include.

"Where is the source?"

1.15 ▶ *Other ways this might be phrased:* "lacks authority"; "provide a source".

Tutors write this where a student has made an assertion without providing the necessary evidence to support that assertion. This is particularly a problem in relation to assertions of law, where the evidence must be in the form of a case or statute. For example:

> There is only one ground for divorce, namely irretrievable breakdown of marriage.

This is quite true, but it is an assertion of law (i.e. the student is stating what the law is on that point) and therefore needs to be proved by stating a legal authority (i.e. a primary source of law). The legal principle given here about divorce comes from s.1(1) of the Matrimonial Causes Act 1973. It is also important to demonstrate your use of secondary sources books, articles, etc. clearly in your work. Failing to do this meticulously may be perceived as plagiarism.

"Insufficient application to the facts"

Other ways this might be phrased: "too general"; "more specific advice is needed"; "how does ▶ **1.16** this affect our parties?".

This mistake is applicable to problem questions which ask you to provide advice to a particular party or a number of parties, and arises where the student writes a general essay on the area of law without saying how it affects (i.e. *applies to*) the party he or she has been asked to advise.

Application is a very important skill for a lawyer. Clients coming for legal advice do not want to pay for an hour's worth of waffle on generalities: they want to know how the law affects them, and, depending on the circumstances, whether they are likely to win in court. This is what you need to bear in mind when answering problem questions. Note that this does not mean that you give only one side of the argument—your client wants honest, objective advice!

> **TIPS •** *Check who you are advising about what, then make sure that as well as stating the law and providing evidence to support your statement, you then go one step further: "So in Fred's case, this means . . .". The name of the party you are advising should occur frequently throughout your work. There is more about this in Chapter 2.*

"Too descriptive—lacks analysis"

Other ways this might be phrased: "more depth needed"; "insufficient evaluation". ▶ **1.17**

This is likely to be written on an essay where a student states the law (hopefully with the right authority) but does not go on to discuss the question in enough depth. This is especially needed in essay questions. Description is important, because that is how you explain the relevant law, but in order to get good marks you need to go further than this and provide evaluation—not just what the law is, but why it is like that, what effect this has and so on. This is a skill which you will be expected to develop as you proceed with your studies, and you will also learn about looking at the law from different perspectives. Try to develop a questioning or critical attitude towards the law. (There is more on this in Chapter 5.)

"Mistakes on the law"

Other ways this might be phrased: "contains a number of legal errors". ▶ **1.18**

It is, of course, vital that in order to succeed in your assignments you must have a thorough and up-to-date understanding of the legal principles on which you are being tested. That said, this is not as daunting as it may appear because so much of your study time will be focused on making sure that you have grasped the right rules. Therefore a student who works hard throughout the year and attends and participates in classes will have a very sound grounding in this. It is usually only those students who have not engaged with the course who find they are floundering in terms of their knowledge at assessment time. And you don't need to be told that students who don't do the work do badly—that is obvious.

"English needs work"

1.19 ▶ *Other ways this might be phrased*: "your written English is not up to standard"; "you make a number of grammar and punctuation errors".

Communicating effectively means using the standard rules for written English. Failure to do this may make it harder to follow your argument or indeed in a worse case scenario impossible.

> **TIPS** • *Find out what additional support your institution offers to help you improve your English language skills. There is more about this in Chapter 7.*

HOW CAN I REFLECT ON MY OWN WRITING SKILLS?

1.20 ▶ In order to get the most from this book, you now need to stop and think about the steps that *you* need to take in order to improve your own writing, in the light of what you now know about what makes legal writing successful and the factors your tutors will take into account when judging your work. The following activity will help you identify your strengths and weaknesses to help you use the reminder of this book effectively.

ACTIVITY 1.4

1.21 ▶ **Step 1: Successful writing**

What do you regard as the most successful piece of writing you have done to date? (This could be an essay you wrote at school or college, or a project you have done, or perhaps a job application or a short story or a poem.) Note this down.

Step 2: Judgment

On what basis did you make the judgment that it was successful? Was it because you got a high mark/got the job/won a prize? Now dig a little deeper and try to think about *what it was* that made that piece of writing successful. Try to be as specific as you can—for example, was it on a topic that you were very interested in? Did you get a lot of help with writing it? Did you do it in a group? Was it with a clear goal in mind like a job or a prize? Did you do it to a tight deadline? Did you use a particular approach to the writing? Note down any factors you can think of which contributed to your success.

Your first reaction to this might be that you aren't sure, or it was "just luck" but there will have been a combination of factors which led to your success, so really try to pinpoint these. Remember that you need to think about specific factors, not vague statements like "Well, it was an English essay and I was always good at English". Try to be more focused and specific and look for reasons and evidence to support your reflection.

Step 3: Unsuccessful writing

Now think about what you would class as one of the weakest pieces of writing you have done, and go through the same process with this as you did with your best piece, again identifying the factors which affected your writing and how you tackled it.

Step 4: Skills

Thinking back to what we suggested earlier about focusing on the purpose of different types of writing, what was the purpose of the writing you did in your most successful piece and your least successful piece? What skills were they testing? Again, note these down. If you get stuck on this, perhaps look at the list of "criteria" we gave earlier in the chapter to see if that gives you ideas for what the pieces of writing were aiming to test.

Step 5: Analysis

You should now have two lists: one relating to the factors and skills of your most successful writing, and the other covering the same for your least successful writing. Can you see any *patterns* emerging as to what skills you already have, what skills you need to work on, what things help you to do well and what things hinder you?

There are not necessarily any "quick fix" solutions but if you are able to focus on what is right for you then this will help you make the most of this book. All we can do here is provide general advice and tips—we do not know you and we have not seen your work—based on the things we know about what students find difficult and what helps them to resolve these difficulties. Having a clear idea of what you need to work on and what things you are already good at will help you target the problem areas most effectively. In other words the strategy for improving your own writing has to come from you.

SUMMARY OF CHAPTER 1

- The key to successful legal writing is good communication, which in turn depends on having a clear understanding of the purpose of the writing.
- You will be expected to demonstrate that you can write in a variety of different situations.
- You need to be clear about the purpose of each different type of assessment you are set.
- Your work is likely to be judged against some form of criteria, which will vary from institution to institution.
- You will learn more about how to avoid common student mistakes in legal writing throughout the rest of the book.
- You should reflect carefully on your existing strengths and weaknesses to make the most of the advice in the rest of the book.

▶ 1.22

▶ 2
The process of writing

WHAT IS THE PURPOSE OF THIS CHAPTER?

2.1 ▶ You are likely to find studying and learning at university different from studying and learning previously. Higher education forces independence on you: it may be the first time you are making decisions about where to live, when to get up, whether to attend classes, how much time to spend studying, and how much time to spend on other things. Similarly, the way in which you tackle your assignments is your responsibility. As you've chosen to read this book, it seems likely that you want to review how you produce your written assignments and that you want help to improve them.

By the end of this chapter you will:

- have had an opportunity to reflect on your existing time management skills and how this impacts on your academic work;
- be able to manage your time effectively;
- have learnt the steps required to manage the process of writing.

HOW CAN I MANAGE MY TIME MORE EFFECTIVELY?

2.2 ▶ Our students, particularly those who feel they haven't done themselves justice in an assignment, often say that with hindsight they realise they managed their time poorly: started too late, left it to the last minute, underestimated the amount of research required and did not leave themselves enough time to check their work through. At university you are in control of your own time to a much greater extent than at school or college. You will be set a number of assignments in different subjects and these may have deadlines which are close together or even on the same day. Therefore it's vital that you take control of your time. In particular don't fall into the trap of thinking that time outside taught classes is free time or a gap in your timetable. The reason you have fewer hours in class is because there is more work to be done outside class. In this section we give suggestions to help you improve your time management.

The starting point is to think about how you do things now and how you prioritise your time. Secondly, you need to look at the decisions you make about what you *do* with the time you have available: in other words, ensuring you are making the most of it by working effectively and prioritising appropriately. Deciding what to prioritise is also part of the independence you have as a university student. Let's think about common barriers to effective time management. Do any of the following apply to you?

- *Underestimating the amount of time it takes to complete a university assignment* – as you will see later on this chapter successful writing involves a number of steps. You will have to do a considerable amount of preparatory work before you can even start writing and you must plan for this. Action: This is an easy one; start sooner. Block out regular chunks of time to make some progress on the assignment – avoid the 'I can get it all done in 1 day' approach.
- *Putting things off*—this is a variation on underestimating the time involved and we probably all do this at some point or another. Sometimes putting things off can be because of a worry about failing. Putting things off is essentially what you are doing if you've ever used the phrase "I can only work when up against a deadline" as an excuse for leaving an assignment to the last minute. What you really mean is that you don't *want* to work up until that point. Be honest with yourself—is it a strategy that works well? Do you really get the marks you think you deserve? If not, then change your approach. Action: Be disciplined and begin to tackle your assignments earlier. Giving yourself enough time to complete will help with worries about failure.
- *Not being able to prioritise*—again, this leads to a failure to spend the appropriate amount of time on the things which are important. Action: read the advice on prioritising later on in this chapter.
- *Getting distracted*—Being able to be a good multi-tasker is often seen as a strength but writing a good assignment requires focus. Having Twitter, Facebook and email open with the television on in the background is just asking to be distracted from your work. Action: Be disciplined – count the numbers of windows you have open on the computer and reduce them to one.
- *Being too available to others*—you need to be assertive in turning people down when you need to manage your own time (for example, "today is just not going to be possible—can we get together at the weekend instead?") and manage the expectations of other people about how much time you have available for them, especially when you are coming up to an assignment deadline. Action: Be firm with others. Don't feel guilty about this— remember the people who care about you want you to do well on your course.
- *Being too perfectionist*—Obviously you want to get the best mark you can but it is better to submit a completed assignment on time than a brilliant first half of an assignment or one that is late. Trying to be too perfect can lead you to spend a long time getting something which isn't actually that important absolutely right, and leaving yourself less time to spend on the important things. Action: Prioritising is going to be the key here – see the advice below. It can help to consider the relative importance of your tasks and to appreciate that not all will need to be done to perfection.

A good starting point is to look more closely at how you spend your time at the moment, by keeping a time log for a few days. ▶ **2.3**

Work out how you spend your time now

Step 1:

2.4 ▶ On a sheet of paper record everything you do and note down when you start and when you finish each activity. For example, if it takes you 15 minutes to walk to the library then note that down. If you play football with your mates for 25 minutes in the afternoon then jot that down. Don't forget to include all your classes. Keeping this kind of log is time-consuming and you may feel a bit daft doing it, but it is really worth it—remember that the key to improvement is reflection and to reflect you need the facts. You only need to do this for a week but by the end of the week you will have a better idea of exactly how you spend your time.

Step 2:

2.5 ▶ Looking at your record identify the things that are really important to you or that need to be done because of commitment to others which you cannot change e.g. work or childcare. Now look at what's left and see if there are any timewasters. For example, there are obvious differences between spending three hours a day online because you need to and spending three hours a day online because you want to. Don't let the "because I've always done it like that" mentality cloud this radical re-assessment of your time.

Step 3:

2.6 ▶ Now think about what possible changes you can make . . . and make them! Don't set yourself up to fail by being unrealistic. For example, by thinking you can manage without any time spent socialising. Remember this may be just as much about changing your attitude as it is about changing what, when and how you do things. If you feel that flicking between writing an assignment and Facebook is genuinely the best way of working, fair enough but in that case be realistic about the extent this will slow you down and therefore you will need to start the assignment earlier to accommodate this. If you find you do simply have too much to do, then you must make decisions about what to prioritise.

> **TIPS** • *Why not try spending one evening working at a particular task without trying to multi-task and then review the experience?*

HOW SHOULD I PRIORITISE?

2.7 ▶ Getting your priorities right is vital in order to make the most of the time you have available for your assignments.

ACTIVITY 2.1

2.8 ▶ Below we've drawn up a sample grid of assessments for a typical first-year law student (yours might not be exactly like this—this is just an example to get you thinking). The grid shows the assessments the student has to prepare during the year. We've left out the exams for now (we'll return to the question of exams in Chapter 9).

Subject	Weighting (how much this assignment counts for as part of the whole grade in this subject)	Type of assignment	Group or individual	Word limit	Deadline
Contract	25 %	Problem question	Individual	1,500	December 15
Legal Theory and Research	100%	Research portfolio	Group	4,000	May 20
Legal System	10 % 10 %	Case analysis Court visit report	Individual Individual	500 500	October 25 March 15
Public	50 %	Essay	Individual	2,000	March 15
Tort	50%	Problem question	Individual	2,000	January 15

How would you advise this student to prioritise their work? Consider the following questions:

- Which assignment is the most important?
- Which assignments do you think are likely to be the most time-consuming?
- Which assignment should you start first?

Activity feedback—here are our thoughts:

Your considerations when deciding on priorities might have included the following:

- Deadline—this helps you assess the *urgency* of any particular task.
- Percentage weighting of overall grade—this helps you assess the *importance* of the task.
- Number of words—this may be some kind of guide (as is the weighting) of the amount of time your tutors are expecting you to spend on this task.
- Group activity or not—this helps you factor in the other members of the group and their priorities.

Did you think of any other factors to take into account?

You probably didn't advise the students to start with their favourite subject because you know as a matter of reason that this shouldn't affect the prioritising of the work. However, when tackling your own assignments, it's much more tempting to make a start on your pre-ferred subject. Priorities can be affected by personal preference. It may feel virtuous to have "got some work done" but if it was work which shouldn't have been a priority at that time then you shouldn't be patting yourself on the back quite so hard. This is true of life in general, isn't it: going out with friends is generally preferable to washing clothes. Washing your clothes only assumes vital importance when (a) you have no clean underwear left, or (b) there is an assign-ment you should be preparing. If the latter, this is a classic displacement activity—in other words you are doing the washing simply to put off doing your assignment. This is a really easy trap to fall in to: do your best to avoid it.

You already know that how much time you *should* spend on something isn't necessarily the same as the time you will *actually* spend on it. For example, looking at the above table, you might find it comparatively easy to advise our imaginary student that he or she should not spend a disproportionate time on the two 500-word Legal System tasks because each only counts for 10 per cent of the whole grade for that subject. This is not to say they should be dashed off without care or attention, but simply that they should not be allowed to overshadow other activities.

In reality, however, because the case analysis *is* still an assignment (and the first one in the year at that), it is only too easy to get this out of proportion. Consequently, a student might spend a week buried in the library, reading texts and writing and re-writing draft after draft, only to find that they've produced 3,000 words worth of material which they cannot use. And now they've also probably missed lectures and tutorials/seminars on the topic of negligence, which is what the Tort assignment is on, plus two group meetings for the Legal Research portfolio—which is 100 per cent of the assessment in that subject.

The two most common mistakes when prioritising are:

● underestimating the amount of time an assignment will take to prepare from start to finish; and
● failing to strike the correct balance between *all* types of work—assignments and other work, such as preparation for and attendance at tutorials for example, which of course are almost certain to be relevant for a later assignment or exam—which you need to be completing.

> **TIPS** • *Missing classes to complete an assignment is simply setting yourself up to fail later on.*

This is likely to be a real issue at the beginning of the course, because managing your own time more *independently* is one of the major differences between school or college and university; you will find you have less time in scheduled classes and more time in which you are researching and working on your own. Make sure you develop this skill as soon as you can—and maintain it throughout.

Priorities tool

2.9 ▶ A useful tool to help identify priorities is to plot importance and urgency on opposing axes as on the diagram on the next page.

2.10 ▶ The idea is that you place tasks in the appropriate quadrant to help you plan when you will tackle each task. You may find it helpful to use the diagram to make a "to do" list showing the order in which you must tackle the tasks you have to do and the time you are going to allocate to them; starting, obviously, with those which are both important and urgent.

For example our student's to do list for January 14 is likely to be very focused on finishing touches to the Tort assignment. This is due on the following day, and therefore *urgent*, and worth 50 per cent of the marks in that subject, and therefore *important*. At this point the

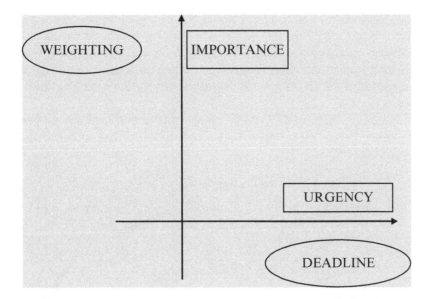

preparatory research for the Public essay, whilst important because it is worth 50 per cent of the subject, is not yet urgent because its deadline is two months away.

If you use this as a tool for planning your tasks, remember to personalise it to your own needs and skills. For example, any group working task is likely to take longer because getting people together for meetings takes time. Or, if you know from past experience that you find answering problem questions easier than essays, you may want to give yourself a bit more time to get to grips with planning an essay.

TIPS • *If you find yourself juggling assignments at the last minute stop and think "how did I end up in this state?" and go back and do the reflective time log again. The only way to improve is to work out what went wrong.*

Now that you have reflected on how effective you are at managing your time, we can now turn our focus to the writing process.

HOW SHOULD I MANAGE THE WRITING PROCESS?

Successful writing requires certain steps which we explain in more detail in this chapter. We explore each step in the *writing* process in the following chapters.

▶ 2.11

In other words, if you adopt the pattern we suggest in this chapter, you will give yourself the best chance of writing at the required standard.

Great authors often have particular habits in relation to their writing. For example, J.K. Rowling famously wrote much of the first Harry Potter book in an Edinburgh café and Roald Dahl always used a shed at the bottom of his garden. These are writers who found something that worked for them. Sadly, this does not mean that if you write in a shed or a café you will produce successful children's books but whatever habits you develop in terms of where, how and for how long you like to write—and finding out what works for you may be a process of trial and error—you will need to carry out a series of steps to complete the overall writing process.

As you go through a particular step, issues may arise which require you to revisit a previous step. This is an important part of keeping your writing under review, so do not think of the steps as entirely separate. This is why the diagram shows the interaction between each step and the centre.

Note that we've described the cycle below as it relates to coursework assignments. We explain the adjustments which are needed to the cycle for writing in exams in Chapter 3 and a dissertation in Chapter 10.

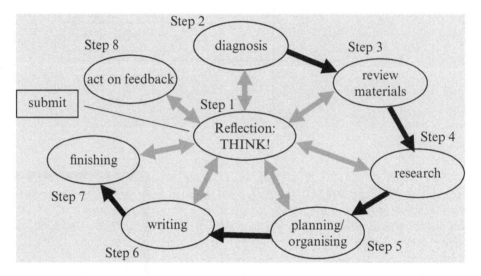

Step 1: Think

2.12 ▶ Successful people—whether writers or anything else—are reflective. This means that they engage in a constant process of reviewing what they are doing and what they have done in order to learn from their own experiences and improve for the future. Therefore, the first step is to review how you *think* you currently write and compare this to any *evidence* you have of the results this produces, for example, previous marks or grades, and feedback from tutors (or peers).

This part of the writing cycle has already been considered in detail in Chapter 1 and you were given the opportunity to undertake an activity designed to do just this. As you develop your skills as a reflective practitioner (this simply means someone who always has at the back of their mind questions like *"How am I doing at this?"* and *"Could I be doing this better? If so, how?"*) then you will find it easier to keep reflecting as you proceed with your work. Whilst you develop this habit, we've emphasised that after each phase, you reflect again: the idea of this reflection as you go along is to evaluate your progress so far and review what you need to do next.

Before you move on to Step 2 you also need to undertake some basic planning by considering the instructions you've been given about the assignment—often called the assignment brief. Understanding these instructions is essential to carrying out the task effectively, so make sure that you are clear on these *from the start*. This guidance might cover, for example, rubric (instructions or specification including word limit), presentation (e.g. word processed, margin sizes, font) or style (e.g. preferred footnote scheme).

- Are there rules or instructions applicable to all assignments on your course? You might find instructions in your student programme handbook and/or your e-learning space/VLE.
- Are there specific instructions for *this* assignment? These might be found in the subject manuals, on your e-learning space/VLE or perhaps in a handout. Alternatively, your tutor may have gone through the instructions verbally in a class.

Draw up a timeline for managing the assignment. Remember to apply prioritising techniques to this in terms of importance/urgency. Look at the word count. Look at the weighting.

Step 2: Diagnosis

In this phase you work out exactly what you have to *do*.　　　　　　　　　　　　　▶ 2.13

We explore the skills you need to diagnose your task—for example, identifying key words, and instruction words, and other techniques for working out the nuances of the question—in much more detail in Chapter 5. We'll look at diagnosis in the context of essay questions and problem questions, and explore how these might differ. The main point to appreciate for now, in order to make sense of the rest of the writing cycle, is that your diagnosis will require you to break the question down into sub-questions/*issues*. The answer to each sub-question will form a part of your overall argument. As you learn more about the topic, you keep in mind whether the questions you posed were the right ones, or whether you need to adjust them. After each phase you continue to keep your diagnosis under review.

Step 3: Review your materials

Once you have an idea of what you've been asked to do, and an idea of why you've been asked　　▶ 2.14
to do it, the next step is gathering your resources together in preparation. Some of these will be resources you already have and some will be resources you will need to carry out extra research to get.

Gather together materials you already have on the assignment subject. This might include, for example: unit manual/subject handbook, lecture notes, tutorial/seminar preparation notes, textbooks, books, cases and articles. And don't forget your reading list (if you've been given one). This will give you a good idea of the sources your tutors think are important for your subject and may well include sources directly relevant to your assessment. See Chapter 4 for more on this.

The goal in doing this is to see how much material you have to help you answer the questions you posted in Step 2. It is extremely unlikely that you will be able to find *all* the answers you need simply by looking at your existing work. In other words, whilst it's the obvious starting point, your existing work can only ever be just that—a starting point. Your lecture

> **TIPS** • *Make sure your existing materials are complete. For example, did you miss a class on the subject? If so, work out how to catch this up—can you ask a friend for their notes or perhaps the notes are available on the internet? Have you ensured that you have all the suggested readings for this topic? If not, get hold of copies.*

notes and the basic textbook are never going to be enough to get good marks in themselves, but think of them as clues—they start you off looking in the right places for further sources. You will be expected to read as widely as you can, but remember in doing so that your goal is to answer the questions you posed in Step 2. This is what you need to keep in mind as you move into your research phase, Step 4.

Step 4: Research

2.15 ▶ The research phase of your writing is where you pursue a wider range of sources in order to find out the answers to the questions you have posed in Step 2. We explore how to plan and carry out your research in much more detail in Chapter 4 and how to remain focused on relevant sources. You will also need to learn how to make notes effectively from the sources you research. Strategies for note-making are also covered in Chapter 4.

When you have completed your research, you will have found answers to the sub-questions you have posed for yourself in Step 2. Perhaps we should put this the other way round: when you have found sufficient material to address the questions you have done enough research—so *stop*. It can be very difficult to draw a line under the research phase and again there is more advice on how to do that in Chapter 4. You are now in a position to start thinking about how to put your assignment together, which is the next step.

Step 5: Planning and organising your assignment

2.16 ▶ You now need to think about exactly how your writing will fit together. A well-written assignment will have an organised structure which flows logically from point to point. Something which students sometimes find difficult is how best to integrate the evidence they have found into their own arguments. In other words, how can other people's words and ideas become part of your own argument? What is an effective argument anyway? These matters are covered in Chapter 5, which will show you how to make the most of your evidence.

You also need to spend time planning your structure carefully.

There is much more general guidance on how to structure your work in Chapter 6, but if you have diagnosed your task effectively, the structure should flow logically from the questions you have posed, and your discussion on the issues that flow from your research.

Once you have put your structure together, *review it*. If you write up your assignment in this way, will it address what you have been asked? If yes then you are ready to move to Step 6.

Step 6: Writing

2.17 ▶ You are now in a position to write your assignment, making sure you are still keeping the question you have been set in mind at all times. When you are given an assignment, the writing stage is probably what you think of immediately, and yet, as you can now see, it appears comparatively late on in the cycle we are suggesting. Unless you have completed Steps 1–5 carefully first, you are not going to be in a position to start the writing phase successfully.

Step 6 is where your communication skills are at their most important, so make sure you fulfil the requirements of effective communication which we suggested in Chapter 1. Chapters 5, 6 and 7 all contain material relevant to this. Remember you will need to:

- use evidence to support assertions and acknowledging those sources so as to avoid a risk of plagiarism, and ensure your arguments form a logical structure (see Chapter 5);
- structure your writing appropriately by writing an effective introduction, main body and conclusion (see Chapter 6);
- write in good English, including use of grammar, your style, sentence construction, spelling, use of legal terminology and so on (see Chapter 7).

Once you have finished writing, it is tempting to think you've finished. Sorry, but you haven't—you now need to reflect on what you've written and make any final adjustments, in Step 7.

Step 7: Finishing

It is vital to factor time for this stage into your planning. This stage in the process includes editing your work, reviewing and reflecting on your work and checking for inaccuracies or irrelevancies and presentational errors, all of which are covered in Chapter 8. You may need to revisit Chapter 7 at this stage to make sure your assignment is written in good English. In addition, remember to look back at any specific requirements you've been set and make sure you comply with those. You can now submit your assignment.

▶ **2.18**

Step 8: Feedback

Although you have now completed and submitted your assignment, in order to make the most of this assignment in terms of learning for the future, you will need to reflect carefully on the mark and any other feedback you get. There is advice on how to do this in Chapter 8.

▶ **2.19**

Having explained the writing process we now explore some possible issues about legal writing at university.

SHOULD I TACKLE PROBLEM QUESTIONS IN THE SAME WAY?

As you already know from Chapter 1, problem questions require *application* of the law in the context of a specific set of *facts*. This means that the most important way in which you hone the advice given in the rest of the book to problem questions is by making sure every stage of the writing process is geared towards this goal of giving specific advice. You will find, therefore, that there is less scope for flexibility, speculation and innovation when answering problem questions than essay questions. When you finish your training and are legally qualified and clients come to see you about a simple divorce, for example, they will not be that keen (or necessarily impressed) to hear your speculations on what the position might be if they had a large property abroad or had been having an affair with Brad Pitt! They want to know what you can do for them in their particular situation—on their facts and in *their* context. In order to provide appropriate advice, you need to be able to identify the issues which arise from their particular circumstances and avoid matters which don't.

▶ **2.20**

Making your diagnosis in a problem question

2.21 ▶ In order to make your writing successful in respect of problem questions, your diagnosis phase must have more specific elements to it. You need to do all of the following:

- Identify whom you are advising about what.
- Identify the parties, and the role of your "client" in the scenario.
- Identify the material facts and the order in which they occur (*chronology*).
- Identify the legal issues arising from those facts.

This is explored in detail in Chapter 3.

Researching a problem question

2.22 ▶ Whatever your writing assignment, your research will be designed to answer questions which you have posed to yourself as part of your diagnosis. This is essential in order to make sure that your research is focused. In relation to a problem question, your research may focus more specifically on primary sources of law, i.e. cases and statutes, because you are being asked to advise about how the law affects a particular person. In your research phase you must make sure that you record the *authorities* for the advice you are planning to give. Remember, however, that your research must focus not on a general answer to your questions ("what is the law on this area?") but on a specific answer as related to the facts you have been given and the client you are advising ("how does the law in this area affect this person?"). There is more advice on how to utilise your evidence in the context of problem questions in Chapter 5.

Writing up your problem answer

2.23 ▶ What does the instruction "Advise Zebedee" mean? There are several things it does not mean:

- giving only Zebedee's side of the case;
- writing directly to Zebedee;
- writing generally on the topic instead of providing advice;
- sitting on the fence with respect to Zebedee's position.

Therefore to advise Zebedee well, make sure you do the following:

Give both sides of the case

2.24 ▶ It is a mistake to interpret "Advise Zebedee" as an instruction to give only those arguments and reasons which support Zebedee's case. If you stop and think about it, telling Zebedee only what he wants to hear (which is essentially what you're doing in that case) is very bad advice. Basically, what Zebedee needs in terms of advice is to be told the truth; the strengths and weaknesses of his case and your reasoned conclusion as to whether overall he is liable/guilty/able to claim compensation, etc.

Keep to an academic objective style unless told otherwise

2.25 ▶ "Advise Zebedee" is the standard way, in legal examining, of asking you to write an academic answer in which you identify the issues applicable to Zebedee's circumstances and relate them to the relevant law. The emphasis here is on the words "academic answer". By this we mean that you should you should write in objective terms and in the third person. Do not begin "Dear Zebedee, my advice is . . .", and continue by framing your answer as if directing it to Zebedee. Instead you are telling the marker what advice Zebedee should be given—"Zebedee should be advised that . . .". Therefore the advice about structuring and writing which you'll find in Chapters 5 and 6 is equally applicable to a problem answer as it is to an essay question.

> **TIPS** • *Check the exact format of the assessment carefully. If in doubt, check with your tutor as to how you are expected to lay out your answer.*

Provide advice rather than an essay

At the opposite end of the scale there is a further potential problem with the writing stage of a problem answer: adopting a completely essay style answer to a problem question. Despite what we've said above about the importance of writing academically, it is still absolutely vital that you make sure that there is *application* in your answer. Remember your goal is to explain how the law on this issue affects Zebedee and his circumstances. A general answer explaining the law on the area without reference to Zebedee or the facts of the question will not score well. In relation to each issue of law which arises you must apply the law to the facts by explaining how this principle of law affects your client.

▶ **2.26**

> **TIPS** • *Check how often the name of your client appears in your answer. If you are applying the law well, then the name should appear in every paragraph. A page without mention of the party you are advising is likely to indicate you've slipped into a generalised answer on the topic.*

Provide an effective conclusion

Writing a conclusion for a problem question may also differ from the process of writing one for an essay question. If you have identified the relevant legal issues and applied the appropriate law with authority to the facts then you should already have reached a series of mini conclusions which need to be drawn together to provide your overall advice.

▶ **2.27**

> **TIPS** • *Bear in mind that if the case actually went to court, the judges would have to find for one side or the other, even if they acknowledge that it is finely balanced. You should therefore be prepared to do the same.*

Students often ask "But it could go either way—do I have to give a definitive conclusion?" It is true that many of the areas of law you will be assessed on will not be settled—you will be asked to provide advice on areas where there are *conflicting* authorities, as this is how your tutors will test whether you understand the nuances of the topic. It can therefore feel risky to conclude one way or the other, in case you get it wrong, but it is a misconception to think that there is necessarily a right or a wrong answer to a legal problem. A good answer will *acknowledge* that there are conflicting authorities and that the law is doubtful on a particular point but then compare the authorities in the light of the facts of the question in order to evaluate which is the better position in relation to these facts. Your tutor is interested in your *reasoning*, and whether you can pursue this logically to a conclusion.

HOW WILL WRITING ASSIGNMENTS AT UNIVERSITY BE DIFFERENT FROM SCHOOL OR COLLEGE?

If you are coming to university straight from school or college in which you did essay-based A levels you are probably used to getting quite a lot of support with your writing from your tutors.

▶ **2.28**

You may perhaps be given a reading list and some generic guidance on the planning of assignments and then be expected to use that with the particular assignments you are set. Because of the independent nature of assignment writing at university it's something you are expected to be getting on with alongside classes in other subjects. Your other lectures/tutorials/seminars will continue as usual exploring topics and points relevant to the final exams. In other words do not expect all your classes leading up to a submission deadline to be focused on that submission; they won't be, although there may well be a class in which the tutor outlines some expectations and gives advice. In addition your university is unlikely to give you repeated reminders that a deadline is approaching. Your tutor may mention it in class or you may get a text or online message with a few days to go. Equally you may just be given a schedule of submission dates at the beginning of the year and be expected to monitor this yourself. Be prepared for this change of approach which is an important part of your development as an independent learner.

I HAVEN'T WRITTEN AN ESSAY FOR YEARS—HOW DO I GET BACK INTO THE SWING OF WRITING?

2.29 ▶ If you are a mature student returning to education, you may be concerned that it is a long time since you have had to write an essay and you may think you have forgotten how to do it. However, this does not mean that you are totally out of practice—think about the writing you have done since, for example at work or helping with schoolwork.

Similarly, you'll have been doing other things which will help you with the process of writing, even if you don't realise it—when you read, or even when you watch the news you will have been developing skills in critical assessment. The actual writing part is only a small part of what you need to do, as we explain in this chapter. Recognising how to utilise your existing skills to underpin your academic study will be an important part of your university life.

WHAT HELP CAN I GET WITH MY ASSIGNMENTS?

2.30 ▶ There will be help available but it is likely to be different from what you have experienced at school/college. For example:

- It is unlikely that your tutors will provide comments on a draft of your assignment (the exception to this is a dissertation/project—the writing process here differs and we talk about this in more detail in Chapter 10).
- It is also unlikely that a tutor will reply specifically to queries about what to include and what not to, beyond the guidance provided to all students. As we explained in Chapter 1 when looking at assessment criteria, your ability to make these decisions for yourself (i.e. diagnose your task) is part of what the assignment is testing.

However, this is not to say that no help is available. There may be a specific lecture in which expectations for the assignment are covered—make sure you attend this. There is likely to be a tutorial/seminar on the same topic as the assignment and whilst this may not focus on the specific question you have been asked it will give you valuable pointers. In addition, there will of course be an opportunity to ask questions and clarify anything you don't understand about the topic in any tutorial offered. Check all the material you have been given—there may be further instructions/guidance/tips/materials either online or in the module handbook. At university tutors do not expect to have to remind you to check whether such material is available. Of course you can still speak to your tutor; their help will probably consist of giving you pointers, as opposed to specific guidance on your own work. Additionally, some law schools build a formal opportunity for formative assessments into their programmes which provides a chance to practice skills relevant to the coursework including writing and receive feedback. If you are offered this opportunity, use it.

Finally, check whether your university offers study support including assignment preparation help that you can utilise.

CAN I WORK WITH OTHER STUDENTS ON ASSIGNMENTS?

It makes sense to talk with your friends/colleagues about the assignments you have all been set. However, if you are going to do this you must be able to distinguish between *collaboration* and *collusion,* in other words what is allowed and what may be construed as cheating. ▶ **2.31**

The Oxford English Dictionary ("OED") defines collaboration as: "United labour, co-operation; esp. in literary, artistic, or scientific work". You may well be encouraged to work collaboratively with your friends on a variety of tasks throughout your studies (indeed collaboration is at the heart of group work) as this can help you to set your assignments in context and provides a good opportunity for you to learn from others and to offer your own ideas. On the other hand the OED definition of collusion is "Secret agreement or understanding for purposes of trickery or fraud; underhand scheming or working with another; deceit, fraud, trickery." So in the context of your academic work, collusion can be defined as being where two or more students work together on a task which you were required to complete as individuals and submit work which is substantially the same. This is likely to be regarded as academic misconduct by your institution. The key is not to cross the line from collaboration to collusion.

Universities may have their own definitions of these words, in particular of collusion as it is seen as wrongdoing, so check your student handbook or course regulations. If in any doubt, ask your tutor about what is acceptable. Generally, you will probably find that it is perfectly acceptable to brainstorm with a colleague or two and even to some extent share some of your ideas and research. However, to avoid any possible suspicion of collusion you must make sure that the work you submit is your own, i.e. not the same or similar to that of another student. So do not write together and do not swap drafts. It should hopefully go without saying that you shouldn't share your finished work with another student no matter how much you trust them. If they utilise *your* work in what they submit *both* of you will be in trouble.

HOW WILL THE PROCESS DIFFER FROM WRITING ASSIGNMENTS IN OTHER DISCIPLINES?

If you are studying a law conversion course, having taken a degree in another discipline, you are likely to find that successful techniques you've developed to write well previously will work here, because whatever the subject, good writing requires independent reflection, research ▶ **2.32** and style. Specific differences will exist in terms of the subject matter and sources, and you may find that certain conventions are adopted which are different from your own subject (for example, in legal writing there is usually a preference for avoiding use of the first person which may have been the norm in other subjects you have previously studied). You are also likely to find that referencing conventions differ. The key is therefore to adapt your existing skills rather than work on entirely new ones.

SUMMARY OF CHAPTER 2

2.33 ▶

- Managing your writing effectively requires you to understand the process involved and to set aside sufficient time to tackle it.
- You can do this more effectively by reflecting on how you currently manage your time and deciding what you need to change.
- Adjusting your priorities can help you manage your time better.
- To write successfully you should follow a cycle of reflection, diagnosis, review, research, planning, writing and finishing, with further reflection throughout. These stages are explained in further detail in Chapters 3–8.
- Although legal writing at university level demands particular skills, you can use your existing writing skills as a starting point for improvement.
- The level of support for writing at university will be different from what you have been used to and you will need to be more independent in managing your writing.

PART 2

Preparing your assignment

▶ 3
What is the question asking?

WHAT IS THE PURPOSE OF THIS CHAPTER?

We've already seen that it is vital to successful writing to consider why you've been set a particular assignment. Understanding what a particular type of assignment is testing is going to help you work out how to tackle it.

▶ 3.1

However, there is much more to identifying your purpose than this. As well as understanding generally what an essay is for, and what a problem question is for, the real key to successful writing is to understand *exactly* what the question you have been set is asking you to do. This is Step 2 of the writing cycle—making the diagnosis—and this chapter will help you with this. The reason we draw the analogy with diagnosis is that the question is a bit like the symptoms of an illness—you make your diagnosis of what is needed and the "cure" is the assignment you produce. Making an incorrect diagnosis will mean that the suggested cure doesn't actually help these particular symptoms.

By the end of this chapter you should:

- understand what we mean by purpose and diagnosing the task;
- understand what we mean by "instruction words" and the meaning of the common instruction words used in legal assignments; and
- be starting to work out your own strategies for diagnosing the tasks you are set.

WHAT IS DIAGNOSIS OF TASK?

Imagine going to a restaurant, sitting down at a table, and before you've had a chance to consider a menu or think about what to order, a plate of food arrives. The chef has thought "oh well, they've come in here for food—doesn't matter what kind". Similarly, if you ordered a particular dish, and then a different one arrived, you'd complain, wouldn't you?

▶ 3.2

This is essentially what a student who doesn't take time to diagnose the task is doing to the tutor who has set the assignment. You need to think carefully about what it is the tutor wants. (And remember your tutor is allocating marks to your work: what kind of review would you write of a restaurant which tried to serve you food without reference to what you wanted to order?)

Essentially, diagnosing your task is all about working out *exactly* what you've been asked to do in any particular assignment or question. There are a number of different steps you can take to help you make your diagnosis. First of all, you need to spend time thinking about the question. You should already have an idea from Chapter 1 about the purposes for which tutors set particular types of question which should help you to think in general terms about what the assignment is for. However, you need to narrow it down much more than this in order to produce an effective piece of work.

You do this by working out what *issues* the question is asking you to consider, and then making the correct judgment about the relative importance of these aspects so you can work out how much detail is needed on each one. In other words, good diagnosis involves making decisions in relation to two important elements:

1. coverage (what needs to be included); and
2. depth (which aspects need more detail).

You can see from this that you need to do the following (and the more of them you do, the better your work will be):

● Be clear and organised in identifying the right points.
● Work out which points are the most important (these are your major points which need more detail).
● Work out which other points are relevant to the question but are not as vital as the major points (these are your minor points which will accordingly need less detail).
● Work out whether there are any hidden issues which need discussing even though the question does not directly mention them (your marker may have "hidden" an issue which is important to a sophisticated discussion of the subject matter of the question by not referring to it directly in the wording of the question). These are what legal markers call *oblique* points, or non-explicit points, and identifying these tends to increase your marks because spotting them is difficult: you'll need to learn to distinguish between a *hidden* point and an *irrelevant* point. The former is relevant to a full discussion of the subject matter of the question even though there was no reference to it in the exact wording of the question. Only a student with a thorough grasp of the subject matter is going to be able to spot this. The latter may be peripherally related to the subject matter but is not included within the material required to answer the question.

TIPS • *Always keep your diagnosis under review as you learn more about your subject through your detailed research. To make sure you do this, print the question out and stick it as close as you can get it to your computer screen and make sure you've always got a copy with you for example when in the library.*

This last point raises an important issue in relation to making an effective diagnosis, namely that it is impossible to do this completely without a thorough understanding of the topic. Yet, as we've already seen, your diagnosis gives direction to the research which you carry out on the topic—and it is from that research that you get your thorough understanding. So, how can you diagnose the task beforehand? The answer is that you make a *preliminary* diagnosis and then keep it under review as you research the topic further.

Finally, you will prove to the marker that you have carried out an effective diagnosis by the following:

1. By identifying what the question is asking you to do—a good introduction which expresses the issues and indicates their relative importance will help show the marker you have done this.
2. By then performing the tasks you have identified—in the main body of your essay, discuss the issues you indicated were relevant, weighted appropriately to their relative importance.
3. By taking a final position in relation to the question asked—you do this with an effective conclusion weighing up the evidence.

On the following pages, we'll work through some examples to help you understand how to do this.

WHY IS DIAGNOSIS IMPORTANT?

The sorts of mistakes which result from a poor diagnosis of task include:

▶ 3.3

- Advising the wrong person in a problem question or advising them on issues which do not relate to the legal problem presented.
- Providing a general discussion of the law rather than specific advice in a problem question.
- Being too descriptive in an essay question which requires analysis.
- Including irrelevant material.
- Missing out important points.

If you look at the section on mistakes to avoid in Chapter 1, you'll see that many of these result from a poor diagnosis of task. If you get comments which seem similar to any of the above, then you need to focus on this in order to improve.

Diagnosing a task if you don't feel that you know enough about the subject in order to do it effectively can seem difficult. The temptation is therefore to think "I'll read around the subject first and then come back to the question later". This is a fatal error, because your research will be unfocused and you will therefore waste a lot of time; you may become expert in an area not specifically required, which then leads to the further mistake that rather than waste all that work, you think of a way to "get it in somewhere". You're now well on the way to writing the essay you *wish* you'd been asked to write, rather than the one you *have* been asked to write.

A student who performs a good diagnosis will find that much of the rest of the work falls into place. Diagnosing the task is a skill, not a gift. You can still master it through practice and by following some tips and suggestions.

HOW DO I MAKE A DIAGNOSIS ON AN ESSAY QUESTION?

3.4 ▶ We've established that a diagnosis involves making sure you understood what the question is asking you to do. As problem questions ask you to display different skills from those which are needed for essay questions, it is logical that the techniques you use to diagnose the task are different as well. We're going to consider techniques for diagnosing essay questions first, and then later in the chapter we'll look at diagnosing problem questions.

> Techniques for diagnosing an essay question include:
> ● making sure you understand the question;
> ● picking out keywords and instruction words;
> ● looking for the position presented in the question; and
> ● making a list of sub-questions.

A. Make sure you understand the question

3.5 ▶ As discussed in Chapter 1, an essay title commonly takes one of the following forms:

1. Question:

> Is X true?

2. Statement (hypothesis):

> "X is true". Discuss.

3. Instruction:

> Critically assess the extent to which X is true.

> **TIPS** • *Read the question carefully. If there are any words or terms you don't understand, look these up before you go any further.*

All the above are effectively asking you to take a critical evidenced position in relation to X. In other words they are asking the same thing. You may find it easiest to diagnose the direct question format, as this makes more overt exactly what you have been asked to do. However, if you look at the statement and instruction formats, you can see that what you have to do is analyse the strengths and weaknesses of the position taken, with appropriate evidence, and this therefore involves the same skills and techniques as answering the question format. Do not make the mistake of assuming that you are expected to agree with the statement in a statement-style title.

For example:

> "The voting system used at UK General Elections requires reform to reflect the values of a liberal democracy". Discuss.

This is a title to which we will return to in much greater detail later in the chapter, but in very brief terms, you can see that it is asking whether the voting system used at UK General Elections requires reform to reflect the values of a liberal democracy. It would be quite easy to rephrase the title into a question:

> Does the voting system used at UK General Elections require urgent reform to reflect the values of a liberal democracy?

In the second example it is clearer that you are being asked take a position. In other words, your conclusion should make it clear to the reader whether you believe the answer to be yes or no. Your view must be informed and evidenced; in other words you must demonstrate the ability to acknowledge and evaluate both sides of an argument. If you are in any doubt about this, remember that the original format of the title was a statement asking for your critical assessment. Critical assessment involves looking at the strengths and weaknesses of any particular position. Therefore, what you have to do in this type of situation is to argue both sides but conclude which side of the argument (i.e. the "yes" side or the "no" side) is stronger. Turning the statement into a question is a good starting point to help you get to grips with what you have been asked to do, and can be a useful technique to try to get initial ideas flowing about what is involved in the assignment topic.

B. Pick out key words and instruction words

The next step is to pick out *key words* and *instruction words*.   ▶ **3.6**

Key words (also sometimes called topic words) are words which *relate to the subject matter* and instruction words are words which tell you *what to do with the subject matter*.

For example:

> "The law that a **squatter can acquire a title** merely **from occupying land for 12 years** is **outmoded**."
> *Discuss* this statement with *particular reference to the* **Land Registration Act 2002.**

The key words, which define and/or modify the subject matter, are outlined in bold. The main topic of the essay relates to squatters and how they gain title to land (adverse possession), and the particular focus within this topic is on whether it is "outmoded" that a squatter can acquire title after a particular length of time; this modifies the key subject to indicate the scope of your work, or to put it another way, the slant your essay has to take, rather than simply being a general discussion of adverse possession. A further key phrase is the statute which is specifically mentioned. The instruction words are highlighted in italics: you are asked to *Discuss* the statement, and this is further modified by a specific instruction to make sure the 2002 Act is included within your discussion (this is something of a clue: an alternative form of the question might omit this on the basis that inclusion of detail on the recent Act is implicit in answering the question effectively).

It would therefore be a mistake—although not an uncommon one—to do any of the following in an essay on this topic:

- Discuss adverse possession generally, without reference to the specific hypothesis posed that it is "outmoded".
- Fail to discuss the content and impact of the 2002 Act on the law on adverse possession.
- Merely describe the law on adverse possession and/or the 2002 Act rather than engaging in a discussion of them.

All essay titles will have key words. Whether or not the title also has instruction words will depend on the way it is asked—if in the form of a simple question then you will have to infer the instruction word. For example, supposing you had been asked:

> Is the rule that a squatter can obtain good title to land after squatting for 12 years outmoded?

Although the subject matter is the same here, there is no instruction to "Discuss" the topic. However, since it would be difficult to answer this question without entering into a discussion of the relevant issues (a simple description of the rule, for example, clearly does not answer the question because there would be no attention to the issue of whether the rule is out of step with modern thinking, which of necessity demands some evaluation or discussion of the law), then the word "Discuss" or "Analyse" can be *inferred* as the instruction.

As well as *Discuss*, more instruction words which you might come across include:

> Analyse
> Critically assess
> Evaluate
> Criticise
> Explain
> Compare and contrast

Note that although it is possible to define these words so as to highlight different nuances, in practical terms, in legal examining the first four terms are usually used interchangeably. So (unless your tutor instructs you differently), *Analyse*, *Critically assess*, *Evaluate* and *Criticise* are all similar to *Discuss* in that they require you to examine any propositions made or implied in the question or statement given and look for the strengths and weaknesses of those propositions, relying on appropriate evidence. The key here is to explore both sides of the question but move to a conclusion which takes a position.

Explain is asking you to clarify a rule or situation, and would usually be accompanied by an instruction to do something else as well (for example, "Explain the recent reform proposals and critically assess whether they will achieve their object").

Compare and contrast is used in relation to two situations or positions, for example an existing law and a planned reform, or two different theories. A compare and contrast instruction (as you would expect) requires you to take these two situations and identify similarities and differences between them.

On the other hand, you are unlikely to come across an instruction merely to *Describe*.

This is because describing is a lower level skill—it simply involves summarising a factual situation rather than applying any other cognitive skills to that situation. This is not to say that description is something to avoid. In order to explain the effect of a rule, you will certainly need to *describe* that rule. However, the trick is to be as concise as possible. A common student mistake is to focus on a lot of descriptive detail (for example, giving exhaustive accounts of the facts of a string of cases) at the expense of going on to make *judgments* about the material and draw conclusions about it. Getting this balance right is considered further in Chapter 5.

Now try spotting instruction words and key words for yourself.

ACTIVITY 3.1

Consider this essay title:

▶ 3.7

> 1. Critically assess the extent to which the Practice Statement 1966 allows development of the law.

Which of the words listed below are the key words/phrases and which are the instruction words?

Critically assess	Practice Statement 1966
Development of the law	Extent
Allows	

Activity feedback—here are our thoughts:

Critically assess—this is an instruction phrase.

Extent—this is modifying the instruction and indicates the slant which is needed to your critical assessment.

Practice Statement 1966—this is a key phrase because it defines the subject matter.

Development of the law—this is a key phrase because it refines the subject matter of the essay: instead of generally looking at the pros and cons of the Practice Statement (for example) the focus must be on whether it permits change.

Allows—this is also a key word which modifies the discussion of the Practice Statement, suggesting there must be some consideration of the nature of the power granted by the Practice Statement.

ACTIVITY 3.2

We've already seen that, sometimes, an essay title may be in the form of a question in which case there is no instruction word. For example:

▶ 3.8

> 2. Does the Practice Statement 1966 allow sufficient development of the law?

However, we've also seen that within this type of question, an instruction to "discuss" or "critically assess" the issue is implicit. Would you say that this question is asking you to do the same as the title in the previous activity, or something different? As a reminder, the previous title was:

> Critically assess the extent to which the Practice Statement 1966 allows development of the law.

Activity feedback—here are our thoughts:

We'd suggest the answer is yes, the two essays are asking the same thing. Our reasoning for this is that:

1. both have the same key words/phrases (Practice Statement 1966, development of the law);
2. the instruction words *Critically assess* in the first question mean "examine whether the Practice Statement allows development of the law", and in the second, this is directly asked in the form of a question;
3. the word *extent* in essay 1 quantifies the "critically assess" instruction by asking *how much* the Practice Statement allows development of the law. This is matched by the word *sufficient* in essay 2, which is essentially asking "is it enough?"

You might have thought that the above reasoning means the essays are *different* because essay 1 is asking *how much development of the law the Practice Statement allows* whereas essay 2 is asking *how much development of the law the Practice Statement allows and is it enough*? This is a fair point: asking the price of something is not the same as asking whether it is good value for money, is it? It sounds like essay 2 is asking you to make more of a judgment about the Practice Statement—in other words, draw some conclusions about how much development of the law is actually desirable and then compare the amount allowed by the Practice Statement with the "desirable" standard you have set.

However, if we go back to your instruction phrase in essay 1: *critically assess*, we can see that this is not just asking you to *describe the amount* of development: critical assessment involves making (informed) *judgments*, so in fact, it is implicit that this question is *also* asking you to compare the amount of development permitted by the Practice Statement with some sort of "desirable" standard: in other words the question "is it enough?" is implied by the instruction phrase *critically assess*. Therefore, it seems these two essays are really asking you to do the same thing.

ACTIVITY 3.3

3.9 ▶ Now look at this title:

> 3. "The Practice Statement 1966 impedes the proper development of the law because so few cases reach the Supreme Court". Discuss.

Do you think that this is asking the same as, or something different from, the first essay titles we've already considered?

The first essay was:

> 1. Critically assess the extent to which the Practice Statement 1966 allows development of the law.

Which of the following points comes closest to your view?

A. It is a different essay because although the subject matter is the same, the instruction word is *Discuss* rather than *Critically assess*.
B. It is a different essay because it includes reference to only a few cases reaching the Supreme Court so I would have to make specific reference to that within the discussion of the development of the law.
C. It is the same essay again because although there is a reference to cases reaching the Supreme Court, this is a red herring because the Practice Statement only applies to the Supreme Court anyway so this must have been implied in the other titles.

Activity feedback—here are our thoughts:

If you chose answer A: We'd agree with you that it is a different essay, but not because of the different instruction word: *discuss* and *critically assess* tend to be regarded as interchangeable in legal examining. Essay 3 is directing you to a slightly different emphasis in your discussion of the Practice Statement through an additional topic word rather than an additional instruction word.

If you chose answer B: We agree. This issue would also have been relevant in the first essay but here you are specifically directed to it so the issue would assume more prominence in the answer.

If you chose answer C: We can see your point about the Practice Statement only applying to the Supreme Court, but actually what makes the essay different is that it is asking you to concentrate on a particular angle of the idea impeding the law, namely that the Supreme Court can only reform the law in the few cases which come before it. It is certainly true to say that the other essay was asking you to focus solely on the Supreme Court (because the Practice Statement doesn't apply to any other court) but even so the phrase "because so few cases reach the Supreme Court" adds a further slant to the discussion.

C. Look for the position presented in the title

Essay titles, particularly those which contain a statement and an instruction to *discuss* or *critically analyse*, will take a position which will almost invariably be based on one or more *assumptions*. Part of your diagnosis will involve spotting the assumptions so that you can research them effectively and then support or challenge them using the evidence you've collected.

▶ **3.10**

ACTIVITY 3.4

Let's return to essay 3:

▶ **3.11**

> "The Practice Statement 1966 impedes the proper development of the law because so few cases reach the Supreme Court." Discuss.

Delving deeper into the question, the statement in this essay title makes two *assumptions*. What do you consider these to be?

Activity feedback—here are our thoughts:
The two assumptions found in the title are:

1. that the Practice Statement impedes the proper development of the law;
2. that this is because so few cases reach the Supreme Court.

> **TIPS** • *You will often find that a "statement" question will make assumptions with which you have to agree or disagree, arguing your case with reference to appropriate evidence. Being able to pick out assumptions from the question is vital.*

You are asked to "discuss" these assumptions. Therefore, you need to critically assess whether they are true. In other words, does the Practice Statement impede the development of the law? If so, is it due to the reason suggested or is it due to other reasons? You can see that the answer to the former question will bear a very strong resemblance to the answer to the question asked in the previous activity—*Does the Practice Statement allow proper development of the law?*

However, although the questions are very similar, the slant is still different. The current example takes the lack of cases reaching the Supreme Court as a starting point: it therefore has to be front and centre in your answer. In the other answers it would have been *part of* your argument but not necessarily central to it.

D. Make a list of sub-questions

3.12 ▶ Next, a good technique is to pose a series of sub-questions, which need to be answered in order to take a position on the title of the question. You can use this as the basis for your research phase, and as you carry out your research, you would gain understanding of which questions need more detail.

This will enable you to classify these into major and minor points in order to work out the amount of *depth* you need to devote to each of them.

ACTIVITY 3.5

3.13 ▶ In this activity we are returning to essay 1:

> Critically assess the extent to which the Practice Statement 1966 allows development of the law.

Have a look at these questions below, which are all related in one way or another to the doctrine of precedent, and try to pick out the ones which help answer this particular essay title.

● What was the Practice Statement 1966?
● What difference did the Practice Statement make?
● What are the advantages of the Practice Statement?
● What are the disadvantages of the Practice Statement?

- What was the position before the Practice Statement?
- What has happened to precedent since the Practice Statement?
- What has happened to precedent in the Court of Appeal?
- What are the dangers of allowing development of the law?
- What are the dangers of impeding development of the law?
- How much development of the law is a good thing?

At this stage we're just brain-storming: this is not yet an essay plan and we aren't yet trying to classify these into major and minor points—we're just trying out a few preliminary ideas. Brainstorming can be a good way to generate lots of ideas/questions on a specific question when trying to diagnose your task. Once you've narrowed it down to the questions you think are relevant, then the next step is to rank the relative importance of the questions.

Activity feedback—here are our thoughts:

Here are our thoughts about the brainstorming questions above:

- *What was the Practice Statement 1966?*
  This is important introductory information but it is factual and therefore should be given concisely. It is a good technique to ensure your introduction defines relevant terms, and therefore a brief outline of what the Practice Statement 1966 was should be included here.

- *What difference did the Practice Statement make?*
  This is a vital question to consider as it is directly relevant to the idea of the extent to which it has allowed development of the law. Essentially, it involves comparing the respective positions before and after the Practice Statement.

- *What are the advantages/disadvantages of the Practice Statement?*
  Although this has some relevance—you might for example be planning to argue that allowing or failing to allow development of the law is an advantage or disadvantage of the Practice Statement—this very general brainstorming question needs some care, as it could easily lead to a "write all you know" approach.

- *What was the position before the Practice Statement?*
  This is an essential requirement preparatory to thinking about what change it has achieved. Caution is always needed with historical background but here it is necessary: the purpose of the Practice Statement was to allow some flexibility in development of the law, so here the history has direct relevance to the question.

- *What has happened to precedent since the Practice Statement?*
  Yes, this is vital factual information to underpin discussion of whether it has allowed sufficient development of the law. Note that a comparison of your answers to this question and the "position before" question provides the answer

to the question what difference did the Practice Statement make, so essentially that question has been broken down further into these two "before" and "since" questions.

- *What has happened to precedent in the Court of Appeal?*
  Absolutely not! The question is asking you to consider events in the Supreme Court/ House of Lords only (although you might draw on arguments used by Lord Denning in the Court of Appeal, who had much to say on the subject. It is acceptable to use the *argument*, because that could have happened anywhere).

- *What are the dangers of allowing/impeding development of the law?*
  This is an excellent evaluative question. The answer should help you take a position in relation to the question considered below—how much development of the law is a good thing.

- *How much development of the law is a good thing?*
  This is implied within the idea of critically assessing how much development is per-mitted. We've already discussed that you need to conclude whether there is sufficient development, and you can only evaluate this if you have an idea of how much flexibil-ity there should be. What makes this more difficult is that this is a matter of debate. You therefore need to take a position on the flexibility/certainty debate, backed up, of course, by suitable evidence. This may not feel as obviously relevant but it is, because this question is a necessary underpinning question in order to reach an overall posi-tion on the use of the Practice Statement.

So, this leads us to the following sub-questions:

- What was the Practice Statement 1966?
- What was the position before the Practice Statement?
- What has happened to precedent since the Practice Statement?
- What are the advantages/disadvantages of the Practice Statement?
- What are the dangers of allowing/impeding development of the law?
- How much development of the law is a good thing?

Producing a list of sub-questions in this way will help focus your research, and will also assist you with structuring your arguments later.

Worked Example

3.14 ▶ So far, we've spent a lot of time looking at examples of different essay titles in Legal Method/ System, which is an area you are likely to have studied at an early stage in your course and will therefore be familiar with. To improve your skills in making a preliminary diagnosis, try the fol-lowing example, which is drawn from another subject area which tends to have a strong emphasis on essay writing skills, Public Law (Constitutional and Administrative Law). Even if you have not yet covered this subject, attempt this as it should improve your confidence that there is a certain level of diagnosis you can make even without a detailed knowledge of the subject matter.

Consider this essay title:

> "The voting system used at UK General Elections requires reform to reflect the values of a liberal democracy". Discuss.

We're going to use this essay title as a worked example.

Understanding the question

Our starting point is to check the meaning of any words in the essay title we do not understand. ▶ **3.15**
We can note that this is a *statement* kind of title. It can help to turn the statement into a ques-tion, as we saw earlier, for example, *Does the voting system used at UK General Elections require reform in order to reflect the values of a liberal democracy?*

This makes it easier to see that this essay is asking you to assess: does the voting system used at UK General Elections demand reform or doesn't it?

Instruction words and key words

The instruction word here is *Discuss*. We know that a tutor will use this word to require a critical assessment of the position taken in the statement. It is vital to present both sides of the argu-ment; in other words, you have to demonstrate the extent to which the proposition (that the voting system at UK General Elections needs reform to reflect the values of a liberal democ-racy) is true, and the extent to which it is false.

The key words/phrases are:

- *"voting system used at UK General Elections"*—this is your general subject matter: the topic involved.
- *"reform"*—this shows a particular element which you are required to discuss—in other words, you need to think not just about the strengths and weaknesses of the existing law but propose solutions to any problems you identify, to indicate how the law could be improved in the future. It is common for legal essays to include some reference to the prospect of reform. Reform questions always involve a *comparison* between the current system and possible alternatives.
- *"values of a liberal democracy"*—you can see that an explanation of principles is going to be involved and this therefore makes it clear that this is a theoretical essay.

The position presented

The underlying assumption implied in the question is that the voting system used at UK General Elections does not accurately reflect the values of a liberal democracy.

Sub-questions

These "values" are going to be the measuring stick against which you evaluate the current system and any proposed reform.

From your key words, you can begin to identify the knowledge and understanding you are going to need in order to tackle the question by breaking the question into sub-questions. Try this yourself, and then read on to compare your suggestions with the ones below.

- What are the values of a liberal democracy?
- What are the issues which influence judgments about voting systems?
- What is the current voting system in UK General Elections?
- What alternative systems could be used instead?
- Would the alternative systems be "better" than the existing system in relation to the values identified?

These are the issues which you can see need to be addressed simply from looking at the title, with no knowledge of the subject whatsoever. When you start to learn about the topics you'll be able to make a more detailed list. Everything on the list should be *relevant*. You may find it helpful to plot this out in a grid or a list to help you keep track of the sub-question posed and the evidence you find during your research.

By this stage you are in a position to carry out your research, remembering to keep your diagnosis under review. Your diagnosis and your list of sub-questions will also help you to make an essay plan when you move to that stage of your writing. There's more on how to do this, and we return to this particular question in Chapter 5.

HOW DO I MAKE A DIAGNOSIS ON A PROBLEM QUESTION?

3.16 ▶ In a problem question, you will be given a set of circumstances in the form of a case study involving a number of people, and asked to advise one or more of them about how the law applies to them. The vital word here is *applies*. The aim of your diagnosis in a problem question is to relate your understanding of the area of law in question specifically to the circumstances and the people who are involved in the scenario you have been given.

There is a particular skill to answering problem questions effectively, and you may be advised by tutors to use a particular technique to make sure that you are covering the points required to provide effective "advice" to the client. The most common technique usually recommended in legal teaching is the IRAC method. IRAC is simply a mnemonic to remember the steps in the technique required (Issue, Rule, Application, Conclusion):

ISSUE – this is the step that corresponds to the diagnosis phase, where the possible claims or matters which need to be discussed are identified. This corresponds to the sub-question approach we have suggested you use when diagnosing an essay question, since these issues can usually be framed as sub-questions in a problem question (see below).

RULE – this requires identification of the corresponding legal principles or rules which affect the issues or matters identified. This will usually be in the form of case authority. Note that on some matters there may well be conflicting case law or a lack of clarity as to how a particular authority might apply to the circumstances of the case scenario given. This tends to be an indicator that the issue is a more major one requiring more discussion in the final answer, in the form of arguments and counter-arguments at the application stage.

APPLICATION (sometimes referred to as ANALYSIS) – this is the vital step of a problem answer which distinguishes it from an essay question, and means applying the relevant legal rules or principles identified in respect of each issue to the facts of the scenario given. In other words, this is saying how the law affects *this* person in *this* scenario. Without this step, it is impossible to give "advice" – instead the answer would simply be an essay-style discussion of the issues. It may help you to think of this step as being a little like the "workings out" you would give when tackling a maths problem.

CONCLUSION – following from the application, it should be possible to form a mini-conclusion in relation to each issue identified. Where the application of the legal rules to the scenario is clear-cut (perhaps in relation to an issue of settled law, or where the facts of the case relate very closely to a relevant legal authority) then it will be possible to give a firm conclusion. Where there is conflicting case law, or a lack of case law directly relevant to the facts of the scenario, then your conclusion will be less positive. Nevertheless it is important to make some effort to give a conclusion even if you cannot be categorical. You will often be asked to discuss grey areas and moot points, and you are being tested on your ability to propose a viable solution in the form of a conclusion.

There are numerous other mnemonics sometimes used to cover the same set of steps, for example:

IPAC – Issue, Principle, Apply, Conclude or ILAC – Issue, Law, Application, Conclusion.
You can see that both these correspond almost identically to the steps of IRAC.
CLEO – this stands for Claim, Law, Evaluation, Outcome.
IDAR – Issues, Doctrine, Application, Result.
Although the wording used is rather different you can see that the same sequence of steps is covered.

A few points about IRAC and similar techniques before we go any further:

1. All of these methods are tools to help you rather than intended as an additional headache. Don't get too bogged down in the acronyms; the important thing is what these steps help you achieve, i.e. the planning and delivery of an advice-style answer, as opposed to an essay. We have suggested the use of grid below to help you carry out the IRAC steps but if you find the grid restrictive, then simply make a list, or use a spider diagram to work through the steps.

2. IRAC and similar techniques do have their critics. One criticism is that they are too simplistic, and may discourage students from exploring some of the critical nuances required in writing a successful problem answer. We've already pointed out the importance of identifying major Issues, usually indicated by conflicting authorities at the Rules stage, and that this will require discussion of arguments and counter-arguments at the Application stage which may then lead to a less certain Conclusion. As long as you bear this in mind and take care to look for these areas of conflict then following IRAC will not lead to a simplistic answer. It may help you to think of the A as standing for Application (and if Applicable, Analysis) to remind you that some issues require discussion in greater depth.

3. Finally, in relation to IRAC, as well as helping you plan your research, the steps of IRAC will also help you to structure your final answer. We will return to this point when we think about the writing stage of your assignment in Chapter 6.

Identifying the Issues

The diagnosis phase of the writing cycle for a problem question corresponds to the ISSUE phase of IRAC. In other words you need to make sure that you identify the issues correctly. As discussed in Chapter 2, this requires the following:

- Identify whom you are advising about what.
- Identify the parties, and the role of the party you are advising in the scenario.
- Identify the material facts and list them in chronological order.
- Then, from this, you can identify the legal issues arising from those facts.

For example, supposing you were asked to consider the following problem question:

Alicia Atherton has recently begun an enterprise creating bags which she knits from recycled supermarket plastic bags in her front room. She collects the bags from a number of local supermarkets, who are happy to let her have as many of their old plastic bags as she needs for recycling. Alicia found that she could produce the bags quickly. She decided to try selling the bags over the internet to raise money for green charities, calling them Permabags.

She placed the following advert on the internet website GreenProducts.com on February 1:

"FANTASTIC OFFER! Keep Green – buy a Permabag today!
Don't want to use a supermarket plastic bag for your shopping? Use lots of them instead! I do! My Permabags are made from recycled plastic bags and will last you at least a year. And they are only £5 each! Do your bit for the planet by ordering one right now by emailing me on ilovemypermabag@hotmail.com. Help me replace all the plastic bags in the world with Permabags!"

Ben Barker runs a small shop called Barker's Bark, selling woodland products. Having received complaints from customers that the bags he offers (made from recycled wood pulp) are not strong enough for heavy items, he decided he would like to order a batch of the Permabags to offer to customers. He emails Alicia on February 10 saying "I'd like to sell your marvellous bags in my shop – I'll order 100 if you can offer me a discount to £400. In peace, Ben."
Alicia had gone away to a festival and did not access her hotmail account for several days. Ben was anxious to get the bags as soon as possible so sent a further email on February 17 saying "I would like to order these bags and have delivery as soon as possible".

Alicia meanwhile decided to abandon her enterprise and join a protest camp to protect a forest. She tweeted on February 20 saying "Permabag products on hold – sorry for any inconvenience #savetheplanet". She then checked her hotmail account and read Ben's email, and replied saying she couldn't supply the bags. Ben replied that he expected the 100 bags for £400 "as agreed" as soon as possible.

Advise Alicia.

A. Identify whom you are advising about what

In this example, we are advising Alicia about whether a binding contract has been formed. This is your *core issue*. Always check this core issue first, so that you read the rest of the question with this in mind, looking for the facts and law that specifically affect Alicia's position. However, do remember what we discussed in Chapter 2 about the meaning of "Advise"—you must identify the strengths and weaknesses of Alicia's case here, not simply tell her what she wants to hear.

B. Identify the parties and the role of your client in the scenario

In the example, Alicia is in the position of defendant—i.e. she needs advice on whether she has to supply the bags, which as stated above involves working out whether there is an enforceable contract between them. The other party is Ben Barker who is in the position of claimant—he wants to establish that there is a contract.

These two points are quick to identify, but you need to make sure you do it before trying to analyse the question any further.

C. Identify the material facts and list them in chronological order

From your first reading of the scenario, you need to identify the *material facts*, i.e. the ones that you consider are of importance and/or of particular relevance to this question. This will help you diagnose your task and identify the area(s) of law which need to be discussed. A good technique is to read through the question scenario carefully underlining the words and facts that you consider might later prove to be relevant. Keep these under review: remember they are only material if they make a difference. So, for example, it might well be material that Alicia is a small scale manufacturer but the name of the product is unlikely to be material. Place the material facts in a chronology (i.e. in order of what happened when). In certain topics (and offer and acceptance is such a one) exact dates are crucial so we have included them within our chronology below.

You might come up with the following (these are just indicative of the process: we aren't trying to produce a model answer here):

- Alicia is running a small-scale enterprise in her front room.
- She has a good potential supply of raw materials (in the form of the supermarket bags) and can produce her product quickly.
- She advertised the products on a website on February 1, giving details of the price and how to place an order.
- Ben emailed her as instructed in the advert on February 10, saying "I'll order 100 if you can offer me a discount to £400".
- Ben emailed again on February 17 saying "I would like to order these bags and have delivery as soon as possible".
- She gave the notification of the suspension of her production via a different means (Twitter) on February 20.
- She read Ben's email after this on February 20.
- Ben states he wants the bags "as agreed".

D. Identify the legal issues

From your identification of the material facts you go on to the next step of classifying the legal issues arising from these facts. Remember that your diagnosis of the core legal issue (what you are advising Alicia about) sets the basic legal framework which will always be required on a question on a particular topic. Here, it is the general principle that in order to form a valid contract, offer and acceptance are required. This principle forms the framework of any similar contract question. However, to make sure your answer is specific rather than general, you must say whether, *in these particular circumstances*, these requirements are satisfied. Here we return to the idea of posing sub-questions to help make your diagnosis.

To do this, the factual points must be generalised into legal issues, on which your sub-questions will be based. Finding the answers to these sub-questions, as in an essay question, will form the basis for your research. As long as you have some understanding of the principles of offer and acceptance in Contract, then you are likely to be able to identify sub-questions along these lines:

- Does the advertisement on *greenproducts.com* constitute an offer or an invitation to treat?
- [If it is an offer], then does Ben's email of February 10 constitute a counter-offer or is it merely a request for further information?
- [If a request for information], then does Ben's email of February 17 constitute acceptance?
- [If so], when is this deemed to be received by Alicia?
- [If there is an offer] Is Alicia's tweet capable of constituting revocation of the offer?
- [If so] is it made in time to revoke the offer?

These are our core issues. We may uncover more detailed issues which we need to discuss as we research and apply the facts of the question, so we need to keep them under review. Of course, as you research more about the law on this area, you will be able to work out whether these questions are major points, minor points, or not at issue at all (even posing the questions in this way may help you to eliminate irrelevancies; sometimes your tutors will include matters as deliberate "red herrings" and you need to be on the lookout for these). Keeping your diagnosis under review, which is just as important on a problem question as on an essay question, will also help you identify whether there are any questions (i.e. legal issues) which you have missed.

It can be helpful at this stage to start plotting the issues you've identified into a grid, which you can complete as you go through the other steps of the IRAC technique. Remember IRAC is just a tool to help you, so if you don't find the grid approach helpful, then make a list instead.

CORE ISSUE: IS THERE AN ENFORCEABLE CONTRACT IN TERMS OF OFFER AND ACCEPTANCE?

ISSUE (sub-question)	RULE (case or statute)	APPLICATION (how this rule would apply to the scenario given)	CONCLUSION (answer to the sub-question posed as the issue)
Does the advertisement on greenproducts.com constitute an offer or an invitation to treat?			
[If it is an offer], then does Ben's email of February 10 constitute a counter-offer or is it merely a request for further information?			
[If a request for information], then does Ben's email of February 17 constitute acceptance?			
[If so], when is this deemed to be received by Alicia?			
[If there is an offer] Is Alicia's tweet capable of constituting revocation of the offer?			
[If so] is it in time to be revocation?			

As you carry out your research you can begin to complete the R, A and C columns of your grid. So for example here, in relation to the first issue identified, of whether the website advertisement is an offer or an invitation to treat, you are likely to identify the cases of *Partridge v Crittenden* [1968] 2 All E.R. 421 and *Carlill v Carbolic Smoke Ball Co.* [1893] 1 Q.B. 256 as being the crucial authorities which need to be discussed. Further investigation will reveal that these are authorities which potentially conflict when applied to the facts of our scenario and therefore these need to be discussed and applied carefully to the facts (in other words, a situation where the Application step requires some careful Analysis as well). Consideration may need to be given to which of the conflicting authorities should prevail (we discuss conflicting evidence further in Chapter 5). This means that we would give a qualified rather than firm conclusion on the point of whether this is an offer or an invitation to treat. Note that logically (as indicated in the issues column) the question of whether the offer has been accepted and whether or not it could be revoked depend on a conclusion that there is actually an offer, in answer to the first question. If the conclusion is that the advert is definitely only an invitation to treat then there has been nothing to accept (or revoke). A logical progression through your issues and mini-conclusions is essential, particularly at the writing-up stage.

So, the top row of our grid could look something like this:

ISSUE (sub-question)	RULE (case or statute)	APPLICATION (how this rule would apply to the scenario given)	CONCLUSION (answer to the sub-question posed as the issue)
Does the advertise-ment on green-products.com constitute an offer or an invitation to treat?	*Carlill v Carbolic Smoke Ball Co.* [1893] 1 Q.B. 256 – an advert may constitute an offer if it is sufficiently certain and demonstrates intent

Partridge v Crittenden [1968] 2 All E.R. 421 – magazine advert was only an invitation to treat – exception is if it is made by a manufacturer | Discuss which of these authorities is most applicable to Alicia's case:

– Are the terms of the advert sufficiently certain? (consider terms of advert)?

– Could Alicia be deemed to be a manufacturer? (She might argue she is only a small-scale operation and therefore the main rule rather than the exception in *Partridge* should apply to her). | Qualified rather than definite conclusion as there are arguments on both sides. Arguable that this would be considered an offer as *Carlill* is an authority from a higher court and there is some certainty to the terms; additionally Alicia might be regarded as having set herself up as a manufacturer. |

By completing the grid for the other issues you would be able to give an overall answer to your core issue of whether there is an enforceable contract, which would form the basis of your final conclusions.

ACTIVITY 3.6

3.17 ▶ In this activity we want you to use the same approach to a different problem question, this time in relation to the tort of negligence:

> Zebedee has been suffering from persistent headaches about which he has consulted his doctor. One morning he is driving to university when he suffers a sudden seizure and collapses at the wheel. His car veers towards Abdul who is standing on some scaffolding and jumps off it to avoid the impact of the car, suffering a broken wrist and ankle when he hits the ground. Zebedee's car ploughs into the scaffolding and on into the path of an oncoming bus. Brenda and Carl are both passengers on the bus and are standing next to each other. Carl is carrying a firework which the crash impact causes to explode, injuring Brenda. Brenda suffers severe burns. The police arrive at the scene and as the police officers are escorting people off the bus the scaffolding collapses altogether, injuring Dan, a spectator who was trying to take photographs of the incident on his mobile phone. Dan suffers injuries to his head. He has now suffered a personality change, and has attempted suicide, causing him further injury.
>
> Advise Zebedee about his potential liabilities.

How could you apply the four diagnosis steps to this problem?
Remember the steps are:

- Identify whom you are advising about what.
- Identify the parties, and the role of the party you are advising in the scenario.
- Identify the material facts and list them in chronological order.
- Then, from this, you can identify the legal issues arising from those facts.

Activity feedback—here are our thoughts:

Zebedee has been suffering from persistent headaches about which he has consulted his doctor. One morning he is driving to university when he suffers a sudden seizure and collapses at the wheel. His car veers towards Abdul who is standing on some scaffolding and jumps off it to avoid the impact of the car, suffering a broken wrist and ankle when he hits the ground. Zebedee's car ploughs into the scaffolding and on into the path of an oncoming bus. Brenda and Carl are both passengers on the bus who are standing next to each other. Carl is carrying a firework which the crash impact causes to explode, injuring Brenda. Brenda suffers severe burns. The police arrive at the scene and as the police officers are escorting people off the bus the scaffolding collapses altogether, injuring Dan, a spectator who was trying to take photographs of the incident on his mobile phone. Dan suffers injuries to his head. He has now suffered a personality change, and has attempted suicide, causing him further injury. Advise Zebedee about his potential liabilities.

A. Identify who you are advising about what
   We're advising Zebedee, about his liability in the tort of negligence.

B. Identify the parties and the role of the party you are advising in the scenario
   Zebedee is the defendant in this situation and the other parties involved are Abdul, Brenda, Carl and Dan, who are all potential claimants. Our overall goal is to establish whether Zebedee is liable to these other parties.

Note that negligence is established through four essential components: duty of care (in law and in fact), breach of that duty, causation of damage which is not too remote, plus the consideration of the availability of any defences (see the spider diagram in Chapter 4 for an outline of the topic of negligence).

C. Identify the materials facts and put them in chronological order.
   Your list should have included the following (you may have identified others):

- Zebedee has been suffering from headaches.
- Zebedee knew he had some kind of health problem.
- Zebedee is a driver.
- Zebedee has collapsed at the wheel.
- Abdul is on scaffolding at the side of the road.

- Abdul suffers injuries jumping off the scaffold.
- Brenda and Carl are road users.
- Carl is carrying a firework.
- The firework explodes because of the impact with Zebedee's car.
- Brenda sustains injuries from the exploding firework.
- Dan is a spectator.
- Dan suffered head injuries.
- Dan has suffered a personality change.
- Dan has sustained further injuries after attempting suicide.

D. Identify the legal issues which arise from the question.

Identification of the legal issues is the hardest part of the diagnosis, but is crucial to a successful use of the IRAC technique. Remember that the identification of issues should grow from your identification of the material facts.

For example:

Relevant material fact	Corresponding Legal issue
Zebedee has been suffering from headaches	Does a pre-existing medical condition affect the liability of a driver in negligence?
Zebedee is a driver	Does a driver owe a duty of care to other road users?
Zebedee has collapsed at the wheel	Does collapsing at the wheel constitute breach of any existing duty?
Abdul is on scaffolding at the side of the road?	Does a driver owe a duty to people at the side of the road
Abdul suffers injuries jumping off the scaffold	Is the damage sustained of a type for which a claim can be made?
Brenda and Carl are road users	Does a driver owe a duty of care to other road users?
Brenda sustains injuries from an exploding firework	Is the damage sustained of a type for which a claim can be made?
Carl is carrying the firework	Does this constitute an intervening act?
The firework explodes because of the impact with Zebedee's car	How does this relate to the chain of causation?
Dan is a spectator	Is there a duty of care to a spectator?
Dan suffered head injuries	Is the damage sustained of a type for which a claim can be made?
Dan has suffered a personality change	Is a personality change following an incident within the boundaries of remoteness?
Dan has sustained further injuries after attempting suicide.	Is the damage sustained of a type for which a claim can be made?

Once you have identified the issues, then you have carried out the first part of the IRAC problem solving approach, and can continue to the Rule, Application and Conclusion steps, remembering always that as you carry out further research, you keep your diagnosis (i.e. your list of issues) under review in case they need to refined as you learn more about the detail of the topic area.

There are some further issues to bear in mind when diagnosing a problem question:

The limits of acceptable speculation

Students sometimes comment that they find it difficult to identify the answer to the core legal question posed in a problem question because of a lack of sufficient facts. The temptation here is to invent or imagine facts to fill these gaps, but this is not appropriate; instead, comment on the fact that an informed opinion cannot be reached because of the facts that you do not know and briefly mention the alternatives. Remember, if there is an ambiguity in a question it is deliberate, so don't go behind the facts you have been given. Essentially this involves drawing a distinction between acceptable speculation and making up facts to suit your interpretation. It is vital that you do not make up facts.

▶ **3.18**

To illustrate this, look back at our scenario involving Alicia and her permabags. One of the facts we were given in that scenario was the wording of the advertisement. This wording is important for the potential discussion required about whether it could be construed to be an offer, as the certainty of the terms is a relevant legal consideration.

If the wording of the advert had **not** been given in the question, and you therefore did not know whether it contained essential information like the price, then this would constitute a gap in the facts, and it would be necessary to speculate on the certainty of the terms. What you should do in this situation is cover both bases: explain that it would depend on (for example) whether the price was specified and whether instructions were given on how the permabags could be obtained and give the likely consequence of each situation.

It would be wrong to do either of the following:

- Ignore the importance of the advert altogether on the basis that you haven't been told the wording—state that you would need to know more and explain why; or
- Jump to an assumption that the advert includes certain terms (or vice versa) and answer accordingly—here, you are inventing facts which would make your advice incomplete: you must acknowledge the gap in the facts and provide advice accordingly.

Returning to the facts of the scenario as actually given, where we know the advert specifies that the price is £5, it is *not* acceptable to discuss alternatives. In other words, in relation to the scenario as given, you should not write "However if the price had not been specified in the advert . . ." since on the facts it was. This is not speculation but rewriting the given facts.

It can be difficult to get the balance right in relation to speculation because you see the judges speculating in their judgments—it is where we get *obiter* from—but in a problem question answer you are not expected to give obiter. So deal with the facts as they are given. Speculate only in the event of a gap in the facts.

Adapting the facts of a well-known case

3.19 ▶ Your tutors may well set a question which uses facts of well-known cases in their invented scenario but with a few important material facts changed. Your identification of the material facts is going to be vital to make sure you do not get caught out by this. You would need, in this situation, to highlight the material facts which make your facts different from the facts of the case in question, so that you can then go on to argue that the ratio of the case is not binding.

Addition of a "compare and contrast" to the advice you are giving

3.20 ▶ Just as we've seen that you might be asked to compare and contrast on an essay question, you might be asked to do the same in a problem question. However, be alert that the *words* "compare and contrast" might not be used.

Two common ways in which a compare and contrast angle can be added to a problem question are as follows:

1. How would your answer differ if the facts were slightly different, for example: *Would it have made a difference if Zebedee had not been suffering from headaches?*
2. How would your answer differ if new legal reforms had been brought into force, for example: *Would it make a difference to your answer if the proposals in the Legal Reform Bill 2011 were in force?*

In both of these situations, you are asked to compare and contrast the facts as given, or the law as it stands, with the alternative facts given or the new law. In both cases, the question will have been asked for a reason—in other words, it is likely that there are significant differences for you to identify which would have an important effect on your answer. However, this is not an automatic rule: sometimes this *compare and contrast* would be set simply to test that you understand that in this particular instance, there would be no difference (as in the first question above).

SUMMARY OF CHAPTER 3

3.21 ▶
- Diagnosis of task is all about working out exactly what the question is asking you to do.
- A correct diagnosis is vital to tackling the question in the right way.
- In an essay question, a good starting point is to put the title in the form of a question, and then work on breaking this down into sub-questions.
- In a problem question, you need to identify the material facts and from these work on a series of legal questions or issues.
- The issues you identify for discussion in a problem question form the I of IRAC (Issue, Rule, Application, Conclusion), a tool or technique you can use to tackle legal problems successfully;
- By framing your issues as question you can see what research you need to carry out and it is helpful to put these questions in a grid format.
- You need to keep your diagnosis under review as you learn more about the subject area.

▶ 4
Planning and carrying out your research

WHAT IS THE PURPOSE OF THIS CHAPTER?

Once you have diagnosed your task, and worked out what you need to do to complete your assignment, the next stage is to carry out a review of your existing materials. Completing out this exercise, together with the questions you have posed in your diagnosis, will help you define the scope of the research which you need to do. Remember that you must *not* assume that you can complete your assignment from your existing materials: you will always need to carry out some element of additional research.

▶ **4.1**

Finding relevant cases, books and articles for your research can be a challenge and this chapter will help you do the following things:

- Review the materials which you already have at your disposal and consider how these will help you write your assignment.
- Understand the difference between the various types of source material and how you can use each type (use of evidence in your writing is also considered further in Chapter 5).
- Identify gaps in your research material, find new sources, and evaluate the quality and relevance of what you find (your tutors will have helped you with this stage when providing you with recommended reading, but it is a vital stage when you are searching yourself).

By the end of this chapter you should:

- understand the importance of planning your research;
- understand the importance of organising your sources;
- be beginning to develop ways of logging/recording your research; and
- be considering the best way for you to organise your information and thoughts before starting to write.

HOW DO I REVIEW MY MATERIALS?

By the time you begin to carry out your materials review, you should already have made your diagnosis of the task you have been set. As you know, you have to keep this under review as you

▶ **4.2**

learn more about the topic and improve your understanding, so that you can pick up any additional nuances to the question which passed you by at the first stage. However, to get to this improved understanding, you have to carry out some research and before you do that, you should review your existing materials on this topic.

To carry out your materials review, gather together all the material you have relating to the subject matter of the assignment you have been set. This is likely to consist of all or some of the following: notes made in a lecture, notes made from your textbook in preparation for a lecture, tutorial or seminar, notes made during the tutorial or seminar, copies of articles or further reading recommended by your lecturer or tutor (perhaps with your own notes on them, or maybe highlighted photocopies) and a reading list specific to this assignment. You may find that (particularly at the later stages of your degree) you are set assignments on topics which have not been covered in taught classes, so that you are expected to do more independent research yourself.

> **TIPS** • *Check any coursework guidance you have been given—where you have been given a reading list, see whether the list is meant to be exhaustive or just designed to get you started. If there is no guidance on this point, then use your common sense and compare the reading list to your diagnosis. A recommendation with a couple of textbooks on it is likely to be meant as a starting point, whereas a tutor who gives you a list with 40 lengthy articles on it may well be expecting you to narrow this down to a relevant selection.*

This can be daunting, but think of your essay preparation as a fitness campaign. Imagine you are trying to improve your fitness by replacing some of your daily bus journey home from university with a walk. The bus part of the journey is the guidance you get from your tutor about your assignment, and the walking part of the journey is the research you do independently. When you first start, you go most of the way on the bus and just get off a stop or two before home, but as you get fitter (i.e. as you progress with your studies and get better at researching and writing your assignments) you get off the bus at an earlier and earlier stop. You can imagine that if you were really trying to get fit then by the end of your fitness drive you could walk the whole way. In these terms your materials review is working out how far along the bus route home you have got with the materials you have already amassed.

Note that your purpose here is *not* to amass a huge pile of paper and therefore feel proud of yourself but rather to gauge how much and what you need to do in terms of the next step of your writing, which is the *research* stage. It may give you a sense of having got on with your essay, but this is a false sense, because all you have done is compile information, when the marks are available for what you *do* with the information and not how much you have! By the end of your diagnosis of task, you should have posed a number of questions to yourself which you need to research in order to tackle the question you have been set. So, review the materials you have *critically* in order to work out what gaps you have and work out a strategy to tackle those gaps. This will involve a combination of two different levels of reading:

1. General reading—which help you gain an understanding of the topic and help you hone your diagnosis of task and therefore your assignment plan.
2. Particular reading—once you have carried out the general research so that you understand the topic, you are in a position to review your diagnosis from a more informed position (we look at reading critically later in this chapter). At this stage

you will be able to fine-tune your diagnosis, to identify further specific questions which you need to address, and therefore by implication, more specific sources which you need to find. The provision of a suggested reading list will help you with this—the specific sources you need (probably articles) may be on it— but keeping your diagnosis under review is nevertheless vital in helping you work this out for yourself in relation to any given question.

> **TIPS •** *Before you go any further, ask yourself: how good is my general understanding of this topic already? This will help you get the balance right between general sources and specific sources.*

HOW CAN I FIND RELEVANT FURTHER READING?

We don't have scope within this text to provide detailed advice on legal research skills.[1]   ▶ **4.3** However, here are a few basic tips:

- Follow any advice you have been given, in a student handbook or guidance pack, as to how to get the best from your university's law library. Most universities have a specialist law librarian and there is likely to be some formal class contact—perhaps a demonstration in a lecture theatre or smaller workshops in computer labs, or a combination of both—as part of your induction or as part of a skills or research methods course. It can be tempting for busy students not to give research training the priority it deserves, dismissing it as "not something we get assessed on". This is completely missing the point—research training is a skill which underpins *all* your assignments, so it is vital you make the most of any training or advice you are offered. You are assessed on your ability to research every time you submit an assignment.
- Learn to use both paper and electronic sources. Electronic sources are easier to access, as you don't have to trek to the library and you can download them to read later if you like, but there will be various materials which are available only in print form which you will also need to be familiar with.
- Start from the right place: a quality resource. Steer clear of Google, at least until you have more confidence in how to evaluate sources for quality and relevance (see below). These days, we are used to thinking of Google or other similar search engines as the quick way to find the answer to almost anything, but remember that in academic work, you are not looking for a quick answer to a factual question—you are presenting an argument based on evidence. Use of Google Scholar or similar filters will help to some extent, but it is much better to utilise the specialist legal databases your university has paid vast licence fees to bring you, as you are immediately then ensuring some measure of quality (academic articles go through a review process before they are published; anyone can put anything on the worldwide web).

> **TIPS •** *Searching on Google for the answers to assignment questions is the internet equivalent of wandering up to a random person at a bus stop and asking them to explain Contract Law to you, in preference to going along to your Contract Law lecture.*

---

[1]   See John Knowles, *Effective Legal Research* (3rd edn, Sweet & Maxwell 2012) for a detailed discussion.

- Make sure your sources cover the right legal jurisdiction—in other words if you are writing an assignment on English law, make sure your sources relate to English law. As more materials become available electronically it is easy to make a mistake here and find yourself reading an Australian judgment avidly without realising its jurisdiction.
- Learn more about research terms and how to link them, for example by use of what are called Boolean search terms. Again, you will find more detail on this in a legal research text but there is a basic summary below.

Boolean search terms

4.4 ▶ These are words and characters which can help you search the web more effectively by allowing you to specify which words and letters are included in or excluded from the search. These searches are carried out using linking words or *operators*, such as AND, OR, NOT, which determine how the search terms are treated.

1. If you use AND between search terms then this means that both terms must appear somewhere in the entry text.

   > A Boolean search for legal AND writing is a narrow search that will find entries containing both the words legal and writing, thus avoiding any legal material which is unrelated to writing, and material related to writing which is not legal.

2. Using OR between two or more search terms means that either or both of the terms can appear in the entry text.

   > A Boolean search for legal OR writing is a much wider search and will find entries containing either or both of these search terms. (You might be reading all day!)

3. Using NOT before a search term will mean that that term must not appear anywhere in the entry text.

   > A Boolean search for legal AND NOT writing is a slightly narrower search that will find entries containing the word legal, but will exclude any entries which contain the word writing, even if they do mention legal.

4. It is also possible to use truncation or wildcards when searching. For example: the asterisk symbol (*) can be used as a wildcard, taking the place of several unspecified characters. This allows you to broaden a search.

   > A search on leg* will enable you to find material including legal and legality (as well as, potentially, material on legumes and legwarmers).

> **TIPS** • *If your initial search generates a lot of results, don't just start reading them one by one: narrow your search down before proceeding.*

You can only use the wildcard symbol to represent letters at the end of a word, not the beginning.

However you choose to conduct your search, the vital thing is that your search terms are related to your diagnosis of what the question is asking for. A general search on "consideration" or "negligence" will generate a lot of material and you will get so bogged down that you will find it hard to start your writing. Add additional search terms relevant to your diagnosis to narrow your search.

HOW DO I RATE WHAT I FIND?

This will be a task proportional to the effectiveness of your search techniques: for example, a search in the Legal Journals Index section of Westlaw using key search terms is going to produce a narrower field than typing random words from the assignment title into Google, and those sources which are generated are much more likely to be of good quality. So, improving your search technique is the key here, as we've already explained. ▶ 4.5

Always keep in mind the *purpose* for which you are compiling resources. You want *quality* sources which are *relevant* to the question. We have also seen that you will need some sort of balance between general and specific sources, depending on how good your general under-standing of the topic already is, and you will need sufficient *coverage* to meet the requirement of your diagnosis (i.e. to help you answer the questions you have posed), which is something you will have addressed in your materials review.

Essentially this is a form of quality control where you are filtering out sources which are not going to help you either because they are not quality materials or because they are not relevant to the question. When you get more confident about using sources, you will carry out this filtering stage as a matter of course, particularly in respect of quality, and will spend more time checking for relevance. However, for the time being we will look at both issues, starting with quality.

How to rate the *quality* of a source
Rate your proposed source against the following questions: ▶ 4.6

1. *Where did you get it?* Is it published by some reputable source, or it is just the views of someone on the internet? Of course there are quality sources available on the internet, but you have to be cautious. Similarly be cautious with newspapers: tabloid newspapers (or what used to be called tabloid newspapers, like the *Sun*, the *Daily Mirror* and the *Daily Mail*) should *not* be used as a source (unless your assignment is on misrepresentation of the law in the tabloid press or similar); even quality papers like *The Times* and *The Guardian* have a reputation for some degree of political bias which you should bear in mind, although it should not prevent you from using them as a source where appropriate.
2. *Who wrote it?* Is it someone you would expect to have knowledge and understand-ing of the issues involved, for example a legal academic, practitioner or judge? Is the author even named? Be careful with anonymous pieces unless you are confident of the source, such as the editorial of a quality newspaper. Is the author someone who might be biased or have an axe to grind, for example, a member of a pressure group or an aggrieved claimant?

Note that being a reputable author in a reputable journal does not mean that the article will automatically be good, but answering these questions is a vital first step in evaluating material: if the quality looks suspect you will be wasting your time even reading it. Once you have done a quick quality check, then the second part of the filtering stage is to check for relevance.

How to rate the *relevance* of a source

4.7 ▶ It is really important to make sure that when carrying out your research, you remain focused on the specific issues you need, rather than becoming side-tracked by information which is only of vague relevance to the question you have been set. Think of this as being a sifting process: you need to sift out the irrelevant or less relevant material. You cannot possibly read everything, so you will need to make selections. If you are working from a specific reading list, then your tutor has already carried out this part of the exercise for you. If not, you will have to learn to do it yourself. When checking for relevance you should always have the assignment brief and your diagnosis research questions in front of you. Assess relevance against these by

- checking the title of books;
- checking the contents and/or index pages of books;
- reading the abstract or summary provided at the start of articles;
- scanning headings of chapters or sections.

As you make these decisions during the research phase, keep in mind the length of the piece you have been asked to write. Reading eight full-length books and six articles will yield much more than you could utilise in one 2,000-word piece of coursework as well being too ambitious in terms of the amount of time it will take.

TIPS • *Rate the relevance of the material with reference to your diagnosis, and remember that you determine whether to include some general material to improve your basic grasp of the topic by reference to your materials review.*

Finally, once you've amassed your materials, revisit your diagnosis. Have you got sources to help you answer each question you have posed? If not, then carry out further searches to find the gaps. You are now ready to begin reading in more depth, but remember to keep reflecting as you do so on whether you need to fine-tune your initial diagnosis.

HOW DO I KNOW THAT I'M NOT MISSING SOMETHING?

4.8 ▶ By definition, you will be missing a lot. This is an entirely good thing, because you cannot possibly read everything there is on a particular topic. Having bundles of photocopied sheets or printouts may well have a "security blanket" effect and will have certainly have cost you a lot but it will not help you write effectively. If you have been honest and reflective about your general level of understanding so that your diagnosis is accurate, and then by use of effective techniques you have designed searches to answer the questions you posed in your diagnosis, then you should be confident that all you have missed out on are irrelevancies, poor quality materials and wasting your own time.

Before you start your research phase, set yourself a time-limit when you will stop looking for further materials. Again, this is a matter of confidence—it is tempting to carry on to make sure you don't miss anything. But if you think this way, you are still falling into the trap of thinking

that you are being assessed solely on your ability to find information. In other words, this assumes that the research phase
is some kind of treasure hunt in which lucky students (or those
which spend the longest time searching) are rewarded.

> **TIPS •** *Don't adopt a "just in case" attitude to your reading by reading something on the off-chance it may contain something useful. This is simply putting off making an effective diagnosis of what is relevant to your assignment.*

This is not the case. The answer is not hidden in some
remote part of the library waiting to be liberated; to the
extent that an answer can be said to exist, it comes from
what you do with the material. You have to process the
information from your different sources and utilise it to form arguments which answer the
question set and thereby demonstrate your knowledge and understanding.

Imagine setting out to cook a gourmet dinner to impress a new girlfriend or boy-
friend. The length of time you spend merely buying the ingredients is no guarantee
whatsoever of the quality of the final meal. The quality of the ingredients you choose is
obviously going to be a factor, but it is the recipe and the cooking skills which really make
the difference.

HOW DO I RECORD WHAT I FIND?

As you will learn in Chapter 5, it is really important to acknowledge where you use the work ▶ **4.9**
of others as part of your own argument. It's therefore vital that you keep records of key
information of the sources you find so that you can reference them accurately later. There is
nothing more irritating than getting to the finishing stage of the assignment and having to
remove a point because a frantic search through all the material you collated for your
assignment does not enable you to locate the reference. On the other hand, risking leaving
the point in but unattributed risks plagiarism as we explain in a later chapter. Therefore
keeping notes at this stage will save both time and possibly your sanity. For cases make sure
you record the case name, citation and court plus the specific page or paragraph number of
any quotation. For books record the author/editor, title, edition number (if any), publisher
and year of publication plus again the specific page number of any quotation. For journal
articles the author, title of the article, name of the journal, the year, volume/issue and page.
For internet sources, then as far as possible the author and title, the name of the website,
the URL and the date you accessed it. You may wish to consider as part of your note-making
(see below) including a summary of the main topic of the source and its relevance to your
assignment.

HOW CAN I READ EFFECTIVELY?

You should now have, as well as your original material some additional reading material which ▶ **4.10**
you are confident is both of sufficient quality and relevance to your assignment. Next you need
to work on using this effectively in your work, the first step of which will be to read it more
thoroughly.

Reading quality material is an essential part of improving your writing skills. It will familiarise you with what good writing is like; you will begin to absorb its qualities and reproduce
them in your own work.

4.11 ▶ However, reading legal material can be a time-consuming business. Generally speaking, the old adage "practice makes perfect" is true here. The more reading you do, the better you will become at it. In order to develop your skills in reading effectively there are a number of techniques you can adopt.

> **TIPS** • *If you find yourself checking out a lot of sources which turn out to be irrelevant, then reflect on your search techniques— revisit any guidance you've received on this and if necessary seek further help from a research methods text or the law librarian on narrowing your search.*

You will already be aware that you will need to read a variety of different sources as part of your studies. Here are some examples:

4.12 ▶
> Textbooks
> Law reports
> Statutes/statutory instruments
> Journal articles
> Dictionaries
> Websites
> RSS Feeds, updater services

4.13 ▶ Some of the issues that our students have commented on when reading legal material are as follows:

- Having to re-read pages as the words don't seem to go in the first or even the second time (this might be especially true when you first start to read law books).
- That reading legal material takes too long.
- Not "getting it"!
- Finding the language used too complex.
- Not being sure what the point of making notes is, how many to take and of what.

Do these seem familiar? Here are our five top tips to help you improve the effectiveness of your reading:

1. Prioritise

You will need to make decisions about what you will read and when. Prioritise the key cases or materials and rank them so you can tackle them in order of importance. To do this, try the following ideas:

(a) Use your diagnosis of task: which are the most relevant resources to your diagnosis? Which are going to be helpful to you in getting a general understanding of the topic? (Read these first because the better you understand the topic, the easier it is to make informed decisions about which of the more specific resources are the most relevant to the particular question you've been set.)

(b) Review your lecture notes: picking up hints in lectures as to what sources are the most significant on any topic is vital.

(c) Look at reading lists for tutorials as well: these are likely to indicate key cases or materials for that topic, even if they do not give guidance specific to the assignment title (and of course this is essential when you are reading in order to help your revision for an exam).

(d) What part of the textbook have you been referred to on this topic? If you haven't been specifically referred to a particular section, then don't assume it means you don't have to read the textbook: use your initiative! Look at the chapter headings and/or the index to work out which parts to read. The author will have done his or her prioritising too, and you can compare this with your own ideas and the indications from lectures and reading lists.

(e) Ask! Seek clarification from your tutor if you're not sure, but remember your tutors expect you to try and find out information for yourself first. Asking which the most important case is when it has been clearly highlighted in a handout or a lecture is a waste of both yours and your tutor's time. Additionally, you may find your tutor is unwilling to give you much extra assistance with the subject matter of a piece of assessed work, because it is important that all students are treated fairly.

2. Don't just make copies of things

When you are given a reading list, it can be a satisfactory feeling spending an hour in the library on the photocopier or alternatively searching electronically and printing materials out, and think that you "got" everything. A common mistake is therefore to be lulled into a false sense of security that sticking something in your file somehow means you have absorbed the material. Of course it doesn't—you just have a full file!

3. Get right to the end

When we learn to read we are conditioned to read in sequence from the beginning—skipping to the end would "spoil" it. The problem with this is that when time is precious, you end up making notes only on the first page or two of the material. If you find it difficult to get to the end, there are several possible explanations. Whatever it is you are reading might be pretty boring or it might be that you are spending too much time agonising over the detail instead of being more selective. It is more important to get all the way through the key material, even if it is not in quite as much depth as you would like, than making copious notes on only the first page of a couple of items. Learn to skim read—but relate this to the decisions you made about what was the most important. Most of all get right through it! It is better to skim read paragraphs and get some idea of the relevant arguments than to give up. Vital conclusions are likely to be towards the end. Try the following techniques:

(a) Get the idea that looking at the end "spoils the story" right out of your head in university studies. We are not story-telling here; we're drawing reasoned conclusions on the basis of evidence. Cut to the chase and look at the conclusion first. Doing this will help you establish how much of your time the material is worth. Do the conclusions the author draws add to your understanding of the particular issues you're investigating? If so, then go back to the beginning and have a look at the opening sentences of the paragraphs—these should help you isolate the really important points and work out which paragraphs you need to spend your time on. Don't assume that important points will necessarily be near the beginning of the material.

(b) You need to have a clear purpose and read to that purpose: *why* are you reading any particular material? Are you trying to answer a particular question you've been set or advise a particular client? You will not want to use the same reading technique you'd use for reading the latest Booker Prize winner or Harry Potter. Look for key points and skip over material which is not relevant.

(c) Set a time target to complete outline notes, and stick to it.

4. Look for signposts

Good writers indicate the direction of their arguments by using "signpost" words such as "additionally", "further", "however", "in contrast". Recognising these words helps you skim or speed read because you can identify when the writer is continuing to advance an argument, and when the writer is changing tack. (This is also something to bear in mind when you start writing, as you can use signposts effectively yourself.)

ACTIVITY 4.1

4.14 ▶ Match the following terms to the meaning intended by the author.

1 Additionally	A This example is the opposite of what I've previously explored
2 Further	B I am extending my argument
3 In contrast	C I am adding further examples to my argument
4 However	D I'm now going to argue a different angle to the same argument
5 Alternatively	E I'm now going to present a different point of view

Activity feedback—here are our thoughts:

1–C, 2–B, 3–A, 4–E, 5–D. These are to some extent a matter of personal style, so don't worry if your judgment was different on the distinction between "additionally" and "further" as long as you got the essential point that they both indicate a *continuation* of the same argument— by means of further views, examples, or evidence. Likewise, "in contrast", "alternatively" and "however" all indicate that the author is now offering an opposite or conflicting perspective. You may not have chosen exactly the same nuance of meaning as we did but the main thing is that you understand that all these terms point to a shift in direction.

We'll return to this in Chapter 6, as signposts are important in your writing as well as in your reading.

5. Don't just read things

Most people do not learn effectively simply by reading material through in detail—once you have made your decision about which parts of which material you need to prioritise, then tackle them either by highlighting or underlining points (on your own copies only, of course!) or making separate brief notes. You may find it helpful to write down the purpose you've identified for your reading at the top of the page to help you stay focused. There are further suggestions for making effective notes and recording what you've read below.

HOW CAN I IMPROVE MY NOTE-MAKING?

Some of our students find the idea of making notes daunting: they don't know why, how or when they should make notes. Notes can take many forms—scribbles, line drawings, bulleted lists, notes on index cards, spider diagrams and so on. It is important to remember that the goal in making notes is to help you utilise the information later, so whatever technique you currently use for your notemaking, use this section to reflect on whether you can improve on it. If you are new to university study then you are likely to find that the amount of note-making which is needed at university level is significantly more than you have been used to—again, this is part of the process of adapting to independent study.

▶ **4.15**

> **TIPS** • *If your experience of making notes is that you end up with a lot of paper but no idea how to incorporate it into your assignment then you need to review your approach: notes should help you rather than hinder you.*

The purpose of note-making

The primary reason for making notes is to help you to remember.
Other reasons include:

▶ **4.16**

- To help you understand—you can go back over your notes to check your knowledge and understanding.
- To make connections between differing ideas, themes and debates.
- To act as a record of your reading/research.
- To reduce large amounts of material into more manageable chunks.

How to practise note-making

We're going to divide this into two steps—the first is making general notes on a reading and the second is making more focused notes.

▶ **4.17**

1. General reading

Find a piece of writing that you need to read for an assignment. Don't overwhelm yourself by picking something complex for the purposes of this exercise—aim to pick something more straightforward. You are the best judge of what is manageable for you.

Then break the piece into definable "chunks" of text, which might be sections or paragraphs. Read to the end of the first one. When you finish reading that chunk, write down in your own words one sentence which sums up the content. Then repeat this for each successive chunk until you have reached the end of the text.

You may find this hard to do—especially if you are new to reading academic texts—but persevering with this method will really help you to tackle complex texts in an organised way. You will end up with a précis, or brief summary, of the entire text. This will not necessarily be enough to inform the writing of your assignment but will give you a clear sense of the overall content, which in turn provides the basis for a more detailed, focused reading of the same text and for taking helpful and informative notes on the exact areas most relevant to your assignment. You won't have to do this task every time you take notes. Once you have mastered the skill of making effective notes from focused reading (see below) then this generalised approach to reading may not be needed.

2. Focused reading

A sheet of paper with a vertical line drawn down it about one third of the way across can be used to make more in-depth notes. Look back over the same text you used for the previous activity and use the space to the right hand side of the line to set out these new notes. Remember what you are trying to do this time is to make a compact and correct record of the information you have read. You might choose to include your own comments in the space to the left-hand side of the line by way of brief notes or sub-headings but the important thing is that your notes reflect what you have read and the views contained within those texts.

Some people make so many notes that they are soon drowning in paper and can't work out which to use when it comes to sitting down and doing the writing. This is usually caused by two common errors when note-making. Either you have written down too much of the original text or you haven't been discriminating enough when it comes to choosing topics to take notes on. To fix these problems you need to be more selective. This is the first step in only using the *relevant* in your writing. You need to think more and write less. Interrogate the text so it gives up what you need. Be ruthless—less descriptive and more analytical. In addition, you must stay focused on the purpose you are reading for. For example, if it is for an assignment, write out the question on a piece of paper and pin it up over your desk when you are reading. It should stay clearly in your mind and this may help you to stick to the directly relevant material when note-making.

Tips for note-making

4.18 ❱

- Before you start, make a note of the title, author, and other essential information. You will need these when referencing your work later.
- Write clearly, leaving spaces between each note/comment, and write on only one side of the page.
- Consider using coloured pens to help discriminate between points/issues.
- Don't try to write complete sentences. You will find that as you progress through your studies you will devise relevant legal abbreviations that will help you to be brief and concise in your note-making. For example AC: for Appeal Cases, SC for Supreme Court, CA for Court of Appeal and LQR for *Law Quarterly Review*. As well as these recognised abbreviations you will develop your own shorthand as you go through your course which will help your note-taking, for example Ct for court, Cl for claimant, D for defendant, J for judgment and so on.
- Devise a logical layout. Headings, sub-headings and numbering help you to take in the information and to remember it when needed.

> **TIPS** • *Keep a "key" to your abbreviations—it's no good if you suddenly think of an abbreviation at the start of your note-making and go on to use it extensively if when you come to review your notes you have no idea what it means!*

Here's an example of notes taken from Chapter 18 of *Davies on Contract*.[2]

Davies on Contract—10th edition Upex and Bennett

Chapter 18 Breach:	"A br of c occurs where a pty fails to perform or evinces an intention not to perform, one or more of the obligations laid upon him by the contract".
Forms of breach	e.g. *actual* (non-performance or defective performance or non-truth of a statement that is a term of the c) or *anticipatory* i.e. occurs before the date of performance (explicit and implicit)
Effects of breach	can sue for damages. Plus may be extra right to treat yourself as discharged if you wish NB NOT rescind see *Johnson v Agnew* (1980) HL so c still valid.
Anticipatory breach	Used to b: always = contract discharged BUT see *Decro-Wall* (1971) CA = same test as for actual breach . . . *innocent pty must act so as to make plain that he claims to treat the contract as at an end*.

(See also: *Frost v Knight* (1872) on repudiatory breach and *The Mihalis Angelos* (1971) CA)

Alternatives to linear notes

Notes do not just have to be in a linear form. For example, if you are a visual learner, you may prefer to utilise a spider diagram or mind map to set out your notes. Please see the next page for a spider diagram we prepared on the topic of negligence in Tort giving a broad overview of the topic.

▶ **4.19**

You may find it helpful to use a combination of linear and spider diagram notes—perhaps a spider diagram to help you get an overall sense of the text, or for revision notes, but with linear notes for closer analytical reading.

Other alternatives to linear notes include underlining or highlighting a text (as long as it is not a library copy!) or flow diagrams. If you have yet to find an approach to note-making that works for you, now is the time to try out some alternatives.

---

2   R. Upex and G. Bennett, *Davies on Contracts* (10th edn, Sweet & Maxwell 2008).

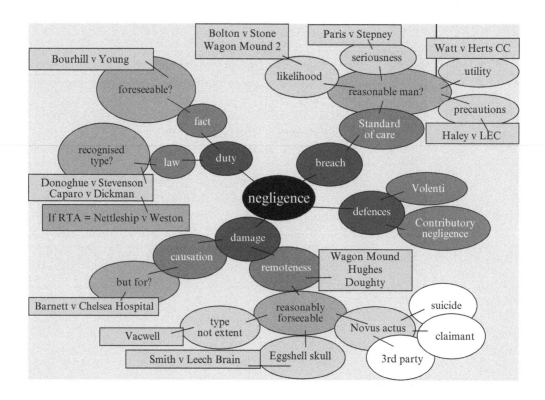

Organising your sources

4.20 ▶ In order to ensure you can keep track of your notes as you move from researching your assignment into planning the writing, you need to devise a system for summarising and recording your sources.

One possible approach to summarising that you could adopt is a *note card* system. In this approach each sentence, idea or quote from a judgment that you find in your sources is paraphrased in your own words and written down, in brief note form.

See for example:

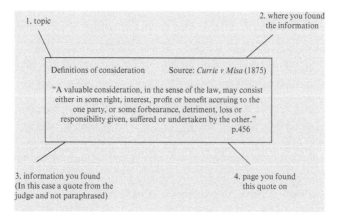

1. The *card topic* is the title or name of the card. Here it is "Definitions of consideration" but it could be "Cases on mistake" or "Comment on privity". What you are trying to do when you give a piece of information a title or topic name is to categorise it. This will help you focus on the relevant aspects.

2. The *source title* tells you where this piece of information came from. Here it is a case but it could be a statute, textbook or article, for example. Here we have named the case but if you are using a wide range of secondary sources then you might consider using a numbering system instead. So instead of writing the title out on each card when you use information from it, you simply list all your sources on a separate sheet of paper. Number your sources here and then use those numbers on your card to identify which source provided the fact/comment/quote.

Example Source List

1. *Davies on Contract*: Upex & Bennett
2. *The Law of Contract*: J. C. Smith
3. *Smith & Thomas: A Casebook on Contract*: J. C. Smith
4. *Exclusion Clauses and Unfair Contract Terms*: Richard Lawson
5. *Damages for Breach of Contract*: Jill Poole
6. *Contract Law*: Anne Ruff.

Remember: this is not a complete works, cited bibliography or reference page. You will need to add the publication information and use the correct citation form when referencing your actual answer.

3. This is the *paraphrased information* or brief quotation that you discovered in your research. You might actually find it easier to do this summarising while you are making notes from your research. What should be clear is that if you paraphrase reliably at this early stage then you run a lower risk of plagiarising someone else's work by chance and being penalised because of an accident.

4. Being accurate with the precise location (*page/paragraph numbers*) of your item of information, fact or quotation is obviously very important as this will help you to find the correct citations which you will need when starting to reference your work correctly. So, you are keeping track of all your sources to save time later and to avoid any charge of plagiarism. "EndNote" is a software package which helps you to manage your sources by creating bibliographies for your work automatically. Many universities have site licenses for EndNote and training may also be available through the library. It is worth familiarising yourself with this package, if it's available, as early on in your university career as possible. The time spent now (before you have any assignments to submit) will pay dividends as a deadline fast approaches. If you do not have access to EndNote, create a document on your computer to manage your references instead. (See Chapters 5 and 8 for more information on referencing and creating a bibliography.)

As you are reading and making notes from your sources, you must also ensure, as well as just summarising information, that you carry out a critical evaluation of your sources in order to make use of them in your own arguments later. This is considered in the next section.

HOW CAN I READ CRITICALLY?

4.21 ▶ Once you have identified quality, relevant materials, you read these in more depth in order to utilise the ideas (properly acknowledged and referenced of course) in your own work. Do not use your sources simply as a source of information, by accepting the facts and arguments within them at face value and replicating them in your own work. This will tend to result in tutor comments on your writing like "too descriptive" or "insufficient analysis". In a critical evaluation you are not simply summarising the position of the writer, but going on to identify strengths and weaknesses in the arguments and positions adopted. You can then begin to develop a much more sophisticated writing style in which you compare the arguments and positions of different writers and make judgments about the material. Essentially, you are moving from saying "A says X" and "B says Y" into "A says X, but this position can be criticised as illogical, and incompatible with Y, the view put forward by B, which is a stronger argument, as it reflects . . ." and so on. There is more on how to construct a logical argument in Chapter 5. Here we discuss the purpose of reading critically and how to do it.

The purpose of critical reading is to form judgments about what you are reading so you can utilise the material effectively as part of your own work (with appropriate acknowledgement). Basically, this means taking a questioning approach to what you read. Being *critical*, in an academic sense, is not just about being negative: essentially you are interrogating the material and evaluating its strengths and weaknesses. By developing your skills in this area, you will also develop your ability to evaluate your *own* work.

ACTIVITY 4.2

4.22 ▶ The purpose of this activity is to test what you understand by critical assessment or critical evaluation. What sort of questions would you ask yourself if you were critically evaluating an article or text?

If it helps, think about something about which you have to make critical judgments in your work or home life. How do you decide if a TV programme is any good? How do you judge whether your football team played well at the weekend?

You won't use the same criteria for legal materials, but it may help you to think about how to develop a critical *attitude*. It may help you to think of this as "marking" the material you are reading. If there are a number of good points, then you will want to use these, perhaps by using a quotation or paraphrase. But be ready to spot any weaknesses in the arguments as well, so that you can make an appropriate judgment about whether the author's conclusions are valid. This is the same process that your tutors will go through when they look at your assignment, looking for the strengths and weaknesses.

Write down three questions you could pose yourself about the material you read, which you think would help you *critically evaluate* it. Your questions should be capable of acknowledging strengths as well as weaknesses (remember that critical assessment in this sense does not just mean finding things wrong with the piece you are reading). You may find it helpful to reflect back to the exercise in Chapter 1 where you considered what makes a good piece of writing.

Activity feedback—here are our thoughts:
Paul and Elder suggest a number of different questions which you could pose in order to critically evaluate an article or text. The following questions are loosely based on Paul and Elder's suggestions, but you may wish to look at their comments in full for further ideas.[3]

- Why do you think the author wrote this material?
- What is the key question the author is trying to answer in this article or text?
- What is the author's conclusion?
- What evidence is advanced to support the conclusion?
- Does the author make any assumptions? If so, what are they?
- What is the opposite point of view from the one the author is advancing, and do you know of anything from your reading which supports this opposite point of view? Has the author acknowledged the opposite point of view?

Now we want you to consider what types of judgment should form part of a critical evaluation.

ACTIVITY 4.3

Consider the following statements and judge whether each could form part of academic criticism of a piece of writing:

▶ **4.23**

Statement	Possible academic criticism?—yes or no
A. There is little or no evidence presented	
B. The argument is logical	
C. The piece is mainly descriptive	
D. The piece is largely anecdotal	
E. There are spelling and grammatical errors	
F. The piece is from a reputable source	
G. The author is well-respected in the field	
H. The piece is boring	
I. The print is too small	
J. The author seems to have an axe to grind	
K. The author of the piece is not identified	
L. The piece uses emotive language	

---

[3]   R. Paul and L. Elder, *The Miniature Guide to Critical Thinking* (4th edn, Dillon Beach: Foundation for Critical Thinking 2004).

M. I do not agree with the writer
N. Unjustified assumptions are made
O. The piece is factually accurate
P. The piece challenges the established thinking in the field
Q. The piece is vague in its conclusions

Activity feedback—here are our thoughts:

A. There is little or no evidence presented—yes: looking at the quality of evidence is a vital part of critical assessment.

B. The argument is logical—yes: although it is a favourable comment (which might lead some to conclude that it is not critical) analysing the logic of an argument is a vital part of critical assessment.

C. The piece is mainly descriptive—yes: this is basically saying that there is not enough analysis in the piece.

D. The piece is largely anecdotal—yes: again this is criticising the text for being lacking in evidence, or the right kind of evidence to justify its conclusions.

E. There are spelling and grammatical errors—this is probably a "maybe" as it might indicate that there has been no editing process and that therefore the quality of the source might be questionable. However, it isn't something you would actually use as a critique in an essay.

F. The piece is from a reputable source—yes: this would tend to add weight, but does not automatically guarantee its quality.

G. The author is well-respected in the field—yes: as above.

H. The piece is boring—no: this is just opinion and not very constructive at that!

I. The print is too small—no: this is nothing to do with the quality of the piece as an academic authority.

J. The author seems to have an axe to grind—yes and no: noting the possible bias is a relevant issue but the informal phrase "axe to grind" should not be used to express it. Bias is a better word.

K. The author of the piece is not identified—yes, potentially, if it is some random piece off the internet, but there are some situations in which you would not expect an author to be identified, for example a newspaper editorial.

L. The piece uses emotive language—yes: this may indicate an overly journalistic approach rather than an academic approach. Why is the author relying on emotion rather than logic to sway the audience? Is it because there are faults in the logic or evidence being presented?

M. I do not agree with the writer—another yes and no: you can certainly be critical of the author's position, but you would need to express this in objective terms and with supporting evidence ("The author's position can be criticised because . . ."). You should not use the statement in the form given here.

N. Unjustified assumptions are made—yes: identifying where the author is leaping to conclusions is an important part of critical analysis.

O. The piece is factually accurate—yes: assessing the accuracy is an important starting point in critical analysis.

P. The piece challenges the established thinking in the field—yes: this is higher level critical analysis because it involves having an understanding of the literature on an area *and* being able to draw parallels between the arguments of different authors on the same subject.

Q. The piece is vague in its conclusions—yes: if the piece is not specific in what it is saying, why is this? Is it because the author has failed to make a case by appropriate use of evidence?

There is more about logic in relation to your own writing in Chapter 5—as we have seen before, the skills needed for reading are very closely linked to the skills needed for writing.

SUMMARY OF CHAPTER 4

- Reviewing your existing materials will enable you to plan the research you need to do to answer the questions you have posed as part of your diagnosis.
- You should ensure that the materials you read are good quality and relevant.
- Effective reading is a vital component of good research.
- Making useful notes of the material will be key to utilising them effectively in your writing
- Interrogating your reading will help with becoming more "critical".

▶ 4.24

▶ 5
How to use your materials in the writing process

WHAT IS THE PURPOSE OF THIS CHAPTER?

5.1 ▶ The purpose of this chapter is to show you how to use the material you have found and read in constructing your own arguments. This is a particularly challenging part of the writing process, because here you really start to *think* about what your answer is going to be like; in other words, this is the point at which you start forming conclusions about the questions you have posed yourself, drawing on the research you have carried out.

> **TIPS •** *What is said in this chapter about logical argument in your writing is equally applicable to the sources you read—using the same techniques will help you to evaluate your sources as well as improve your own writing.*

Your goal is to *utilise the sources* you have read as *evidence* to help you *answer the question*, whilst fully *acknowledging* where you have drawn on the views of others by appropriate *referencing*.

More specifically, by working through this chapter you will learn:

- what makes a good argument and the concept of logical progression of ideas;
- how to use evidence to support the assertions you make;
- how to draw on your reading to compare, contrast and synthesise the ideas of others;
- how to paraphrase and quote the arguments of others in support of your own conclusions; and
- how to acknowledge the sources you have used through appropriate referencing and so avoid the academic offence of plagiarism.

5.2 ▶ It might be helpful, before we go any further, to outline two common student mistakes in relation to using research material in the writing process:

1. *Failing to acknowledge your sources in the mistaken belief that you will get more marks if you can fool your tutors into thinking you thought of all this yourself.* This is a mistake for two reasons—first (and most obviously), this is *plagiarism* (there is much more detail about this later in the chapter). Secondly, it shows you do not understand what academic work is about, which is essentially using other materials and analysing them. The starting point is the primary source (e.g. a case); a writer writes

about the source, thereby making a secondary source. The next person comes along and looks at the primary source *and* the secondary source, and produces a further secondary source. Somewhere later in the chain, you come along and look at the primary source and all the various secondary sources you have found and draw on them to produce your own work on the subject (in the context of your particular question).

It may help you to get your head round this to think of these other secondary sources becoming something a little like "precedents" in a case. Just as you cannot walk into court and say "I think the law on this area should be as follows . . ."—you need evidence in the form of existing precedents—existing academic views on a topic are *evidence* on which you base your own arguments.

Therefore there is nothing to gain by pretending that the views of others are actually your own, but much to gain by showing (through appropriate acknowledgement) that you can work with these materials: in doing this you are working *academically*, as the previous writers on the topic have done.

2. *Production of an essay which is a collection of quotes or a collection of paragraphs merely describing the academic views which have emerged from your reading*. These may be linked together something like "Smith says . . . And Khan suggests . . . But McAllister says . . .". The student in question may be quite pleased with the end result, because, after all, it demonstrates that he or she has "done a lot of reading", and this is true, it does. However, simply providing a collection of quotes or summaries is not going to gain the best marks, because it is essentially descriptive. To make the most of the time spent researching all this material you need to make more *judgments* about the material: in other words, did Khan's view conflict with Smith's? If so, which is the better view in the context of the specific question or circumstances? As is more likely, perhaps Khan and Smith had some areas of agreement, and some areas of disagreement; being able to highlight these more subtle implications of their arguments—a process sometimes called *synthesising* their views—and turn them into effective arguments of your own is going to demonstrate your understanding of the topic at the highest level.

There is more about how to avoid both these mistakes in this chapter. To begin with, as this chapter is all about using your materials to support your arguments in your writing, we'll start by exploring the concept of an argument.

WHAT IS AN ARGUMENT?

The term *argument* means something different in academic writing than it does in ordinary language. In ordinary language, an argument means a disagreement or a row, whereas in academic writing, what is meant by an argument is taking a *position* (essentially reaching a conclusion, or a series of conclusions). This is done by making an *assertion* (i.e. a point) and backing this up with *reasons* to justify that point, and *evidence* to support the reasons. To form arguments in your writing, you work *backwards* from the evidence you have read to formulate the reasons for your overall conclusions or position. This will be much easier if you have diagnosed

▶ 5.3

the task properly because you will be looking at the relevant evidence and, more importantly, looking at it from the right perspective in order to utilise it in an argument.

This is the process to follow:

1. You diagnose the task and set yourself sub-questions which inform your research.
2. You then carry out research to find out the answer to the questions you have posed.
3. You review the answers you have found to the questions (and of course, bearing in mind that you keep your diagnosis under review, as you research further into the subject you keep checking that you asked the right questions) to form a conclusion.
4. When you write this up by putting it together as an argument, your answers to your sub-questions form the reasons for the conclusions you have reached, and the material you have researched provides the evidence for those reasons.

This may be easier to understand in the context of an example. Look back at the problem question on negligence at the end of Chapter 3. In diagnosing that task, various sub-questions emerged for consideration, one of which was, *does Zebedee owe a duty of care to the people in the scenario?* If you were really completing this as an assignment, then you would have carried out your research in order to provide the answers to all these sub-questions, and we're going to take this particular one about the duty of care to the other road users as an illustration.

Let's suppose that you have carried out a relevant search, or perhaps looked at lecture or textbook notes, and from this you have identified that *Nettleship v Weston* [1971] 2 Q.B. 691 is the crucial case on this point (see the spider diagram notes in Chapter 4), because it establishes the legal principle that a driver owes a duty of care to other road users. Because this is a problem question, you then need to *apply* this to the case in point: from the general (a driver owes a duty of care to other road users) to the particular (*this* driver, Zebedee, owes a duty of care to *these* road users A, B and C). This becomes your *conclusion* on this point, your *reason* being that a driver owes a duty of care to other road users (which is an assertion of law) and your *evidence* (or authority) being the case of *Nettleship v Weston* (the evidence for a proposition, or assertion, of law must always be a case or a statute).

In other words:

A driver owes a duty of care to other road users	PRINCIPLE / RULE
Zebedee is a driver, and A, B and C are other road users	APPLICATION
Zebedee owes a duty of care to A, B and C	CONCLUSION

This is what is known as a *syllogism*, which is a form of logical reasoning. In a syllogism, the principle or rule would be identified as a *major premise* and the application as a *minor premise*, but in terms of your legal study, it is probably more helpful to stick with thinking of these as *principle (or rule)* and *application*, as this is more likely to keep you on track with your writing. This also corresponds with the technique or tool for problem solving we considered in Chapter 3, the IRAC method—remember that once the Issues have been identified, the remaining steps are Rule, Application and Conclusion.

TIPS • *Whenever you state a legal principle, you are making an assertion of law, which must be supported by legal authority. There is more on this later in the chapter.*

The process of translating your diagnosis and research into your writing can be represented as follows (still using the negligence case as an example):

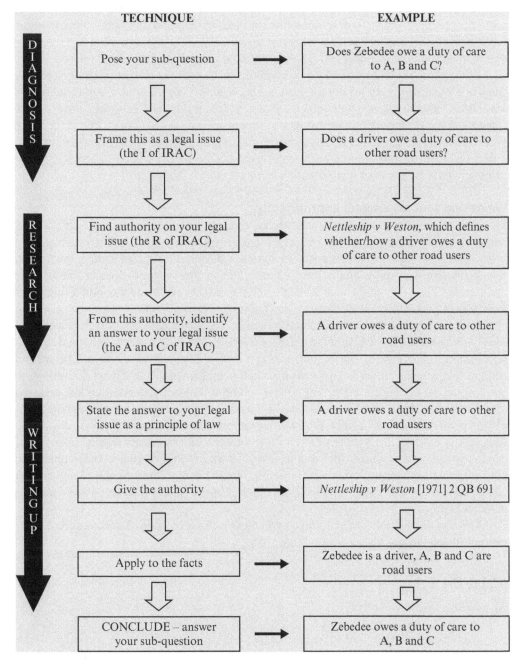

TECHNIQUE

EXAMPLE

DIAGNOSIS

Pose your sub-question → Does Zebedee owe a duty of care to A, B and C?

Frame this as a legal issue (the I of IRAC) → Does a driver owe a duty of care to other road users?

RESEARCH

Find authority on your legal issue (the R of IRAC) → *Nettleship v Weston*, which defines whether/how a driver owes a duty of care to other road users

From this authority, identify an answer to your legal issue (the A and C of IRAC) → A driver owes a duty of care to other road users

WRITING UP

State the answer to your legal issue as a principle of law → A driver owes a duty of care to other road users

Give the authority → *Nettleship v Weston* [1971] 2 QB 691

Apply to the facts → Zebedee is a driver, A, B and C are road users

CONCLUDE – answer your sub-question → Zebedee owes a duty of care to A, B and C

This diagram represents the *broad process*, and you can see here that the IRAC technique is not used only for planning your answer but also for ordering the material when writing up your answer. The RAC steps are identified for the Issue under discussion; this same structure would be repeated for each of the issues identified in a logical order. Of course, when you "write up" your answer there is some scope for flexibility: for example, as a matter of style you may give your conclusion, then your reasons (the principle of law) and authority, rather than (as represented in the diagram) stating the principle and authority and then moving to the conclusion. Similarly, it is often unnecessary to separate the application stage from the conclusion, where the facts are straightforward. In other words, you do not necessarily need to spell out the "Zebedee is a driver" part—where the facts are sufficiently simple (as here) you could simply move from the principle and authority to concluding that this means Zebedee owes a duty of care to A, B and C. However, we've specified the application stage as separate from the conclusion in the diagram to help you understand the process. As you become more practised at legal analysis and problem solving you will find it easier to make decisions about which parts of the process need to be spelt out more clearly.

Weighting your arguments appropriately

5.4 ▶ Bear in mind also that as you complete the research to inform the questions you have posed as part of your diagnosis, you need to keep in mind the need to *rank* of the issues into major and minor issues. Research into this particular issue (i.e. a driver's duty of care to other road users) should confirm that the example we've chosen here is one which is uncontroversial: it is "settled law" (i.e. a confirmed legal principle with very little or no room for doubt) that a driver owes a duty of care to other road users. This is therefore a comparatively minor point: it is an important preliminary step to the establishment of Zebedee's liabilities (which is what you have been asked to do) because of the nature of the particular topic of negligence (and so *must* be included in your answer), but not one on which you would spend a lot of time. Of course, in relation to much of your writing, you will be asked to explore issues which are *not* settled; in other words the evidence is *conflicting*. This would be the case if your research had revealed some authorities stating a driver owes a duty of care to other road users, and some stating that a driver does not owe such a duty. We saw an example of this in Chapter 3 when considering whether Alicia Atherton's website advert for Permabags might constitute an offer or an invitation to treat, and we suggested then that thinking of the A of IRAC as being not just Application but also Analysis where appropriate may help you remember that some aspects of your answer will demand more depth of discussion than others. How to deal with conflicting evidence is pursued further later in this chapter.

We now need to think in more detail about the process of using evidence to form arguments. The following activity will help you do this.

ACTIVITY 5.1

5.5 ▶ Consider the following question:

> Which is the best football team?

If you are a supporter of football, then an instinctive answer may spring to mind; in other words what you are giving is your *opinion*, based on the team you support. In order to develop an argument, you must be able to specify *reasons* to support this opinion. In other words *why* is Manchester United/Chelsea/Liverpool/Arsenal/Manchester City (or whichever) the best football team? Again, the football supporter's answer might be "because they are" but this kind of "it's obvious" reason is not an argument at all. In order to be an effective reason, it must be based on *evidence*.

If you are not a supporter of football, then you are much more likely to have given an answer which is based on evidence, as you are not starting from a position of *bias*. This is important in developing your skills in making an academic argument, where objectivity is crucial: instead of giving opinions or gut reactions you form arguments on the basis of evidence—and the evidence is the material you have gathered as part of the research stage of your work in coursework, or the material you have revised for an examination.

In order to evaluate this question of "which is the best football team" in a more reasoned way, you would need to find some sort of criteria to measure what makes a good football team (you would also need to determine the parameters of the question—is this the best team in the world? The United Kingdom? England and Wales? Professional teams only or amateur? Men's football, women's football or both? National sides or club sides?). The criteria might relate to recent competitions won, or loyalty inspired in their supporters, or good play or whatever (of course, with a subject like football, this would be a matter of some controversy!). These would form the basis of your sub-questions. Having posed the sub-questions, you would then carry out your research, to find out the answers to these questions, remembering to keep your diagnosis under review, in case, when finding out more about football, you discover that a key issue in how to rank football teams is something you had not included in your original list of sub-questions, perhaps for example track record in competitions over a number of years to indicate consistency (you might well have other views on what criteria should be used to judge a football team).

Of course, it is unlikely with a question like this one, which particularly appeals to a gut reaction answer, that you would have delved so deeply. However, we're going to stick with this example for some further exercises to show you how to develop effective arguments. For the sake of the worked example which follows we are setting the parameters of the question as the professional domestic (England and Wales) men's game.

HOW DO I DEVELOP EFFECTIVE ARGUMENTS?

In order to help you develop your argument, you must have supporting reasons for your conclusions. Effective reasons are those which are *accurate*, *relevant* and *based on evidence*. ▶ **5.6**

ACTIVITY 5.2

Let's return to the football question. Supposing you wanted to argue, in answer to the question posed, that Manchester United is the best football team. Have a look at the following statements and decide which of them are effective arguments in this respect: ▶ **5.7**

> Manchester United is the best football team.

> Manchester United is the best football team because they just are.

> Manchester United is the best football team because I've always supported them.

Activity feedback—here are our thoughts:

We already know that in order to develop an argument, you need supporting reasons, which in turn must be based on evidence. Simply stating *Manchester United is the best football team* is not an argument—it is an opinion, and one which is not supported by any reasons.

Manchester is the best football team because they just are—again, this is an opinion, supposedly supported by a reason, but "they just are" is not really a reason at all, it is simply a restatement of the position that they are the best (this might be described as a circular argument). You will note that there is no evidence presented and therefore no objective basis for the opinion.

Manchester United is the best football team because I've always supported them. Again, this is simply a restatement of the opinion, represented as the reason.

Conclusion: None of these statements represents a valid academic argument.

ACTIVITY 5.3

5.8 ▶ What about these statements—are they any better?

> Manchester United is the best football team because the team has won the Champions League five times.

> Manchester United is the best football team because the team is based in Manchester.

> Manchester United is the best team because everyone thinks so.

> Manchester United is the best football team because the team has won the Premier League title more times than any other team.

If you are not very familiar with football, then in order to carry this activity out, it will help you to know that the Champions League, previously known as the European Cup, features the best club teams from across Europe, culminating in a knock-out competition, and the Premier League, or Premiership, is the most prestigious league in England and Wales (it replaced a league called the First Division in 1992, and therefore represents recent domestic success).

Activity feedback—here are our thoughts:

Manchester United is the best football team because the team has won the Champions League five times.
Your view on this one will depend on whether football is something you know very much about. On the face of it, this looks like a valid argument, because it is based on a reason, namely

success in the Champions League, which as we've explained above is a prestigious European competition, and this sounds like a valid "yardstick" in ranking football teams, so it seems to be a *relevant* reason. However, if you know something of football, you may have stopped short when reading this argument: because in fact Manchester United has not won the Champions League or European Cup title five times (at the time of writing in 2014). This is therefore not an effective argument because the evidence on which it is based is not true. So, to be an effective argument, your reasons must be *accurate*.

Manchester United is the best team because the team is based in Manchester.
Bearing in mind what we've just said about accuracy, your first thought should be whether this statement is accurate (and just in case football geography is not your strong point, it is—the team name is something of a hint). However, accuracy in itself is not enough to justify an argument—looking at this statement, do you think it is based on a relevant reason? In other words, is location of the team essential to rating its quality? In order to make sure that you are relying on reasons which are relevant, you should refer back to the sub-questions which you have set yourself following your diagnosis. In relation to the football example, these were questions setting possible criteria for rating the quality of a team, for example relating to competitions won and so on. Is location of the club an appropriate criterion? If not, then this is not a relevant argument.

Additionally, the reason must not support an *alternative* conclusion. Followers of football will know well that Manchester has another team, Manchester City. If being located in Manchester is a valid criterion for determining the best team, then it must equally apply to this other team, and therefore cannot be used as valid evidence that Manchester United (and not Manchester City) is the best team.

Manchester United is the best team because everyone thinks so.
There are several problems with this one. First of all, your first reaction (particularly if you are not a Manchester United supporter) might have been something along the lines of "who thinks so?" In other words, you are challenging the accuracy of the reason. And more specifically, what is problematic about this statement is that there is no evidence to support it—where are the opinion polls indicating that everyone thinks Manchester United is the best team? If such evidence had been provided, then the reader could at least acknowledge that the reason is accurate—without it, this is not an adequate argument.

Supposing that this statement did offer some evidence in support (maybe a survey that 100 per cent of people think Manchester United is the best team—however statistically unlikely this might be), then although the statement is then *accurate*, you might again question whether public opinion is necessarily the best evidence to put forward in response to an evaluation of who is the best football team. Again, this comes down to whether *who is popularly rated as the best team?* was one of the questions you set yourself to help you evaluate who the best football team is. Do you consider this to be relevant?

We asked you to think about this particular statement for

> **TIPS** • *Avoid sweeping statements which overstate your case without accompanying evidence in support. It is a good idea to check your work through very carefully for this specific fault.*

two reasons: first, to illustrate that statements like "everyone thinks so" tend to be indicative of poor argument—they are what is called *sweeping statements*, i.e. broad assumptions made without evidence in support. Essentially, what the writer is arguing in this situation is that it "goes without saying" that a particular position is right or correct. In fact, in academic writing, anything which forms part of your argument needs to be articulated and evidence needs to be supplied: it does not "go without saying". "Everyone says . . .", "It is commonly accepted that . . ." and "It is a well-known fact . . ." are similar statements which will set off alarm bells in a critical reader (including the marker of your assignment), who will immediately be thinking *who says?*

> **TIPS** • *Be cautious with the use of popular opinion to justify your position.*

The second reason for including this example is to encourage you to reflect on the appropriateness of using *popular opinion* as evidence in support of your arguments: even if you can prove what popular opinion is on a particular point, it is not necessarily appropriate evidence in an academic essay (unless perhaps your essay is something to do with the nature of democracy, or the role of public opinion in influencing law reform, for example).

Manchester United is the best team because they have won the Premier League title more times than any other team.

Here we have a reason which would certainly seem to be relevant, as long as it is true (which it is, therefore this reason can be said to be accurate). We could criticise this statement for a lack of authority—there is no evidence given to prove that that this statement is true (it is, at the time of writing in 2014)—but this could be argued to be *common knowledge*, in which case authority is not required. We will discuss common knowledge, and what counts as common knowledge, later in the chapter. Apart from this point, we seem to have a good argument here, because it is accurate, and also relevant, since winning the Premier League would seem to be a valid measure for assessing a football team.

So we now know that the reasons which support your arguments must be *relevant*, *accurate* and based on *evidence*. This is all very well in the context of football, but we need to think about this in the context of law and legal writing.

WHAT EVIDENCE DO I NEED TO USE IN MY ARGUMENTS?

5.9 ▶ In academic writing, it is essential to use evidence to support any points you make. As a law student you are expected to back up the points you make by reference to *authority*. In other words you cannot simply make claims without having reasons and evidence. This evidence might be a primary source of law (i.e. a case or a statute) stating what the law *is*. Alternatively you may refer to a secondary source, such as a textbook or a journal article, to support an argument *about* the law or about a particular legal theory.

The basic rules about providing evidence or authority for your reasons are as follows:

● An *assertion (or proposition) of law* needs a case or statute (i.e. a primary source) as authority.
● An *assertion of fact* needs a secondary source (wherever you found the fact) as authority.

● An assertion which is *common knowledge* or *common legal knowledge* does not need authority.

Assertions of law

Many of the assertions which you make in legal writing will be assertions of law—essentially where you state what the law actually is on a particular point, in other words giving a legal rule. These are also sometimes referred to as statements of legal principle or propositions of law.

▶ 5.10

> The courts can use *Hansard* as an aid to statutory interpretation provided certain criteria are satisfied.

This is an assertion of law, because it states what the law is on this issue. Assertions of law must always have a primary source as evidence (a primary source, in legal terms, means either a case or a piece of legislation). The source for the assertion of law given above is the case of *Pepper (Inspector of Taxes) v Hart* [1993] A.C. 593; this information could be included within the text or added via a footnote, depending on the referencing system you are using for your assignment.

> **TIPS** • *Whenever you state a legal rule, you must cite where that rule comes from. There is more information on how to cite your evidence later in this chapter.*

Assertions of fact

You may, in the course of legal writing, find yourself making certain *assertions of fact*, for example: "The number of mortgage repossessions by the lenders has continued to fall year on year since 2008" or "The Government has stated that it is committed to reform of this area". Alternatively your assertion of fact might be summarising the position of an academic writer, for example: "Santos argues that . . ." or "In Thompson's view, this is a useful development . . .".

▶ 5.11

You must provide evidence for any assertions of fact which you make, unless the fact can be considered to be one of *common knowledge* (see below). So for example our statement about the fall in the number of mortgage repossessions can be evidenced by information from the Council of Mortgage Lenders.[1] Where your assertion relates to summarising the view of a writer, then of course, your evidence will be the secondary source by this writer from which you obtained these views. Note that you provide this evidence regardless of whether you have quoted directly from the work. Other possible sources for assertions of fact in a legal context could include judicial statistics, Law Commission reports, reports of official inquiries, or *Hansard*.

Matters of common knowledge or common legal knowledge

You do not have to provide evidence of matters of *common knowledge* (for example, you do not need evidence for an assertion that the Battle of Hastings was in 1066) or within the general sphere of legal knowledge for example stating that the Supreme Court is the final court of

▶ 5.12

---

[1] Council of Mortgage Lenders, *Arrears and repossessions still falling, cites CML* (Council of Mortgage Lenders. November 13, 2014) *www.cml.org.uk/cml/media/press/4063* [Accessed November 13, 2014].

appeal in the UK for civil cases. (It's the "It's obvious!" factor.) However, be careful with this: just because something is obvious to you, having researched it, it is not necessarily obvious to your reader. This is linked to the idea of writing for a particular audience: when writing a legal assignment, you are writing for an intelligent reader who understands all the general issues of law but is ignorant of the particular subject matter of your assignment. Suppose you were answering a problem question which involved looking at a Supreme Court decision. In this context, it is a matter of common legal knowledge that this is a strong precedent, although the Supreme Court could use its power under the Practice Statement 1966 to depart from it if it wished to do so, and you would not therefore have to take time out in your assignment to explain this. However, supposing the subject matter of your assignment was directly related to matters of precedent in the Supreme Court, then the ability of the Supreme Court to depart from its own previous rulings could no longer be regarded as a matter of common legal knowledge. You would be expected to explain this rule and give its source (i.e. the Practice Statement 1966).

ACTIVITY 5.4

5.13 ▶ Which of the following statements would need evidence?

> The Supreme Court will not use the Practice Statement often.

> There are several exceptions to the principle that the Court of Appeal is bound by its own previous rulings.

> The Lord Chancellor is Chris Grayling (at time of writing in 2014).

> Zander asserts that the literal rule is "defeatist and lazy".

> The literal translation of the phrase *stare decisis* is "let the decision stand".

Activity feedback—Here are our thoughts:

> The Supreme Court will not use the Practice Statement often.

Although this might seem an obvious statement, it is not so "obvious" that it could be considered common knowledge, even for a law student. This is a statement of fact, so you would need to provide authority, such as statistical information or point to a source where the use of the Practice Statement is discussed.

> There are several exceptions to the principle that the Court of Appeal is bound by its own previous rulings.

This is an assertion of law and therefore must be supported by evidence (here, the authority is the case of *Young v Bristol Aeroplane Co Ltd* [1944] K.B. 718).

> The Lord Chancellor is Chris Grayling.

This does not need a reference. It is a statement of fact, but it is one which counts as within the sphere of legal knowledge: in other words, to a lawyer, the fact that the Lord Chancellor is Chris Grayling (as at November 2014) is as much "common knowledge" as the fact that David Cameron is the Prime Minister would be to anyone else.

> Zander asserts that the literal rule is "defeatist and lazy".

This is an assertion of fact, because it is stating what the views of the writer Michael Zander are. This therefore needs evidence, in the form of a reference to the work where Zander makes this statement which is *The Law Making Process* (6th edn, Cambridge University Press 2004) 145. Note that giving Zander's name, and therefore acknowledging that this is his idea, not yours, is not enough in itself: you have to give exact details. Your goal should be that your readers can find this quote for themselves, based on the information you have given.

> The literal translation of the phrase *stare decisis* is "let the decision stand".

This is a statement of fact, but one which would be considered to be within the sphere of common legal knowledge because it is a standard legal term, and you would not be expected to reference a Latin/English dictionary to support it.

> **TIPS •** *If you fail to reference your sources properly, at best your arguments are weakened, because you have not given your evidence, and at worst you may commit plagiarism. In particular, if you are new to university study, you may find that the emphasis placed on giving your evidence, acknowledging your sources and avoiding plagiarism is very different from what you have been used to previously, so you need to get yourself into a new way of thinking and new habits straight away. There is more guidance on plagiarism later in the chapter.*

Although we can be categorical about the need to reference assertions of law, and about the need to acknowledge the words or ideas of others, learning to recognise matters of common knowledge is less easy to provide clear-cut advice on: it really is a matter of experience, so if in doubt, give your evidence.

Now that we have considered the type of evidence you need to give, we need to explore further how to integrate this effectively into your writing.

HOW DO I INTEGRATE EVIDENCE FROM OTHER SOURCES INTO MY OWN WRITING?

You can do this by: ▶ 5.14

- paraphrasing a point made by the author; or
- quoting from the work directly.

Paraphrasing

This means taking someone else's idea or theory and including it on your own essay, but   ▶ 5.15
instead of doing this by use of a direct quotation in quotation marks, you integrate it into your own argument by putting it into your own words. It is easy to get confused (especially in the light of warnings about plagiarism) about whether paraphrasing is "allowed" or a "good idea"

> **TIPS** • *What you are doing when you paraphrase is making a statement of fact (about the author's view or position) so cite the evidence accordingly.*

but do not be afraid to do it providing you give the appropriate references: paraphrasing positions taken by other authors is a good way of demonstrating that you have understood those positions. So, the rule is that it is good to paraphrase as long as you reference properly.

Effectively, when you paraphrase, your goal is to sum up (or restate) the position of the author on that particular point in your own words. In doing this, you should be looking to identify the core point that the author is making on a particular issue: if you paraphrase a side issue or an illustration, then you run the risk of taking comments out of context.

ACTIVITY 5.5

5.16 ▶ Have a look at this quote from Lord Denning's book, *The Discipline of Law*,[2] and then consider what you think the main position in this section is:

> In almost every case in which you have to advise you will have to interpret a statute. There are stacks and stacks of them. Far worse for you than for me. When I was called in 1923 there was one volume of 500 pages. Now in 1978 there are three volumes of more than 3,000 pages. Not a single page but it can give rise to argument. Not a single page but the client will turn to you and say: "What does it mean?" The trouble lies with our method of drafting. The principal object of the draftsman is to achieve certainty—a laudable object in itself. But in pursuit of it, he loses sight of the equally important object—clarity. The draftsman—or draftswoman—has conceived certainty: but has brought forth obscurity; sometimes even absurdity.

Which of the following do you think is an effective paraphrase of Lord Denning's *position*, as evidenced by this quotation?

> Lawyers today have to work much harder than Lord Denning did to interpret statutes.

> The number of reported cases rose from enough to fill 500 pages in 1923 to 9,000 pages in 1978.

> Certainty is incompatible with clarity but both are equally important objectives.

> Problems with the methods of drafting statutes have caused a huge rise in the number of cases in which statutory interpretation is an issue.

Activity feedback—here are our thoughts:

> Lawyers today have to work much harder than Lord Denning did to interpret statutes.

---

2 Lord Denning, *The Discipline of Law* (Butterworths 1979) 9.

Lord Denning does allude to the fact that the volume of cases has made the position of the lawyer today more difficult (assuming that this is who he is addressing when he says "you"—from this quote, it isn't entirely clear). However, do you think it really sums up the core point Lord Denning is making? It would not be wrong to include this kind of statement within a lengthier paraphrase of Lord Denning's work, as long as that core point was also clearly represented.

> The number of reported cases rose from enough to fill 500 pages in 1923 to 9,000 pages in 1978.

Again, Lord Denning does imply this in his discussion of the number of pages which are found in law reports these days. However, there are a couple of reasons why this would not make an effective paraphrase: this is simply an illustration which Lord Denning is giving as he moves towards his core point and in any case this is a simple question of fact. Lord Denning's statements are hardly the best evidence of how many pages there are in law reports.

> Certainty is incompatible with clarity but both are equally important objectives.

This would need a little work to be an effective paraphrase. Yes, Lord Denning does say that certainty has come at the expense of clarity and he does say that clarity and certainty are "equally important". However, his comments are clearly made in the context of statutory interpretation and the drafting of statutes in recent years, and therefore as it stands this is not an accurate paraphrase because it does not specify this context. Simply adding "In statutory interpretation" brings this much closer to representing Lord Denning's position.

> Problems with the methods of drafting statutes have caused a huge rise in the number of cases in which statutory interpretation is an issue.

This comes closest to being an effective paraphrase because it gets to the core point which Lord Denning is making about the nature of legislative drafting. However, although accurate, this particular statement does illustrate one of the difficulties with paraphrasing, which is striking the right balance between stating the position concisely, and yet giving sufficient detail to be of value. Arguably here, although the position is accurately summarised, the flavour of Lord Denning's argument does not really come across.

A really effective paraphrase might therefore need a little more detail. Suppose a student had written the following:

> Lord Denning pointed out in his book about the discipline of law that statutory interpretation has become a much more significant issue for today's lawyers; there has been a huge rise in the number of cases in which statutory interpretation is an issue, which he argues is because the drafting process prioritises certainty (which he acknowledges is important) over clarity (which in his view is equally important).

A student writing a paragraph like the one above has represented Lord Denning's position accurately, and has therefore shown that he or she is getting to grips with what Lord Denning is getting at. However, there are two things missing here, both of which are covered in more detail later in this chapter:

1. A reference is needed to Lord Denning's book, and exactly where within it the material used in this paraphrase is located; and
2. the student needs to add his or her own judgment on Lord Denning's position in order to move from *describing* what Lord Denning said to *evaluating* what he said.

Using quotations

5.17 ▶ Quoting from a work can be a good way of integrating your research into your own arguments. However, there are several things to bear in mind with quotations:

1. Quotations are someone else's words, not your own, and the marker will award marks only for your *own* words. Yes, you can gain marks for your *choice* of quotations, and what you do with them, but not for the quote itself. Despite this, it is likely that quotes will count towards your allowed word limit on an assignment, so every time you include one you are using up your word count with material which cannot contribute directly to your mark. This is not to say that you should avoid quotes, but you should certainly be sparing with them, and keep them as short as possible.

   > **TIPS** • *Before including a quote, ask yourself "Could I paraphrase this instead?"*

   This is especially true with secondary sources—unless the author's position can be summed up in a short, punchy quote, then a paraphrase is usually better.

2. Learning to paraphrase the ideas in secondary sources rather than quoting directly from them can be a challenge, because of course a learned author is likely to have made their point particularly well, and you may well feel that you cannot improve on it. However, you *can* usually improve on it because the author was not writing in response to the specific assignment you have been set, whereas you are. On the other hand, if the quote perfectly encapsulates what you want to say, and is short, then by all means use it—but remember to explain why it is relevant to your argument (see below).

   > **TIPS** • *In your assignment, show clearly when you are using someone else's words by indenting a quotation, using italics or inverted commas. Check whether your institution has any particular specifications on how to delineate quotes.*

3. One area where a quote can be particularly useful is where you are quoting from a primary source, in the form of a case (direct quotes from statutes are rarely needed), particularly in order to explore the implications of the case with reference to the facts you are considering. Again, however, keep your quotes as short as possible.

Making the most of paraphrasing and quotes

5.18 ▶ Remember that just paraphrasing or quoting from the source is not enough in itself to get you really high marks: you also need to make *judgments* about the material. This is the difference between the following types of statement:

A. *This is Smith's position* (which is *describing* Smith's position), and might be done by paraphrasing or giving an illustrative quotation; and

B. *this is the implication of Smith's position for my argument* (which is *evaluating* Smith's position in the context of your assignment) and would involve you making a judgment about what Smith has said.

A weaker essay will contain more statements of type A than type B. Type A statements are certainly needed (if you want to use Smith's position in your argument, then clearly you need to say what it is) but should be as concise as possible (and of course accurate). However, such statements show only that you have been able to *find* relevant material: they do not show that you have *understood* the material fully and can really use it as part of your own arguments. To show this, you need statements of type B.

So a good essay will have a balance of A type statements and B type statements, with the A statements presented con-cisely and as *evidence* for the B statements; in other words, a B statement about the implications of Smith's views is illus-trated by an A statement of what those views are. You should do the same with case law: type A statements will be concise representations of the relevant points decided in the case, and type B statements will critique the decision, or explain how the legal position taken by the court affects your argument through application to the facts of a problem question.

> **TIPS** • *Even though you are building your own arguments by reference to the evidence, keep your language objective—avoid writing in the first person (in other words, don't say "I think . . ." or "In my opinion . . .").*

Always remember that a quote or paraphrase only *illustrates* the point you are making; it is up to you to *make* the point. If you find this difficult, try asking yourself why you want to include this quote or paraphrase in your assignment. Articulating the reason for your choice to yourself should help you move towards an appropriate evaluative statement and help you to get your point across.

Using a source found within another source in my writing

By this we mean the sort of situation where you read a book or an article by author X and it gives you a reference to another source by author Y, which you want to use. We are going to refer to this as an indirect source. This is something which occurs frequently in research, and yes you can use it but you always need to acknowledge the ideas of others. Here the idea of using author Y's source (the indirect source) came from author X, not from you. It is a common mistake to think that you only need to reference author Y in this situation, when you need to also acknowledge author X.

▶ **5.19**

The starting point is that if you want to make a significant use of the indirect source (i.e. the material written by author Y) then you should find it and read it for yourself, rather than relying on second-hand information about it (i.e. the views of author X). However, where you are only going to make a minor use of the text then you may not, realistically, have the chance to chase up every reference which is thrown up in your research. Therefore, it is acceptable to make use of an indirect source provided that you acknowledge both the original author, and the author who found that source for you.

For example, supposing as part of researching material for an essay about the interpre-tation of *ratio decidendi*, you wish to draw on the work of Holland and Webb in *Learning Legal Rules* (their references omitted)[3]:

---

3   James Holland and Julian Webb, *Learning Legal Rules* (8th edn, Oxford University Press 2014) 186.

There is no set single test for defining what is meant by *ratio* or for establishing the *ratio* of a particular case. As Cross stated: "It is impossible to devise formulae for determining the ratio decidendi of a case." But before you lose heart altogether, Cross also stated that "this does not mean it is impossible to give a tolerably accrate description of what lawyers mean when they use the expression" and we shall see that that is true. Like so many things in law this problem of identification is not unique to legal studies. Think of the plot to a book or a film. The facts are clear, the storyline can be described but if some people were asked to say what the film, etc. was *about* then opinions would vary. Some might see the film as nothing more than, say, an adventure film; others might see a social or political message in it; others might think the director was clearly paying tribute to an earlier famous director. Even if the writer or director was asked to spell out the meaning, the purpose, of the film (equivalent to reading the judgment of a case) the onlooker's reply could still be: "You may have meant that, but you produced something different."

Thus to the student who asks "how do I spot the ratio?" Twining and Miers would respond:

"Talk of *finding* the ratio *decidendi* of a case obscures the fact that the process of interpreting cases is not like a hunt for buried treasure, but typically involves an element of choice from a range of possibilities."

It is unwise, therefore, to presume that there is one and only one possible ratio to a case.

Now, if we were to pick out what ideas Holland and Webb have had in this passage, the obvious one is the film metaphor. So, if we wanted to borrow that idea it would certainly have to be acknowledged.

But they have two further ideas:

1. That what Cross has to say supports their general argument that there is no easy answer to the question "what is the ratio"; and
2. that what Twining and Miers have to say also supports this general point.

They support these by using quotations from the work of Cross, and from Twining and Miers. Therefore if you borrow these quotations to support *your* argument, then you must acknowledge where you found them, which is in *Learning Legal Rules*, rather than in the original texts. In this situation, Holland and Webb are author X, and Cross and Twining and Miers are all in the position of author Y.

ACTIVITY 5.6

5.20 ▶ Have a look at the following passage. If this had been written by a student, which statements within it would need to be referenced?

Twining and Miers point out that the ratio isn't "buried treasure" and it is therefore simplistic to assume that there is only one possible formula for finding the ratio. The reason for this is that there will be a number of possible formulations for any given

> case, and therefore opinions might vary as to which of them is actually the ratio of the case. Holland and Webb liken this to the range of different opinions which might be given by a group of people who have just watched a film as to what the film's meaning was—and not even the director knows the "right" answer. In other words, expressing the ratio means selecting a possible ratio out of range of principles, any one of which is capable of being the ratio.

Activity feedback—here are our thoughts:

This paragraph does three things which need referencing:

1. It summarises Twining and Miers's quotation including giving a direct quote of the words "buried treasure".
2. It borrows the "formula" idea from Cross, although without a direct quotation.
3. It paraphrases Holland and Webb's idea of comparing the ratio to saying what a film is about.

All three require acknowledgement, and therefore a reference. The form of the reference will depend on whether our student drew all their information from Holland and Webb.

If so, then as well as acknowledging the three "ideas" listed above, the student would need to make clear that this paragraph draws on the ideas of Holland and Webb for *all three* of these sources. This is done by acknowledging Author Y, and adding "cited by" or "quoted in" Author X, for example:

> William Twining and David Miers, *How to do things with rules* (5th edn, Cambridge University Press 2010) 306 cited in James Holland and Julian Webb, *Learning legal rules* (8th edn, Oxford University Press 2013) 186.

This demonstrates to your reader that this was an indirect source and acknowledges that Holland and Webb did the work of finding these useful quotations rather than you.

WHAT IF I FIND CONFLICTING EVIDENCE IN MY RESEARCH?

It is extremely likely, as we acknowledged earlier, that the evidence you find may point in differ- ▶ **5.21** ent directions. This is especially true in relation to areas of critical debate and obviously these areas are popular choices for assignment questions. First of all, if you find conflicting evidence don't panic, you have uncovered evidence of a critical debate and capturing this debate is likely to strengthen rather than weaken your assignment. The skill your tutor is likely to be looking for is that you can acknowledge the alternative strands of the debate but reach an evidenced conclusion in relation to it.

So you need to spot any conflicts or alternative positions when you are carrying out your research. Next, you have to evaluate the conflicting positions and work out which is the

> **TIPS** • *Try applying the following technique to your research:*
> 1. *In relation to each of your sub-questions, try to sum up in a nutshell what the position is of each of your sources in relation to that sub-question.*
> 2. *Compare these positions: which broadly complement (i.e. essentially agree with) each other, and which conflict with each other?*
> 3. *From the opposing positions, which is the better view?*

better view, which then informs your conclusion. To make a really good argument, you must acknowledge the contrary evidence, and explain why, in spite of this, your conclusion or position is still valid.

If you can do this, then you are really developing your skills in argument. Dealing with a conflicting in evidence is something which is especially important in legal study, because it is essentially what, in legal practice, is involved in anticipating your opponent's case and stating why, despite the contrary arguments which your opponent may use in support of his or her client's case, *your client's case* is still the stronger one.

We're going to return to the previous football example to illustrate the point (and although earlier we speculated on a variety of possible sub-questions, to keep this illustration straightforward, let's stick to ones which have an objective, verifiable answer). So, supposing that in researching the question *Which is the best football team?* you had posed the following sub-questions, and found out the following answers:

Possible sub-questions	Answer
Who has won the most Premier League titles?	Manchester United
Who has won the most Champions League/European Cup?	Liverpool (assuming we're still concentrating on domestic sides)

The problem that we now have is that the research into our sub-questions has provided a conflict in evidence: depending on which sub-question you rely on, we have so far proved that the best football team is either Manchester United or Liverpool. So which of them is it? The answer would depend on further reasoning as to which of those sub-questions is the best indicator of footballing success.

The structure of the argument might be:

1. If consistency in the Premier League is the most important factor in rating football teams, then Manchester United are the best.
2. Alternatively, if success against European teams marks a quality team then the domestic team with the best record is Liverpool.

Your conclusion would therefore have to be based upon a decision (supported by reasoned argument as to whether success against European teams is the best indicator of quality, therefore success in the Champions League (or European Cup) is the key yardstick, and therefore Liverpool is the best football team, or whether consistent domestic success is the best indicator of quality, in which case Manchester United's track record in the Premier League would be judged the best team. The important element is that whatever position you take, you *justify* it with evidence.

Applying this to legal writing, there will frequently be competing positions in what you write, and part of the art of writing successfully is to evaluate them in order to make a decision on which position is the strongest. What you need to do, in order to demonstrate that you understand your evidence and can make effective use of it, is to acknowledge these competing positions and tailor your argument accordingly. The best writing acknowledges, rather than attempts to hide, the opposite point of view, but demonstrates how this opposite point of view is weaker than the writer's position. In other words, you deal with conflicting evidence by evaluating it.

Evaluating your evidence

In order to do this, you need to consider the *weight* and *quality* of your evidence. To give another non-legal illustration, consider a remark like: "My uncle smoked 40 a day all his life and lived to be 90 so smoking can't be bad for you." Is this a convincing counter-argument in respect of the huge weight of medical evidence that smoking is bad for you? Balancing the weight and quality of the evidence from this example would give us: ▶ 5.22

Smoking is bad for you	Smoking is not bad for you
Hundreds of objective medical studies (which if you were really pursuing this in an academic study you would have researched, of course)	One anecdotal example

From this example, we can see that the weight (there's more of it) and quality (scientific studies are better than anecdotes) of evidence is strongly on the "smoking is bad for you" side. It can often be helpful to draw up a table in this way, and use it to list the arguments for and against a particular position. This will help you to judge where the weight of evidence lies. However, remember that you are not just looking for the longest list of "pros" in order to pick the "winning" argument. You must also bear in mind the *quality* of your evidence: if your table of conflicting evidence produces a ratio from the Supreme Court on one side, but an obiter from the High Court on the other, the numbers are even—but clearly the Supreme Court's ratio is stronger.

Dealing with conflicting evidence is a skill which is likely to be especially needed in legal writing when you are using cases as evidence. As well as ranking the cases according to which court they were decided in (in relation to the hierarchy of the courts) and whether the evidence you are relying on forms part of the ratio or is merely obiter, it will usually be appropriate to rank the relevance of the cases to the particular facts in your question. For example, a case with exactly the same material facts is more valuable evidence than a case with only some similar material facts.

> **TIPS** • *The point of giving the facts of cases is:*
> 1. *to demonstrate the relevance of a case to the point you are making;*
> 2. *to highlight similarities/differences between the facts under discussion and the cases being discussed.*
> *Remember that case facts are simply descriptive, so limit their use to the above situations, and even then be as concise as you can.*

You must also ensure that the way in which you deal with conflicting evidence is logical. This is explored in the following activity.

ACTIVITY 5.7

5.23 ▶ Returning to our question about which is the best football team, supposing a student argued as follows:

> Liverpool FC is the best football team because the team has won the Champions League/European Cup five times. However, Manchester United has won the Premier League title more times than any other team which is even better.

What is wrong with this statement? If you find it difficult to put your finger on exactly what is wrong with it, then try identifying the conclusion drawn by the author to see if this helps you pinpoint the problem with the statement, and then identify the reasons given to support this conclusion.

Activity feedback—here are our thoughts:

The main problem here is the lack of logic. At first, the conclusion appears to be that Liverpool is the best football team, and there is a reason given for this, namely that they have won five Champions League/European Cup titles. This is fine so far, as it appears that the author has found a criterion against which to measure what makes the best football team, namely success in the Champions League or European Cup. However, the next supposed reason given relates to success in the Premier League, and the author states that this reason is even more important. Logically that must mean that Manchester United is the best football team, not Liverpool.

Of course we already know that you can have more than one criterion to help you carry out an evaluation, and it is entirely appropriate to rank your criteria against each other. However, the problem here is that overall the statement is illogical: if Manchester United ranks best against the "better" criterion, then the logical conclusion is that Manchester United is the better team, yet the statement starts by asserting that Liverpool is. In other words, the writer takes two positions:

1. Success in the Champions League is the best indicator of the best football team; and
2. winning the Premier League is a better indicator than this.

Clearly, these positions are not compatible with each other. There can be nothing better than the best. What the author should have done is acknowledge that both are important ways of rating the best football team but decided which criterion was the better, in order to take one (concluding) position.

So for example:

> Manchester United is the best football team because although they have not won as many Champions League or European Cup titles as Liverpool, they have won the Premier League title more times than any other team, which demonstrates recent domestic consistency.

There are again two competing arguments here, but the ultimate *position* taken ranks one (domestic consistency) above the other (success in the European competition) and is therefore *logical*. Of course this doesn't necessarily mean that it is *right*, but remember that in your legal writing you will only rarely be dealing with issues which have a simplistic "right or wrong" answer, and so logical argument based on quality evidence should be your goal rather than a fruitless search for the "right" answer. There is more about the concept of a logical progression of ideas in the next section.

HOW CAN I MAKE SURE MY ARGUMENTS PROGRESS LOGICALLY?

By now you should understand that the process of answering the sub-questions you have set ▶ **5.24** yourself as part of your diagnosis will throw up conflicts, and you know that you need to rank these to work out which is the better view. You then need to make sure that you structure these appropriately.

If you have ever watched the TV show *Little Britain* then you will be familiar with the character of Vicky Pollard. If this means nothing to you, then for the purpose of this explanation all you need to know is that this character is famous for the catchphrase "Yeah . . . but no . . . but yeah . . . but no . . . but . . ." with which she begins more or less every answer to a question. Basically, your goal in logical progression of argument is to avoid being Vicky Pollard. In other words, if you have a number of conflicting arguments, then don't give a pro, then a con, then a pro, then a con, then a pro, then a con. This will produce the Vicky Pollard effect. It is usually much better to produce an essay which looks at all the pros and then all the cons before proceeding to your conclusion. In a problem answer, this pattern will vary according to the particular "formula" which may apply to tackling questions on particular topics.

The following example of a logical progression of argument is based on the question about democracy which we looked at as an example of diagnosis in Chapter 3.

> "The voting system used at UK General Elections requires reform to reflect the values of a liberal democracy." Discuss.

In order to understand how the arguments in this essay should progress logically, it may help to think of the essay title in abstract terms. In other words, this essay title can be represented as:

> Measured against standard X, which is better—Model A or Model B?

Standard X, in our example, is the values of a liberal democracy—our yardstick for this assignment. Model A is the current voting system; Model B comprises alternatives for reform. (Note that this "formula" can be modified to suit most *do we need reform* type questions.)

Breaking this down into our sub-questions, they could be as follows:

1. What is standard X?   DESCRIPTIVE
2. What is model A?   DESCRIPTIVE
3. What is model B?   DESCRIPTIVE
4. How does A rate against X?   EVALUATIVE
5. How does B rate against X?   EVALUATIVE
6. So, measured against X, which is better—A or B?   CONCLUSION

ACTIVITY 5.8

5.25 ▶ How could the sub-questions listed above be organised into a logical progression of argument?

Activity feedback—here are our thoughts:

Number 6 clearly goes last, because you need the answers to all five preceding questions to answer it—your conclusion must always go last. Similarly, it seems logical to start with number 1 because this sets out your "measure" or yardstick. Further, number 4 has to go after 1 and 2, because the explanation in 1 and 2 is needed before the evaluation in 4 can take place; on the same basis, 5 has to go after 1 and 3.

So therefore, our two possible structures are:

$$1 - 2 - 3 - 4 - 5 - 6$$

or

$$1 - 2 - 3 - 4 - 5 - 6$$

Looking back at the questions, you can see this is a choice between dealing with *all* areas of description first and then moving on to *all* areas of evaluation, or dealing with *all* issues to do with Model A, both descriptive and evaluative, and then dealing with *all* issues to do with Model B, both descriptive and evaluative. If it was you trying to understand it, which would you find most helpful? It is probably best to evaluate Model A while the facts about Model A are fresh in the mind, and then do the same for Model B.

This means that your progression of argument would be as follows:

1. The values of a liberal democracy are . . .
2. The current voting system is . . .
3. The strengths and weaknesses of the current voting system as compared to the values of liberal democracy are . . .
4. Alternatives to the current voting system are . . .
5. The strengths and weaknesses of the reform possibilities as compared to the values of liberal democracy are . . .
6. Conclusion.

Finally, as alluded to in the football example, a logical progression of argument needs a *conclusion*, and you need reasons to support this conclusion. Your reasons should lead logically to your conclusion. In academic writing, you are likely to make a number of conclusions, or sub-conclusions, which lead to your overall or main conclusion.

A common mistake in student writing is to confuse your final conclusion with a *summary*. A conclusion gives your final *position* on your arguments, having evaluated the conflicting evidence to decide which way is the way forward. Returning to our football example (for the final time), a student might finish their consideration of which is the best football team like this:

> So in conclusion, if the best way to judge a football team is by reference to the number of Premier League titles won, then the best team is Manchester United, but if success in the Champions League is a better guide then the best team is Liverpool.

Does this tell you which is the best team? No—so this is not a *conclusion* at all. This is simply a repetition of the conflicting evidence which has (presumably) been given in the main body of the essay and therefore is merely a summary. To be an effective and logical conclusion, it must reach an overall position on which of these conflicting arguments is the better view. In an answer to a legal answer problem questions, the example above is the equivalent of something like "Therefore Fred should be advised that he may win if . . . but he may lose if . . ." You should have already made clear this conflict in your evidence in the main body of your work, so in your conclusion you need to say whether Fred is more likely to win or lose. Simply saying "in conclusion" at the beginning of your final paragraph is not enough to *make* it a conclusion: you must make your final position clear. There is much more help on how to write an effective conclusion in Chapter 6.

We now need to return to the issues of plagiarism and referencing.

WHAT IS PLAGIARISM?

Exact definitions may vary but broadly plagiarism is a form of dishonesty or *cheating*. Alison Bone's *Plagiarism: a guide for law lecturers*,[4] draws on the definition by Ryan[5] that plagiarism is "stealing someone's words or ideas and passing them off as your own". Your university may have its own definition of plagiarism or may class it together with collusion as "academic misconduct". It is vital that you check out your own institution's definition and penalties, which you will probably find in your assessment regulations or student handbook. If you cannot locate a definition, or any guidance which will help you avoid plagiarism, then *ask* where you can locate this information.

▶ 5.26

> **TIPS** • *Find out your university's rules on plagiarism and/or other academic misconduct—don't be caught out by ignorance as it is unlikely to be a valid excuse.*

A further area of confusion is whether plagiarism has to be intentional or whether it can be committed accidentally. The answer is that yes, it certainly can be committed accidentally. Again, this is something that you need to check in your own university's regulations. Of course the safest course of action is to ensure that you do not commit plagiarism at all, whether intentionally or accidentally.

The basic rule is that you must acknowledge where you have drawn on the words or ideas of others in your work, and give a reference to this material so that, if they wanted, the person reading your work could go and find the original source and read it for themselves. This will avoid any risk of plagiarism. We have already explained how you need to give evidence as a matter of putting together a good argument—if you do this properly then you will avoid plagiarism as a matter of course, as well as improving your marks because of the high quality of your arguments. Many universities are now using plagiarism software which can be used

---

4   A. Bone, *Plagiarism: a guide for law lecturers*, (UK Centre for Legal Education) *http://78.158.56.101/archive/law/resources/assessment-and-feedback/plagiarism/index.html/* [Accessed November 17, 2014].
5   J. Ryan, *A guide to teaching international students* (Centre for Staff and Learning Development 2000).

as a detection tool but can also be used developmentally by students to assess whether their work conforms to what is required. If you are concerned, check to see if your university offers this option, or what alternative support is available to help students understand and avoid plagiarism.

ACTIVITY 5.9

5.27 ▶ Consider the statements below. How many do you agree with?:

"Plagiarism can only be committed deliberately."
"It isn't plagiarism to copy from a book as long as you put the book in your bibliography."
"Copying from the internet isn't plagiarism—plagiarism is only copying from books or journals."
"Tutors have too many assignments to mark to spot plagiarism."

Activity Feedback – here are our thoughts:
"Plagiarism can only be committed deliberately."
From what you've read already, you should be aware that plagiarism is plagiarism whether it is committed intentionally or accidentally, which is why it is your responsibility to make sure you understand what it is and how to avoid it.

"It isn't plagiarism to copy from a book as long as you put the book in your bibliography."
This is false. You certainly need to put any books you have used in your bibliography, but that is not enough in itself. You have to make it clear throughout your work whenever you draw on someone else's ideas by referencing it at the appropriate point.

"Copying from the internet isn't plagiarism—plagiarism is only copying from books or journals."
This seems to be a common idea: as long as you can find something on the internet, then it is "ok" to cut and paste it into your work. However, plagiarism is copying from *anywhere* without acknowledging the source (and think how easy it is for your tutors to check up on quotes from the web).

"Tutors have too many assignments to mark to spot plagiarism."
Well, it is certainly likely that your tutors have a lot of assignments to mark, but do not assume therefore that this will make them less likely to spot plagiarism. They have a lot of experience both of the subject matter and sources available and in recognising a change from a student's own words to someone else's. Additionally as mentioned previously many universities now use plagiarism detection software. You may find that your university checks all work through this as a matter of course.

Having ruled out the hope of getting away with it as an option we would want to emphasise again that engaging with the techniques that will ensure you avoid plagiarism also bring the benefit of producing better academic work. Remember that your tutors will want to reward effective arguments—i.e. those that are supported by evidence—so providing references is genuinely to your benefit.

It can be easy to focus on the penalties which attach to plagiarism, without stressing enough the benefits which come from good academic practice: *if you use and cite your materials in the right way this will result in good marks.*

▶ 5.28

> **TIPS** • *Use a highlighter pen to identify quotes or use quotation marks when copying a quote so that it stands out in your notes, but remember you need to acknowledge ideas as well as quotes.*

Remember that we've emphasised throughout this book that marks are not awarded for simply being able to replicate information: the marks are for what you *do* with the information. It follows that being able to show that you can use sources to develop your own reasoning and argument is the best way to improve your writing—and will have the added benefit that you avoid plagiarism!

ACTIVITY 5.10

We are going to return to our quotation from Lord Denning's book, *The Discipline of Law*[6] which we looked at earlier in the chapter when we were looking at paraphrasing. Here is a reminder of Lord Denning's original:

> In almost every case in which you have to advise you will have to interpret a statute. There are stacks and stacks of them. Far worse for you than for me. When I was called in 1923 there was one volume of 500 pages. Now in 1978 there are three volumes of more than 3,000 pages. Not a single page but it can give rise to argument. Not a single page but the client will turn to you and say: "What does it mean?" The trouble lies with our method of drafting. The principal object of the draftsman is to achieve certainty—a laudable object in itself. But in pursuit of it, he loses sight of the equally important object—clarity. The draftsman—or draftswoman—has conceived certainty: but has brought forth obscurity; sometimes even absurdity.

If a student wrote the following in an essay, would you consider it to be plagiarism?

> Statutory interpretation has become much more significant with the rise in the number of reported cases from 500 pages in 1923 to more than 9,000 pages in 1978. Every page may have some issue of statutory interpretation on it, and although the principal object of the draftsman is to achieve certainty—a laudable object in itself—problems with the method of drafting may mean that this is at the expense of clarity.

Activity feedback—here are our thoughts:

Remember that you are looking out for the use of someone else's words or ideas without proper credit.

There are therefore two main problems with this example:

---

[6]   Lord Denning, *The Discipline of Law* (Butterworths 1979) 9.

> **TIPS** • *To avoid plagiarism you need to cite all the following:*
> 1. *Direct quotations, whatever the source.*
> 2. *Paraphrasing of ideas from a source even where you don't quote directly.*
> 3. *Summarising of ideas from a source even where you don't quote directly.*
> 4. *"Borrowed" ideas, such as quotations or case ratios, from an indirect secondary source.*

1. It directly quotes the phrase "the principal object of the draftsman is to achieve certainty—a laudable object in itself" without acknowledgment.
2. The rest of the passage draws very heavily on Lord Denning's ideas, for example about the pages in the law reports, and certainty/clarity. This is therefore a paraphrase. Paraphrases as well as direct quotations must be referenced.

Now let's look at *how* to reference your work correctly so as to avoid any possible risk of plagiarism.

HOW SHOULD MY LEGAL WRITING BE REFERENCED?

5.29 ▶ In this section, we will demonstrate:

> **TIPS** • *Keep in mind your goal in referencing is to acknowledge the use you have made of other people's words or ideas and to enable your readers to locate these works for themselves.*

- how to write citations for primary sources of law;
- how to write citations for printed secondary sources;
- how to write citations for electronic and web-based sources;
- how to reference the same source more than once (a repeat reference).

Time spent learning how to reference appropriately will be well spent as you can reuse this skill in all your assignments. If you use a word processor then it is likely to contain a mechanism for inserting footnotes (or endnotes) for you (in MS Word, it is located in the References menu), which makes life a lot easier. If you are unsure how to use this facility then seek guidance— mastering this will only take a couple of minutes and will save a lot of time later.

It is an extremely good habit to reference as you are writing. Leaving it to the end is an invitation to miss something out which might lead to an incident of inadvertent plagiarism.

Different systems of referencing

5.30 ▶ There are two main systems for citing material. The first is called the Numeric system (sometime also called the footnoting system) and the other is the Harvard or Author-Date system. You will probably already have seen both styles in academic books (although legal textbooks are more likely to use the Numeric system).

1. The Harvard or Author-date system
The author's name and the year of publication are included in brackets within the text, for example:

> There are two main systems for citing material (Higgins & Tatham, 2015, p.102).

The bibliography would then set out in full the reference for the work. The bibliography is an essential accompaniment to the essay because it shows the location of all the material cited (which in this case, we have invented).

2. The numeric system

Numbered footnotes (or endnotes) are used to provide the reader with the location of the material which has been referenced in the main text, for example:

> There are two main systems for citing material.[1]
>
> ---
> [1]   Edwina Higgins & Laura Tatham, *Successful Legal Writing* (3rd edn, Sweet & Maxwell 2015), 102.

It is more conventional for the numeric system to be used in legal writing.

Different conventions for referencing

As well as the two major systems of referencing, there are also different conventions covering how to cite different types of material, of which the most commonly used is the Oxford Standard for Citation of Legal Authorities (OSCOLA), which can be downloaded from *www.law.ox.ac.uk/publications/oscola.php*. This gives advice and detailed rules on the citation of both primary and secondary legal sources.

▶ **5.31**

Guidance on how to reference

Of course your starting point should be whatever your institution requires. Are you expected to use Harvard or footnotes? Are you expected to follow OSCOLA or does your Law School have its own convention? Is there a guide to how you should cite material? If there is, get hold of it and use it. The key is to be *consistent* in your referencing. You will note that the references throughout this book follow the consistent "house style" of the publisher. If your Law School or university has its own house style, this is what you must use. We provide examples based on the 4th edition (2012) OSCOLA convention throughout the rest of this chapter.

▶ **5.32**

Citing statutes

Cite a *statute* by reference to its short title, including the calendar year, and, where needed, specific section number.

▶ **5.33**

> Children Act 1989, s.1(1).

Citing cases

Cite a case by giving its *name* (i.e. the names of the parties) in italics, the year, and the reporting citation. There are two different styles of citing cases, the *neutral citation* and *the law report citation*.

▶ **5.34**

Neutral citations

The neutral citation system was introduced in January 2001[7] and gives each case one unique

---

[7]   Practice Direction (Judgments: Form and citation) (January 11, 2001), [2001] 1 W.L.R. 194, Practice Direction (Judgments: Neutral Citations) (January 14, 2002) [2002] 1 W.L.R. 346 and Practice Direction (Citation of authority) [2012] 1 W.L.R. 780.

individual citation, based on the court and year in which the case was heard, which can be used to identify the case regardless of which series of law reports it appears in.

The standard format when giving a neutral citation is (in this order): *case name* in italics, year of hearing in square brackets, abbreviation of the court, judgment number.
Example:

> *Radmacher v Granatino* [2010] UKSC 42

TIPS • *Find out whether your institution allows or prefers you to use neutral citations where available.*

Here, UKSC indicates the United Kingdom Supreme Court, and the judgment number of 42 indicates that it was the 42nd case to be heard by this court in 2010. Similar abbreviations exist to cover the other major courts, for example:

> UKHL—UK House of Lords
> EWCA Civ—England and Wales Court of Appeal (Civil Division) EWCA Crim—England and Wales Court of Appeal (Criminal Division) EWHC (Ch)—England and Wales High Court (Chancery Division) * EWHC (Fam)—England and Wales High Court (Family Division) *
> EWHC (QBD)—England and Wales High Court (Queen's Bench Division) *
> *For High Court citations, the judgment number is given after the court, and before an indication of division is given in brackets.

Official neutral citations are only available from 2001 (BAILII, the British and Irish Legal Information Institute, have assigned neutral citations to important older cases on their database, available at *http://www.bailii.org* [Accessed November 17, 2014], but these are not authoritative).

Law report citations

TIPS • *Find out whether your institution prefers you to use a citation from The Law Reports where available, or whether you may choose to cite other law report series.*

The standard format when citing from a law report is (in this order): *case name* in italics, year reported in square brackets, volume number (if any), abbreviated name of the law report, number of the page on which the report begins.

Examples:

> *Pepper (Inspector of Taxes) v Hart* [1993] A.C. 593
> *Carlill v Carbolic Smoke Ball Company* [1893] 1 Q.B. 256
> *Re Ellenborough Park* [1956] Ch. 131
> *Law v National Greyhound Racing Club* [1983] 1 W.L.R. 1302

OSCOLA format for citing cases
OSCOLA recommends that where a *neutral citation* is available, this should be given first, and followed by the law report citation from The Law Reports (this means the set of reports

comprising Appeal Cases [AC], the Queen's or King's Bench Reports [QB or KB], the Chancery Reports [Ch] and the Family Reports [Fam]). If the case was not reported in any of these reports, then a citation from the Weekly Law Reports (WLR) should be used, if available, and failing that, the All England Reports (All ER).
Example:

> *Radmacher v Granatino* [2010] UKSC 42, [2011] 1 AC 534

Where a neutral citation is not available (principally, therefore, for cases reported before 2001) OSCOLA's preferred alternative is to use a citation from a law report in the order of preference already given above, i.e. The Law Reports, the Weekly Law Reports, the All England Law Reports. If the case was not reported in any of these, then a citation from a specialist report could be given. Additionally, where no neutral citation is available, then OSCOLA recommends that that the court should be specified in round brackets after the citation (since this is not clear from a law report citation as it is from a neutral citation).
Example:

> *Tatham v Drummond* (1864) 4 De GJ & Sm 484 (ChD)

Citing books

When citing a *book*, it is usual to indicate the following: the author/editor is (if an editor, use (ed) after the name), the title of the book is, the edition number unless it is the first edition, the publisher, date of publication, and (if appropriate) particular pages referred to.

▶ 5.35

Under the OSCOLA system, the author's first name (or initials) and surname, as given on the book cover, are followed by the title in italics in title case, and the information about edition number, publisher and year in brackets, followed by any relevant page numbers. Up to three authors are named; more should be indicated by the first followed by "and others". OSCOLA no longer requires the place of publication to be given.

> An Author, *Title of Book* (3rd edn, Sweet & Maxwell 2014).

Citing journal articles

When citing a journal article, again, the usual rule is to give the information the reader needs to locate the material, so you will need to give the author, and the title of the article, the journal where it is located including volume/edition and page and year where appropriate.

▶ 5.36

Under the OSCOLA guidance an article written by Rebecca Bailey-Harris called "Contact—challenging conventional wisdom?" which was published in the fourth issue of vol.13 of the journal *Child and Family Law Quarterly* in 2001 would be referenced like this:

> Rebecca Bailey-Harris, 'Contact—challenging conventional wisdom?' (2001) 13 CFLQ 361.

Citing web-based materials

5.37 ▶ You are likely to wish to utilise the wealth of legal information available on the web to support your arguments. If you have located cases or statutes on the web, for example through a legal database such as Westlaw or LexisLibrary then simply cite these as you would for printed sources. Do not include the full URL from Westlaw or LexisLibrary.

> **TIPS** • *Don't make the mistake of thinking that web-based material doesn't need to be cited, or that citing 'Westlaw' or 'LexisLibrary' is sufficient in itself.*

Similarly, for articles, where these are simply electronic copies of material which is available in printed copy (most traditional legal journals) then follow the convention for citing the printed copy (as given above). However, for sources available only on the web (not in a printed journal), you indicate that you found the documents on the web, and indicate when and where you located them. Again, there are different conventions for how to cite web-based material, but the key is to give as much information as possible about author and title and so on, as you would in citing printed sources, but additionally indicate the URL (i.e. the web address) where you found the material and the date on which you accessed the information (because web material changes). The example we used earlier on in the chapter should be cited as:

> Council of Mortgage Lenders, *Arrears and repossessions still falling, cites CML (Council of Mortgage Lenders* November 13, 2014) *www.cml.org.uk/cml/media/ press/4063* [Accessed November 13, 2014].

As a note of caution the web obviously contains a mass of information of varying quality, so when you want to use websites to support your arguments you do need to be careful. Remember that if something is published in paper form, this usually (though not always) means that some publisher somewhere thought it was worth publishing; there will usually have been some kind of review process involved. Material from the internet could have been published by literally anyone with no review and no regard for accuracy.

Citing a particular place within a source (pinpointing)

5.38 ▶ You will also frequently need to give a reference to a particular section, page or paragraph of a source. This is called pinpointing, and you must *always* pinpoint a quotation or paraphrase, because your goal in referencing, as we've said, is to provide sufficient information for the reader to find the material for themselves. You can't expect your reader to read a whole book or judgment to find the quotation you've used: you must specify exactly where it can be found.

OSCOLA recommends that pinpointing should be done by giving the specific page or paragraph (see the next section for an example).

Citing the same source on more than one occasion

5.39 ▶ It is very likely that in the course of your legal writing, you will want to refer to the same source more than once. Rather than giving the entire reference every time, it is acceptable to give the full reference the first time you cite it and then use some form of abbreviation on subsequent occasions, but there are lots of different ways of doing it. You may have read in your textbooks use of Latin phrases like *op cit*, *loc cit* and *ibid*. Generally it is best to avoid these as it is confusing, and OSCOLA doesn't recommend them.

Don't reference again if:

- you are referring to the same source several times in a row (for example during the course of a paragraph).

However, **do** reference again if:

- there has been a gap in which you have referred to other sources or moved on to other issues, then reference it again in abbreviated form by indicating the original citation;
- you have previously referred to the source but now need to provide a reference to a different page or section;
- not citing it again might cause confusion—if in doubt, cite again.

Where you are providing a subsequent reference, then the OSCOLA suggests the following:

1. On first reference, give the full citation.
2. On a subsequent reference, where needed according to the suggestions above, give the author's name again and then reference the footnote in which the previous full reference is located. So for example, if you are referring to a work by Smith, previously cited in full in footnote 6, then a subsequent reference would read:

> Smith (n 6).

You need to add specific pages (pinpoint) if you are referring to a different part of Smith's work in this reference, e.g. Smith (n 6 215).

If you are referring back to a case or statute, then simply give the footnote at which the previous full citation is located (as long as you included the name in the original reference: if not give the name of the case, followed by the appropriate footnote number).

Be careful not to use this technique of cross-referencing your footnotes *as you write*, because at the draft stage, your footnotes are very likely to change. When you use the "insert footnote" facility, your word processor will helpfully keep the numbers of the footnotes straight for you. So, if you've got 10 footnotes, but then decide that you need an extra footnote somewhere between 4 and 5, when you insert it, it will appear as 5, and 5 will be renumbered as 6 automatically, 6

> **TIPS** • *Sorting out your repeat references should be the last thing you do before submission.*

as 7 and so on. So far, so good. However, what the word processor *can't* do is keep track of what the *contents* of your footnotes say, so supposing footnote 10 said "Smith (n 6)", you are now pointing your reader to the wrong material because the full citation for Smith is now at footnote 7.

Therefore the best thing to do is insert your footnotes in full as you write. Only when you are absolutely sure that your main text is the final copy should you then go through and sort out your subsequent references, so that you can be certain which footnote is the first reference to

Smith. You can then abbreviate appropriately for all further references to Smith. How to set out your bibliography is explained in Chapter 8, and there is a sample bibliography in Appendix 4.

SUMMARY OF CHAPTER 5

5.40 ▶

- An academic argument consists of reasons supported by evidence which lead logically to a conclusion.
- Weigh up conflicting evidence to conclude which side of the overall argument is stronger.
- You should use a case or statute as evidence to support a proposition of law and a secondary source such as a book or journal to support other propositions, except those which are "common knowledge".
- You must acknowledge where you have used the words or ideas of others to avoid plagiarism.
- Your work must be correctly referenced according to your institution's requirements or other consistent method.

PART 3

Completing your assignment

▶ 6
The writing phase

WHAT IS THE PURPOSE OF THIS CHAPTER?

Once you have carried out your diagnosis and research you need to move to the next stage, ▶ **6.1**
which is to put your pen to paper—or, more likely, your fingers to the keyboard—and begin
writing. The key to a successful writing phase is to understand how a good answer is structured
so you can plan your answer accordingly. The writing phase will also require a good level of
written English which we consider further in Chapter 7. In this chapter we are concentrating
more on the organisation of the material and the style of your writing.

By the end of this chapter you will:

● have developed your skills in planning your writing;
● be able to see the benefits of structuring your writing with a logical flow of
  argument;
● be able to understand the key features of an effective introduction and conclusion.

WHAT DOES *STRUCTURE* MEAN IN ACADEMIC WRITING?

When we talk about *structure* we mean the way in which your assignment is organised: how it ▶ **6.2**
develops from your introduction through your successive paragraphs to your conclusion.
Whether or not your institution awards marks specifically for structure within its assessment
criteria you can still assume that structuring your work will be of vital importance, as it goes to
the heart of successful writing. A good structure lends an automatic air of credibility to your
writing because it means you are communicating more effectively.

A common use of the word "structure" is to refer to a building. The same idea of needing
a foundation in order to support what comes later is equally true of writing. In this chapter we
are going to show you what a good structure to a piece of writing looks like, and how you can
develop the skills necessary to create a workable structure in *your* writing. Whilst the structure
you adopt may differ according to the nature of the writing you are doing, the process of creating a structure for your writing will not.

This is the point at which you will pull together all your work so far by beginning to plan
your assignment.

The importance of writing a plan

Word processing your assignments lends itself to an approach of jumping straight in and ▶ **6.3**
starting writing, and some people find it preferable to begin writing first to have something

"down" and then spend time organising and structuring the material later, or do this in tandem with writing the assignment. This approach does work for some people—this is likely to be those who are particularly strong at diagnosing the task—providing that extra time is allowed for organising and editing later. However, a note of caution is needed: for many, it doesn't work to start writing without a plan. You may find you lose your focus and your assignment will end up being confused. There are two reasons why planning your writing is vital:

1. It helps you get your thoughts in order and focuses your mind on the assignment.
2. Your plan keeps you on track as you do the writing itself.

How to write a plan

6.4 ▶ When you have completed your diagnosis, you will have worked out what the question is asking for and gone on to identify a series of sub-questions. In your research phase you will have identified the answer (as far as there is one) to each question you have posed as well as the relevant authority for each point you want to make in answer to these sub-questions. Next, you will need to make decisions about the relevant weight, i.e. which of these points are major points at the heart of your argument and which are minor points which won't need to be covered in as much detail. In other words you will concern yourself with both coverage and depth. (We looked at this in Chapter 3.) These decisions should be reflected in your plan. The last step is making decisions about the order in which your major and minor points will be made in your answer.

We discussed various techniques for diagnosing essay questions and problem questions in Chapter 3 and to a certain extent you will also need to develop different plans for answering different types of questions. With essay questions your plan, and therefore your structure, will be complete once you have diagnosed the task and made decisions on minor and major points. With a problem question it is the question itself which may well give clues as to the best approach to planning and structure. Any plan needs to adopt a logical style and approach and the very nature of a problem question is that it offers these elements.

Once you have your plan you need to start the writing itself. Remember you don't have to start at the beginning. If it suits you to start at the end and work backwards do so. However, in whatever order you choose to approach your writing, you must remain clear on your goal of answering the question, and in order to do that, effective essays contain the following elements:

- An introduction, which identifies the issues you will discuss.
- A main body, which develops the issues into an argument.
- A conclusion, which gives your final position in relation to the core question asked or implied in the assignment.

We now consider these elements in more detail, beginning with the concept of an introduction.

HOW DO I WRITE A SUCCESSFUL INTRODUCTION?

The key to answering this question is *recognising* a successful introduction.

▶ **6.5**

ACTIVITY 6.1

Below are two example introductions, which both introduce the same question. Read them and see if you can work out roughly what the subject matter of the assignment is, and the type of question which has been set.

▶ **6.6**

Example 1:

> There are lots of different things in Land Law which can be classed as third party rights including freehold covenants, estate contracts and easements. For example: rights of way, rights to light and rights of drainage, etc. can all be easements. The law on what an easement is and whether one has been acquired is complex and we need to examine these closely in order to answer this question.

Example 2:

> Peter needs advice on whether the right retained by David to cross Wayside's vegetable garden can amount to a legal easement (*Re Ellenborough*) and if so whether it has been acquired correctly. The three possibilities are expressly, impliedly or by prescription and each have different requirements which we must apply to our facts.

Activity feedback—here are our thoughts:

Presumably you could see that both these examples concerned the same subject area (land law and specifically easements), but you may have struggled to work out in any more detail than this what the subject matter of the question was from Example 1, which is vague and generalised. There is no indication in this introduction as to who needs advice about what. It is not until we read Example 2 that we can work out that the subject matter of the question must be a problem which relates to the reservation of an easement by David, and whether the arrangements amount to a validly created easement.

If you were marking these assignments (or indeed if you were seeking advice from a lawyer about the acquisition of an easement) which of these introductions do you think does a better job of identifying the issues which need to be considered? By using the names of the parties and beginning to pinpoint the material facts, Example 2 is a much better introduction to a problem question. Example 1 gives no indication of the issues on which the parties require advice. Indeed, if we hadn't told you that these were introductions to the same question, you might have presumed that only Example 2 was the introduction to a problem, and that Example 1 was introducing an essay.

And here is the question these examples were introducing:

> In 2009 David, the registered proprietor of Wayside, sold the vegetable plot to Maria. In the transfer, he expressly reserved the right (for the benefit of Wayside) to cross the vegetable plot to reach the adjacent woods. Last year, Maria sold the vegetable plot to Peter, who also intended to grow vegetables for sale. Last month David sold Wayside to Nora.
>
> Advise Nora who has been told by Peter to stop using the shortcut.

And a suggested introduction:

> This scenario concerns the law relating to easements and specifically whether the right to cross the vegetable plot retained by David, the proprietor of Wayside, when he sold the plot to Maria is enforceable by Nora, the new owner of Wayside against Peter, the new owner of the vegetable plot. The first step is to examine whether this right is capable of existing as an easement by applying *Re Ellenborough Park* [1955]. Then we will consider if and how David retained this right so that it benefits Wayside forever.

An introduction is a fundamental element of any answer and will usually take about 10 per cent of the overall word limit. The introduction is where you impress: you inform your reader about what is to come to encourage them to read further in a positive frame of mind. In a non-academic context a reader chooses whether to continue reading a particular piece of writing, and they will often decide on the basis of the introduction—in other words, the introduction should *invite* the reader to go further. Obviously, with assessed work you can assume it will be read whether the introduction is good or bad, but nevertheless this idea of an invitation is important: you must make a good impression. You do this by demonstrating in your introduction that you have identified the relevant issues (which arise from your diagnosis). The introduction sets the scene and context for the rest of the piece. For example, if your essay is an exploration of a central idea, or thesis, this will need to be defined before it can be developed. Whatever is contained in the essay must relate to this main thesis and so that thesis must be introduced to the reader. Get this right and your work will be read by an interested marker looking forward to hearing what you are going to say in the rest of your answer.

From doing the above activity you will have realised that one fault to avoid is just *writing generally on the topic* rather than getting down to the issue. Other things you need to avoid are: *Restating the question* and *giving a lot of historical background* unless that's required by the question. All of these fail to demonstrate that you have successfully diagnosed the task.

Introductions are sometimes described by students as the hardest part of an assignment to write. Often what these students *really* mean is that the hardest part of writing an assignment is actually to start *writing*. There is no need to confuse writing the introduction with starting to write the answer—if you prefer to write the introduction last, you can. As long as your plan and structure are successful it does not matter in what order you tackle the different elements of your assignment. Of course, in an exam situation or any situation where you are writing by hand as opposed to typing, you have less flexibility: here, it is better to focus on writing your answer from start to finish rather than to mess about with where to start on the paper.

Another reason given by students for finding it hard to write introductions is that they can't see the *point* of an introduction. Why write down something in the introduction when you are planning to say it again in more detail in the next paragraph? This is missing the point of an introduction: it is your chance to specify the *issues* which are raised by the question, to let the reader know where the assignment is heading. You then go on to *discuss* those issues in appropriate detail in the main body of the work.

Your first few sentences need to set out the main issues that have been raised by the question. So your ability to write a good introduction, to a certain extent, relies on having completed the planning and preparation stages satisfactorily. By carrying out the diagnosis of the task correctly you will have identified the thesis and you need to articulate this to the reader. Here we are not talking about discussing the minor issues—you need to highlight the key points or concepts or problems that are at the very heart of the question.

> **TIPS** • *An introduction explains what the answer is going to do. So: reveal your diagnosis of task by setting out the issues you will be examining in your assignment.*

Have a look at the following question, which is also based on land law[1]:

> In their textbook *Land Law*, Cursley and Davys comment that "Land law has tended to be led by the needs of large landowners and investors. The result is that land law . . . generally seeks to achieve 'justice through certainty'."
>
> Critically discuss this statement in the context of co-ownership and severance of joint tenancies.

Your introduction to this question might look like this:

> Historically, the law on co-ownership in England and Wales is certain but people co-own land for a variety of different reasons. The legal rules try to accommodate and balance these tensions and indeed, as long as proper advice has been taken, can work reasonably well in practice. However, in this context, the rules relating to the severance of a beneficial joint tenancy, because of their inherent flexibility, can lead to uncertainty.

This introduction identifies the main issue arising from the question (co-ownership) and indicates the relevance and importance of the rules of severance in terms of their effect on land law attaining "justice through certainty". This is setting the scene for the reader, which means you are showing that you know what you are talking about. This doesn't mean a repetition or rewriting of the question. Neither will your marker expect an historical treatise on the background to the subject area; both of these will tend to indicate a "write all you know" approach. Setting the scene

> **TIPS** • *Tips for writing a good introduction:*
> * *Consider using a "topic sentence" to indicate the main point to you answer.*
> * *Be concise (10 per cent of the total words should be the maximum) and relevant— use your diagnosis as your guide.*
> * *Don't include background history unless it is directly relevant to the question.*

---

[1] The full reference for the textbook cited in the question is: Joe Cursley and Mark Davy, *Land Law* (7th edn, Palgrave Macmillan 2011).

- Don't just rewrite the question in your own words.
- Don't assume knowledge on the part of the reader.
- Don't write a conclusion instead: you are setting out the issues here, not giving a position on those issues.

means something different: you are showing you are familiar with the subject area, you have identified the issues to be discussed and what is expected of you in this assignment. The main body of your answer will then demonstrate that you can fulfil the expectations you have raised in the introduction.

The next activity will help you understand the importance of an introduction.

ACTIVITY 6.2

6.7 ▶ Now read the four passages that follow and consider how well they introduce or set the scene for an essay on another typical land law topic—adverse possession. Use the following questions to help you evaluate the usefulness of the four introductions:

- Is the key issue identified?
- Is it obvious what the subject matter of the question is?
- Does it include authority to support any propositions of law?
- Does it encourage you to read on to find out more?
- Is it clear where the writer is going?
- Is the passage easy to understand?

Passage 1:

> The statement in the question refers to a method of acquiring title to land involving occupation which is adverse (i.e. without permission—*Moses v Lovegrove* [1952] 2 Q.B. 533) to the paper owner for a period of 12 years. The time period identified traditionally applied regardless of whether title to the land was registered or unregistered—s.15(1) Limitation Act 1980. The section clearly states that the paper owner cannot bring an action if 12 years have passed since the right arose to do so. The statute does not operate to transfer the paper owner's title to the squatter but the act of not permitting any action ensures that that is the effect. In their consultation prior to the Land Registration Act 2002 ((1998) Law Com No 254, para.10.18) the Law Commission stated that adverse possession should override registration "where it is essential to ensure the marketability of land or to prevent unfairness". However, in actual fact, the rules contained within the Land Registration Act 2002 mean that since October 13, 2003 it is now much more difficult for a squatter to obtain title even though the required time period has been reduced to 10 years by the same rules.

Passage 2:

> Squatting is dead! The old ways have gone to be usurped by modern doctrines created by quasi-governmental organisations with their own protectionist agenda. The Law Commission's proposals were vague but the new rules are surprisingly clear.

> The final result appears robust but since we have no direct authority on its application so perhaps it is too early to say that the "art" of squatting is dead and buried.

Passage 3:

> The justifications for permitting squatting arise out of ensuring, in the interests of certainty, that actions to recover possession cannot be brought after a certain length of time has passed. Stale claims will not haunt landowners and purchasers forever. The law is merely providing for cases where there is no formal proof of title and thereby ensuring land remains marketable. The main issue with the law on adverse possession has always been the view that people have that legal title to private property that has been bought with "good money" ought to be protected whatever happens. These two aims are in conflict.

Passage 4:

> Land law covers many different concepts and situations such as easements, covenants, mortgages and co-ownership. One which is of interest is the notion of adverse possession. The law regarding the squatting can be found in cases such as *Pye v Graham* and *Buckinghamshire County Council v Moran*. It is clear that this rule required serious reform as it really isn't up to date at all.

Activity feedback—here are our thoughts:

OK, this was a bit of a trick. Bearing in mind what we've said so far about the introduction being where you have the opportunity to demonstrate your diagnosis, your first instinct should have been: *How can I judge which is the best introduction when I haven't seen the question?* In other words, in order to assess the quality of an introduction, you have to work out whether it shows good diagnosis of the question.

So, you need the question. Here it is. It is the same question we looked at in Chapter 3.

> "The law that a squatter can acquire a title merely from occupying land for 12 years is outmoded."
> Discuss this statement with particular reference to the Land Registration Act 2002.

ACTIVITY 6.2.1

Now have another look at the passages. Remember that a well-written introduction should enable you to identify the gist of the question—does this help you evaluate them?

▶ 6.8

Activity feedback—here are our thoughts:

- *Passage 1* provides a clear introduction to the subject area that an average reader with no specialist knowledge would be able to understand. The writer names, defines and explains the rule in the question title. The fact that there has been some reform in this area is identified making indirect reference to the suggestion in the question that the law is outmoded.

- *Passage 2* is written in a somewhat over the top style and makes sweeping generalisations. There is no direct or indirect reference to the question, which makes it very difficult for a reader to identify the parameters of the answer. We know what the reader's position is but we don't really know where the argument is going to go.
- *Passage 3* launches too quickly into the subject without sufficient attempt to "set the scene" or indeed settle the reader. We are given some pros and cons of the law but we are not told what the law actually is.
- *Passage 4* makes some bold factual statements which it does attempt to support with authority but as the relevance of these cases is not explained they are of little use. The last sentence is almost a conclusion and does not fit in an introduction "setting the scene".

> **TIPS** • *Remember that your goal in writing your introduction is to make your reader think: "Here's someone who knows what they are talking about, they have clearly done some research and they are going to answer the question that has been set and not one of their own making."*

6.9 ▶ Before we go on to look at writing the main body of your answer, take some time to reflect on your own practice. Find something that you have written recently, look at the introduction and, bearing in mind what we have said above about what to avoid when writing an introduction, try to rate it. How could you improve it? What would you do differently now if you had to write that same introduction again?

HOW DO I STRUCTURE THE MAIN TEXT OF MY ANSWER?

6.10 ▶ Between the introduction and the conclusion, the main text of your answer is where you develop your arguments. The main text is all about *demonstrating your knowledge and understanding* and may be seen as easier or safer to write than the introduction or conclusion. Creating and then developing an argument have been explored more fully in Chapter 5, so you should now have a clearer idea of how to put this together.

Essentially, the main part of your answer will consist of a series of paragraphs, each dealing with a different point in your argument (as identified in your plan) which will equate—broadly—to the questions raised in your diagnosis (appropriately ordered).

Each paragraph should be centred on an organising idea which gives meaning to that paragraph and is what you are attempting to persuade the reader to accept as true or valid. Without an organising idea or thesis, the writing appears pointless (literally) to the reader. As a general guide, you should only deal with one organising idea per paragraph. It is vital that the opening sentence reflects what is in the rest of the paragraph. A good structure will not make markers search around the rest of your answer to find more points on that issue. Getting to grips with identifying an organising idea and how to support it effectively is one of the most important writing skills you can develop. Knowing how to express and sustain an organising idea is the building block of your writing and will lead to coherent and logical writing overall.

You should draw these organising ideas from the sub-questions you have posed in your diagnosis (see Chapter 5).

To develop a point in your argument you should consider including the following elements in your paragraph:

- A sentence identifying the focus or theme of the paragraph.
- Clarification of any issues which may be unclear.
- Some kind of evaluation or analysis or examination or discussion of the point or issue covered by that paragraph supported by relevant evidence.
- Reference to any implications of that point.

But it is the connections or transitions *between* these paragraphs that are the key to developing a good structure. So although your work will consist of a series of self-contained paragraphs, in order for your writing to reach its potential and achieve the best score possible, these paragraphs have to be connected in some way. You are looking to create a logical progression from one paragraph (and its organising idea) to the next, reflecting the flow of your argument.

Making sure your writing flows

This means linking your writing together, which is sometimes also referred to as having effective transition. Transition means the same in writing as elsewhere, in other words movement or change. It is important in your writing to pay attention to how the writing (and your argument) moves from sentence to sentence and from paragraph to paragraph. You are striving for a clear sense of direction in all of your writing so that a reader can follow your *sequence of ideas*. Transitional words or phrases, sometimes also referred to as signal words, can be used to link together sentences and paragraphs, ensure continuity in your writing and give signposts to the reader about how your argument proceeds from one point to another, one sentence to another, and one paragraph to another.

▶ 6.11

ACTIVITY 6.3

To explore the issue of transition more closely, look at the sample answers to the question on the Practice Statement in Appendix 3 and in particular look at Answers A and C. How would you rate the transition or progression of argument here?

▶ 6.12

Answer A is a good example of a writer who has not taken the time to work on the transitions between paragraphs causing the answer to stop and start a number of times. Here we have a demonstration of how not to do it! For example, virtually every paragraph starts with "Another case where the House of Lords used the Practice Statement was . . ." leading to a list-like approach with no apparent connections between the points being made.

Now look at this extract from Answer C:

> A further example is the case of *Miliangos v George Frank Textiles* where the House was prepared to extinguish from the precedent books a ruling that sterling should be the only currency in which judgment can be awarded, a position which, as Lord Denning asserted in the court of appeal was more appropriate to the days of the empire than to modern global economies.

If it were only in the interests of modernising and developing the law and the need for a legal system to maintain its grip on current affairs that the law lords were prepared to use the practice statement then we might justifiably conclude that the small loss to certainty would be a worthwhile price to pay in order to maintain a modern and vibrant legal system.

TIPS • *If the writing flows and makes good use of paragraph transitions it should be possible to take the first sentence of each paragraph and put them together to get a reasonably clear idea of what the remainder of the argument will consist of. Try this with a piece of your own writing.*

Don't consider the spelling, grammar and sentence construction at this stage; look only at the transition between these two paragraphs. The references to "modern" in the last sentence of the first paragraph and "modernising" in the second emphasises the connection between the two sentences and therefore paragraphs, and the writer's development of the argument. You should be able to see that this writer has a better understanding of the need to link or connect their ideas and paragraphs in order to best demonstrate their understanding.

Making effective transitions

6.13 ▶ Transitions (or connections/links) can be used in a number of ways, and we can group them according to what we may want to achieve. For example, you may use words or phrases such as: *but*; *however*; *on the other hand*; or *yet*, if you want to differentiate between two points or facts. If you are extending a point or an argument you may use words like: *in addition*; *moreover*; *furthermore*; *similarly*; *likewise*; or *correspondingly*. To conclude a topic or a section of an essay or even the whole essay words such as: *thus*; *as a result*; *therefore*; or *consequently* can be useful. So essentially, these kinds of words can tie sentences, paragraphs, and arguments together effectively and make interpretation easier for the reader. You may find it helpful to refer back to Activity 4.1 where we looked at defining these words.

As mentioned in the previous activity, the key transitions are those between paragraphs. You are looking to create a link between the last sentence of one paragraph and the first sentence of the next one.

For example:

. . . So it is clear that in some cases the literal rule is not always the best technique to use when trying to establish Parliament's intention.

In addition, a linked but alternative means that we may wish to consider is the golden rule . . .

This example also uses the technique of echoing a key word—*technique*—which can be effective. However you do run the risk of repetition—a common mistake in student writing.

For example:

. . . The other key element to the formation of a contract is acceptance.

One of the most important elements of contract formation is the notion of acceptance . . .

Sometimes it is easier to write a transitional or linking *sentence*. This will not tell you what is coming next in the writing but will let the reader know that this paragraph is a reversal of the last one.

For example:

> . . . It would seem that the court put an end to arguments on this point.
> However, this was not always the case. In the time of . . .

Don't forget that sentences also need to follow each other in a logical manner, and so because your work must adopt a logical pattern you will be using transitions within and between paragraphs almost continuously.

ACTIVITY 6.4

Read the sentences below and insert the best of the three alternatives in the blank spaces provided. Remember to keep an eye on the relationship between the sentences or the constituent parts of the sentences given and also that punctuation will affect what you can use.

▶ 6.14

1. There are occasions when you might use extremely hot water but .... 26 to 27 degrees celsius is adequate.

   as a rule   *otherwise*   *consequently*

2. Student numbers have increased steadily over the past few years. .... the numbers of staff employed to teach them has declined.

   In contrast   *Above all*   *Correspondingly*

3. Courseworks must be handed in by the deadline, ... they will not be marked.

   obviously   *as a result*   *otherwise*

4. .... it is a comparatively simple procedure, mistakes are always made.

   Nevertheless   *Because*   *Even though*

5. The two Houses of Parliament, ... the House of Lords and the House of Commons, are located next door to each other on Parliament Square in London.

   for example   *namely*   *in particular*

Activity feedback—here are our thoughts:

As we noted earlier in the book it is often a matter of preference which transitional words you use, but here are the ones we suggest for the activity above:

1. as a rule.
2. In contrast.
3. otherwise.
4. Even though.
5. namely.

Now, reflect on your own practice again. Using the same piece of writing you used when reflecting on your introduction, look at your use of paragraphs and any connections or transitions between them.

- First, have you used clearly defined paragraphs? It can be tempting when you are in the swing of writing to write in one long stream but this will make your writing harder to read and to mark, as your organising ideas will be lost. Stick to your plan, with a point per paragraph.
- Next, does each paragraph contribute to the argument? Does each one develop a point? Are they so short that you can usefully combine two or three without losing the flow? Are they too long? If so, consider splitting a paragraph in two wherever you introduce a new point.
- Have you actually connected each paragraph to the ones that come before and after? Or does a reader come to an abrupt stop at the end of each paragraph?

This construction of a logical and flowing argument is not always as easy as it may appear and you may find it helpful to refer back to Chapter 5.

To finish our consideration of structure we need to look at writing conclusions.

HOW DO I WRITE A SUCCESSFUL CONCLUSION?

6.15 ▶ As we mentioned earlier, along with writing an introduction, writing a conclusion is often considered to be the most difficult part of an assignment. Some of our students complain that they have "nothing left to say" having already written the assignment. Or they may feel giving a conclusion one way rather than another risks being wrong. This demonstrates a misunderstanding of the purpose of a conclusion.

The aim of a conclusion

6.16 ▶ The introduction is where you set out the issues to be discussed, so the conclusion is where you provide answers or solutions to these issues. In other words, together with the introduction, a conclusion is the frame around the main body of the work. A conclusion lets your reader know that you've finished developing your ideas and shows them your final position. It is the last word on the points you have made in your writing. In addition, a good conclusion leaves the marker with a good final impression (just as they are about to allocate a mark to your efforts). Always end with a definite statement . . . as this concluding paragraph does.

> **TIPS** • *Tips on writing a conclusion:*
> - *Do make it clear and to the point.*
> - *Do answer the core question arising from your diagnosis.*
> - *Do not introduce completely new ideas.*
> - *Do not conclude with a cliché.*
> - *Do not apologise for anything you have said.*
> - *Do not contradict yourself.*
> - *Do not merely summarise what has gone before: remember that a conclusion is not the same as a summary.*

ACTIVITY 6.5

This complements Activity 6.2 on introductions. Imagine those same four students have also written conclusions to the same essay, as set out below. Bearing in mind the advice above, look at these attempts and evaluate them.

▶ 6.17

Passage 1:

> This essay has attempted to show that the rule that a squatter can acquire a title merely from occupying land for 12 years is indeed outmoded. Several cases have been analysed, although some were slightly out of date (i.e. from before the statute). This essay also examined whether the 2002 Act has made any difference at all. The question of the Act's impact on other aspects of limitation was also discussed but we concluded that this was probably true although we are unable to say for sure.

Passage 2:

> This essay has therefore looked at all the cases concerning adverse possession from before the Act like *Powell v McFarlane* and *Bucks v Moran* and all the cases since the Act came into force. It is interesting to also consider the Act's impact in the area of Human Rights e.g. *Pye v Graham*. Whether the Act has such far-reaching consequences as was originally feared—only time will tell!

Passage 3:

> This piece has looked at the nature and impact of the rule on adverse possession. To a large extent this may now be regarded as historical with the major development of the enactment of the Land Registration Act 2002. What is clear is that the operation of the Act fundamentally alters the laws on adverse possession by restricting the ability of a squatter to gain title merely through length of occupation. As such it is the case that the rules on adverse possession are outmoded as in reality in most cases it now becomes impossible to gain a title as the Act provides paper owners with the right to prevent that.

Passage 4:

> The law on adverse possession is not outmoded and the Act doesn't really have much of an impact after all.

Activity feedback—here are our thoughts:

- *Passage 1:* do you think this writer has much confidence in what they have written? Phrases such as "I have attempted", "slightly out of date" and "unable to say for sure" do not make us trust that this reader knows what they are talking about. It repeats what was in the essay (the Act's impact on limitation generally was also discussed) and indeed doesn't really finish properly. It just comes to an end as if the writer's pen ran out!

- *Passage 2:* this writer adopts the "repeat it again in the conclusion and it'll have more impact" approach to the writing of conclusions. However, there does seem to be some attempt at giving an overview and an attempt to set the points in a wider context.
- *Passage 3:* this conclusion is appropriate. It refers back to the main points of the title and makes a reasoned conclusion based on the question apparently having been answered. It ends positively and leaves us with a good impression.
- *Passage 4:* too brief and bland and incorrect!

You have now considered the approach to take when creating and developing a good structure to your writing. You need to match this structure with a sound grasp of written English. This is considered in the following chapter.

SUMMARY OF CHAPTER 6

6.18 ▶

- Structuring your work with an introduction, main body and conclusion will help you to communicate your understanding to the reader.
- You must plan your writing carefully to achieve a coherent structure.
- The introduction should express your diagnosis of the task by specifying the issues you have identified.
- The main body of your assignment should form a logical and linked progression.
- The conclusion should give your overall position.

7
Writing in good English

WHAT IS THE PURPOSE OF THIS CHAPTER?

We cannot repeat too often that the key to successful legal writing is good communication. In order to communicate well, it is necessary to use language which your reader can easily understand, which in the current context means academic English. Your tutors are likely to require you to do the following:

▶ 7.1

- Use English grammar accurately including appropriate sentence construction (sometimes also called *syntax*).
- Write in an appropriate academic style, including making accurate use of technical legal terms and phrases.

Do not expect your law tutors to be prepared to teach you matters of grammar and sentence construction. This chapter contains a number of exercises and worked examples which we hope will help you to improve your written English, if you need to do so.

By the end of this chapter you should understand:

- the importance of writing in good English;
- the main principles of sentence construction;
- how to avoid common punctuation errors, such as misuse of apostrophes; and
- what constitutes good academic style for your writing.

If you have received feedback which says something like "you need to work on your grammar", "syntax needs improvement" or "make sure you use apostrophes appropriately" then go to the specific sections on those areas.

If you have received more generic comments like "your written English needs improvement" it may be harder to work out where you are going wrong. Reading this chapter and particularly the worked example below will help you get an idea of which rules you already understand and you can then focus on the right advice later in the chapter.

To gauge your existing skills, try the following exercise:

ACTIVITY 7.1

Read the following paragraph and then consider the questions which follow:

▶ 7.2

In 1966, the House of Lord's issued the Practice Statement, its significance cant be underrated. As it allowed the Law Lords' to depart from they're own previous decisions where they thought it was right to do so, this went against the authority of the London Tramways case, who's influence had lasted since 1898. The cases purpose was to ensure that the law would be consistent by making the Lord's decisions binding on themselves, however, it also meant that the law couldnt develop for modern times. Consequently, the Practice Statement reversed the position which gave potential for the Lords to make decisions appropriate for modern day's. But it's main danger is that the law could become uncertain if over-used by the judges and therefore its important to note that the Lord's showed they would only use it sparingly.

How would you grade your reaction to this piece of writing?

A. I did not notice any mistakes.
B. I noticed a few mistakes but the meaning of the paragraph is still clear.
C. I thought the level of mistakes was irritating and interfered with my understanding of the paragraph.
D. I was so irritated by the mistakes that I stopped reading for content and started counting the mistakes.

Of course, there's no right answer to this question; the idea is to gauge your *own* reaction which will probably depend on a number of factors, including:

- whether you were "drilled" in English grammar at school (which in turn depends on where and when you went to school);
- how old you are (there have been trends in the teaching of grammar in state education in recent years);
- whether you have dyslexia, which can make it more difficult to recognise spelling and grammar errors, and consequently more difficult to correct them;
- whether English is your first language (if it is not, this may help you because more attention may have been paid to grammar when you learned English, but conversely you may find it more difficult if you do not have the same instinct for English that you have for your first language);
- whether you are reading this or listening to it through a screen reader or other assistive software which will have done what it can to make sense of the mistakes (but may not have made a very good job).

Activity feedback—here are our thoughts:

Answer A: If you did not notice any mistakes, then you are likely to need to put in some work on your own grammar, punctuation and spelling, as there are a large number of mistakes in this piece, which—to those who regard these matters as serious (a body of people which is likely to include the tutors marking your work, as well as many of those to whom you might be applying for work in due course)—are seriously distracting from the author's message.

Answer B: You clearly have some idea about grammar and punctuation but do not regard these as seriously detrimental to effective communication. Again, as with answer A, you are going to have to put some work in to make sure that mistakes in something you don't regard as particularly important don't affect the rating of your work by those who do regard these matters as important.

Answers C and D: If you felt that the level of mistakes in this paragraph seriously interfered with your attention to the meaning of the paragraph, then you already understand why we are stressing the importance of good grammar and spelling as part of effective communication. The fact that you were able to spot the mistakes is likely to mean that you already have a good standard of written English, so you may find that you are already familiar with the rules covered in this chapter.

If you answered either A or B to this exercise, were you surprised to be offered the choices in C and D? If you have not been schooled to regard accurate grammar, punctuation and/or spelling as fundamentally important, it can be difficult to realise the emphasis which is placed on them by others (and particularly the tutors marking your work) and you will therefore have to make more of a conscious effort to make sure your work meets the standard required. Nevertheless, it is important to recognise the importance of using good academic English.

ACTIVITY 7.2

If you didn't count the mistakes, try doing so now (hint: look out for missing apostrophes, apostrophes used where they are not needed and commas used where a full stop is needed. If you are not sure what we mean by these terms we explain later in the chapter).

▶ 7.3

Activity feedback—here are our thoughts:
On this, version, the basic grammar and punctuation errors have been highlighted. There is more information about this below:

> In 1996, the House of Lord's issued the Practice Statement, it's significance cant be underrated. As it allowed the Law Lords' to depart from they're own previous decisions where they thought it was right to do so, this went against the authority of the London Tramways case, who's influence had lasted since 1898. The cases purpose was to ensure that the law would be consistent by making the Lord's decisions binding on themselves, however, it also meant that the law couldnt develop for modern times. Consequently, the Practice Statement reversed the position which gave potential for the Lords to make decisions appropriate for modern day's. But it's main danger is that the law could become uncertain if over-used by the judges and therefore its important to note that the Lord's showed they would only use it sparingly.

How many did you spot? We counted 16 mistakes, although many of these were the same type of mistake repeated on more than one occasion.

We'll return to this example, and explore what the mistakes are in more detail later on in the chapter. Before we do, we're going to look briefly at a few issues about spelling and grammar which some of our students have raised in the past.

ISN'T WHAT I SAY MORE IMPORTANT THAN HOW I SAY IT?

7.4 ▶ Not entirely, for two reasons:

1. It is a simple matter of communication: maximise the effect of your message by making sure it is easy for the person reading and/or marking it to understand what you are saying.
2. Many Law Schools give specific marks in their assessment criteria for presentation in assignments—check your university or programme regulations to find out whether this is the case.

You are studying a law degree, and therefore clearly your ability in legal interpretation and analysis is important, but the rules of grammar provide a standard framework for communication of your knowledge and understanding. It therefore makes sense to follow the standard rules, so as to give your content the best showcase. Aside from any specific marks which may be allocated to reward good use of English in the assessment criteria, an answer which contains a distracting number of basic grammatical errors simply loses authority.

So, accurate grammar is important because it enables you to communicate effectively with whoever is marking your work. The reason why we place such importance on this is not solely because law lecturers have nothing better to do than sit around the staff room exchanging horror stories about misplaced commas. Grammar is especially important for a lawyer because he or she may have to draft complex documents, and grammar will provide essential signposts as to the meaning of those documents. Even a single error could make a vital difference. Finally, think about those job applications you'll be making later. Which do you think has a better chance of impressing an employer—a well-put together application with correct spelling and grammar, or an application with good content ruined by grammatical errors?

If you want a further reason why it is important to pay attention to grammar and sentence construction, have a think about the following example.

There is a programme called Dragons' Den shown regularly on television—you may have seen it—in which budding entrepreneurs appeal to a panel of millionaires (the "dragons") for funding for an invention or a business idea. If convinced, the dragons provide funding and bargain with the contestant for a suitable share of the business. If not convinced, the contestant leaves empty-handed. One of the panel consistently comments on the standard of dress of the contestants, as he believes that when appealing for funding for a business venture, smart business attire should be worn. Now, you might think, "surely the quality of the venture is what's important, rather than what people are wearing?" This is entirely a matter of debate (just as it is a matter of debate whether we should throw out the old rules of grammar and embrace text message style writing instead) but the crucial point, however you feel about formal dress, is that on this programme, *the dragons are the ones with the money*. Therefore, knowing this particular dragon feels that business attire is important, anyone who goes into the "den" in casual clothes is automatically jeopardising his or her case.

The point here is that *your* views on grammar and spelling are not as important as those of your tutors'! This may sound harsh, and by all means make it your mission to become the Vice-Chancellor of a university and change the rules on the weight to be attached to matters of grammar and style. For the time being, however, bear in mind that a good degree will be of considerable use to you in this quest and therefore it would be wise to follow the rules for the time being. If it is any consolation, mastering only a few relatively straightforward principles is all that is needed to improve.

Finally, we want to make the point that being good at grammar and spelling has nothing to do with intelligence. Some people have more of an instinct for it than others, some have received more thorough schooling on it, some have genuine difficulties with it. However, *paying attention* to spelling and grammar *is* a matter of intelligence. The intelligent student reflects on his or her standard and if it isn't up to scratch, does something about it. Look at it this way: if your work is otherwise very good, poor spelling and grammar might cost you those few marks which could be the difference between a good mark and an excellent mark. On the other hand, if the rest of your work is satisfactory, don't risk tipping it down below the satisfactory level by ignoring your spelling and grammar. That said, you are studying law, not English and/or grammar. You will need to use (and if necessary *learn*) a satisfactory level of grammar so that the meaning of your message is clear. Work through this chapter and you should have an idea of the basics.

SHOULD I MAKE USE OF SPELLING AND GRAMMAR CHECKERS?

If you are using a word processing package like Microsoft Word it will have a facility to check ▶ **7.5** your grammar and spelling. It is also likely to have an "autocorrect" facility. Opinions on the value of these tools differ. A spell checker is a good way of spotting mis-spelled words and typographical errors and if you have one, then do make use of it. It is no substitute for a careful read through, however, because it can only identify spelling errors by means of highlighting words which are not recognised in its dictionary. Hence it wouldn't necessarily pick up errors like *In the Supreme Court, witch is the highest domestic caught* for *In the Supreme Court, which is the highest domestic court* because "witch" and "caught" are both accurately spelled words used in the wrong context, although word processing packages do make suggestions of this type.

If you commonly mis-spell (or mis-type) certain words then you can also use the automatic correction facility in your word processing program (in MS Word, it is called AutoCorrect). These days, it is common for a number of common mis-spellings to be pre-programmed into word processors (for example when I mis-typed *dictionery* in the preceding paragraph, my PC helpfully changed it to *dictionary* for me without being asked because it guessed that was what I meant) but you can add further ones. Alternatively, you can use the "Find" facility to look for words which you know you have a tendency to mis-type (a common one is the word "statue", when "statute" is meant).

Grammar checkers are generally less reliable (perhaps because the rules of grammar are more difficult to apply than highlighting any words not found in the dictionary, which is essentially what the spell checker is doing). Using a grammar check is therefore unfortunately no substitute for understanding the basic rules of grammar and being able to apply them in your writing.

I'M DYSLEXIC—CAN I OVERCOME THIS?

7.6 ▶ Yes. Dyslexia and other learning disabilities make effective writing, including grammar and spelling, more challenging. It does not mean, however, that your institution can be more lenient in what level is expected in student work: we've already seen how important accurate grammar is in the study and application of law and this applies equally to students with dyslexia. What your institution *can* do is to make sure you have the *support* you need to improve and attain a satisfactory standard. Seek advice from your tutors at an early stage as to how you can access specialist help, and if appropriate, assistive software. Other support such as additional time in exams may be appropriate in individual cases. It is very important to realise that this support will be given to enable you to be assessed *on the same terms as everyone else*, so the responsibility is then on you to make sure that you use the support available to meet the right standard.

Activity 7.2 – further feedback

We're now going to return to the example in the earlier activity.

The mistakes in our example fall into the following categories:

- Misuse of apostrophes (using one when it is not needed or missing one which is needed).
- Sentence construction—which includes confusion over when a comma is needed and when a full stop is needed, or to put it another way, not writing in complete sentences, and getting confused about using "But" and "However".

Here is a more detailed explanation, taking it section by section, which will help you see which, if any, of the grammatical rules covered below you need to focus on in order to improve your presentation:

> In 1966, the House of Lord's issued the Practice Statement, its significance cant be underrated.

In this sentence, the first problem is an unnecessary apostrophe. *House of Lord's* does not need an apostrophe because it is simply the name of the court—it should read *House of Lords* (because *Lords* is the plural of *Lord*). Conversely the third problem is a missing apostrophe.

If you didn't spot these, then look at the section on apostrophes below.

The second problem is with the sentence construction. What we have here are two statements:

1. In 1966 the House of Lords issued the Practice Statement.
2. Its significance cannot be underrated.

The two statements are linked together with a comma, but both statements work independently as *clauses* (an independent clause means a phrase which has the necessary ingredients to work as a sentence—about which more below, but for the time being, both of the above are examples), so it is *incorrect* to join them with a comma. Instead a full stop should be used to divide the statements, or a semicolon can be used where you want to retain the link between the statements (alternatively a word like "and" could be used to link the statements). Using a comma to join two separate independent clauses like this is called a "comma splice" or a "run-on sentence" and it is a very common mistake. If you didn't spot it, then make sure you read the section on comma splices below, as you can improve your writing by learning to eliminate this mistake.

> As it allowed the Law Lords' to depart from they're own previous decisions where they thought it was right to do so, this went against the authority of the London Tramways case, who's influence had lasted since 1898.

We have three more apostrophe mistakes here. We already know that an apostrophe isn't needed for a plural, so hopefully you have spotted that *Law Lords'* is highlighted because it is simply a plural—there is more than one Law Lord—so it should read *Law Lords*. There are two further apostrophe errors which have led to spelling mistakes:

1. *they're* when *their* was meant (because the meaning is *the previous decisions belonging to them* rather than *they are*);
2. *who's* when *whose* was meant (because it *the authority belonging to the case* rather than *who is*).

"Their" and "whose" are both examples of *possessive pronouns*—indicating "ownership". (We will see later that an apostrophe is usually required to indicate possession, but not when the word itself is a possessive pronoun as the ownership is already indicated). "They're" and "who's" are both examples of *contractions*—where two words are contracted or amalgamated into one and an apostrophe used to indicate the *omission* of certain letters. It's a common mistake to confuse a possessive with a contraction where the pronunciation of the word is the same. These are discussed in the section on apostrophes below.

As well as the apostrophe errors, there is another problem with the sentence construction. *As it allowed* is not the right way to begin a sentence. On the other hand, *this went against. . .* which follows a comma *is* indicative of the start of a sentence. *This went against the authority of the London Tramways case, whose influence had lasted since 1898* is a complete sentence statement in itself and therefore should not be preceded by a comma. It is another example of a *comma splice* or *run on sentence*.

The essential problem here is that the full stops have been put in the wrong place, which in turns disrupts the sentence construction or syntax. There is much more about sentence construction below, which explains in more detail why these changes are needed.

> The cases purpose was to ensure that the law would be consistent by making the Lord's decisions binding on themselves, however, it also meant that the law couldnt develop for modern times.

Here, there are three further apostrophe mistakes. *The cases purpose* is an example of *possession* (it means *the purpose of the case*) and because "case" is not in itself a possessive word (like "their" and "whose" are) it does need an apostrophe. Therefore this should read *The case's purpose*.

The Lord's decisions is also an example of possession, so it is correct to use an apostrophe, but the problem here is that it has been put in the wrong place because there is more than one

Lord—it should be *The Lords' decision* (decision of the Lords). Always be careful to place a possessive apostrophe in the right place according to whether the "owner" is singular or plural. How to deal with possessive apostrophes is covered below.

You will probably have spotted the missing apostrophe in *couldnt*, which is another example of a *contraction* and therefore needs an apostrophe to indicate the *omission* of the *o* in *could not*. Generally in formal academic writing it is better to use *could not* rather than *couldn't* in any case (there is more on academic style towards the end of the chapter). This is also true of the use of *cant* in the first sentence. As well as missing an apostrophe (it should be *can't*) cannot would be a preferable formal academic term.

There is also a further example of *comma splice* or *run-on sentence* in this example. If you look at what the sentence is saying there are two statements:

1. The case's purpose was to ensure that the law would be consistent by making the Lords' decisions binding on themselves
2. however, it also meant that the law couldn't develop for modern times.

Both these statements are complete in themselves, so should be linked by a semicolon or separated by a full stop. Alternatively, the word *however* could be replaced with *but* which is a conjunction—a word which can correctly be used to join two independent clauses together. As the word *but* cannot be used to begin a sentence, this would mean statement 2 is not complete in itself anymore, and therefore the comma would be appropriate. It is a good tip to remember that in formal academic writing, *however* will often follow a full stop but *but* should not. Follow this up in the sentence construction section later if you need to.

> Consequently, the Practice Statement reversed the position which gave potential for the Lords to make decisions appropriate for modern day's.

Arguably this sentence could be improved with a comma after *position* to make it easier to read, but this can be classed as a matter of taste. The only real error here is another apostrophe where none is needed in the word *day's* which is simply a plural (more than one day), and which should therefore be written *days*.

> But its main danger is that it could make the law uncertain if over-used by the judges and therefore its important to note that the Lord's showed they would only use it sparingly.

You already know that *But* should not be used to open a sentence (you often see it used at the beginning of a sentence, as this particular rule is one which is frequently broken as a matter of style —we have done this ourselves in this book, to achieve a less formal tone—but it is better to stick to the rules in academic work). Having checked that this is a complete statement in itself, then the *But* should be replaced with *However*, to correct the sentence. If it had not been a complete statement, then the "but" should be retained, but the preceding full stop replaced with a comma.

Summary of corrections

WRONG	RIGHT
In 1996, the House of Lord's issued the Practice Statement, it's significance cant be underrated. As it allowed the Law Lords' to depart from they're own previous decisions where they thought it was right to do so, this went against the authority of the London Tramways case, who's influence had lasted since 1898. The cases purpose was to ensure that the law would be consistent by making the Lord's decisions binding on themselves, however, it also meant that the law couldnt develop for modern times. Consequently, the Practice Statement reversed the position, which gave potential for the Lords to make decisions appropriate for modern day's. But it's main danger is that the law could become uncertain if over-used by the judges and therefore its important to note that the Lord's showed they would only use it sparingly.	In 1996, the House of Lords issued the Practice Statement. Its significance cannot be underrated, as it allowed the Law Lords to depart from their own previous decisions where they thought it was right to do so. This went against the authority of the London Tramways case, whose influence had lasted since 1898. The case's purpose was to ensure that the law would be consistent by making the Lord's decisions binding on themselves, but it also meant that the law could not develop for modern times. Consequently, the Practice Statement reversed the position, which gave potential for the Lords to make decisions appropriate for modern days. However, its main danger is that the law could become uncertain if over-used by the judges and therefore it is important to note that the Lords showed they would only use it sparingly.

Next, we're going to follow up the main errors which featured in this example; first, we will explore sentence construction, including use of appropriate grammar and joining words, and secondly, we will look in more detail at the correct use of apostrophes.

HOW CAN I IMPROVE MY SENTENCE CONSTRUCTION?

Although this is not a grammar lesson, a basic understanding of some of the principles of grammar will help you to improve your writing. These days, thanks to the best-selling book by Lynne Truss, a commonly known example of the difference in meaning which a misplaced comma can make is the story about the panda who has a meal and then commits a massacre before departing, because he "eats, shoots and leaves" (instead of "eats shoots and leaves" which would indicate, as intended, the favoured food choices of the panda). Truss's book (it is actually called *Eats, Shoots & Leaves*, if you haven't heard of it)[1] is a humorous but meticulous account of various rules on spelling and grammar and is highly recommended if you really want to get to grips with the subject.

As Truss points out, many matters relating to placement of commas and other punctuation are a matter of taste. However, there are some basic rules and an understanding of these basic principles will improve your writing. One error which has already been mentioned, and which causes annoyance, is the matter of the *comma splice*—using a comma where a full stop or semicolon is needed. This is caused by a basic misunderstanding about what forms a

▶ 7.7

---

[1] Lynne Truss, *Eats, Shoots & Leaves* (Profile Books 2003).

complete sentence—which also leads to misuse of full stops and words like *however*. The ability to write in complete sentences is an important element of expressing yourself clearly and will help your reader (i.e. the marker) to understand your argument more easily.

WHAT MAKES UP A SENTENCE?

7.8 ▶ Here is a basic summary of the principles of sentence construction:

- A sentence is made up of one or more *clauses*.
- Clauses may be *independent*—also referred to as *main* clauses—which we've already seen means (as is pretty self-explanatory) that they may stand alone as complete sentences, or alternatively *dependent* (also called *subordinate*) in which case they must be joined to an independent clause and cannot stand alone as a sentence.
- An independent or main clause which stands alone as a complete sentence is called a *simple* sentence. However, more than one independent clause can be linked together to make a *compound* sentence. A dependent clause *must* be joined to an independent one to form a *complex* sentence. We explain this below.
- To be independent, a clause must contain a verb (essentially, an action) and a subject (someone or something doing the action). The verb must be in a finite form (in other words, not in the infinitive form like *to be* or *to go* but with a tense, for example past, present or future—"she *was*", "she *is going*").

Simple and compound sentences

7.9 ▶ Here we have three statements. Each has a subject and a verb in finite form—the first sentence uses the *past* tense ("submitted"), the second the present tense ("is"), and the third sentence the future tense ("will return"). Therefore each statement is an independent clause so it is quite correct to separate them out into three simple sentences using full stops. Note that a sentence always begins with a capital letter and ends with a full stop (or a question mark or an exclamation mark, if more appropriate to the context).

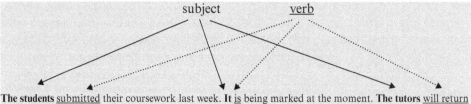

The students submitted their coursework last week. It is being marked at the moment. The tutors will return the feedback in a few days' time.

As an alternative form of punctuation, semicolons or colons could be used *instead of* full stops. Semicolons can be used in the same places as full stops and have the effect of separating the clauses but not as completely as a full stop; the clauses are still linked together. Colons are used between independent clauses to indicate, loosely, that one is the consequence of the previous one, although both are matters of style:

> The students submitted their coursework last week; it is being marked at the moment: the tutors will return the feedback in a few days' time.

Note that this is now one (compound) sentence, so it still begins with a capital letter and ends with a full stop, but after a colon or semicolon a lower case letter is used (unless there is another reason to have a capital letter, for example someone's name).

Avoiding a comma splice or run-on sentence

It is important to grasp that although it is fine to substitute a colon or a semicolon for a full stop, where appropriate to your meaning, it is *not* acceptable to use commas in place of full stops. Therefore the following is wrong:

▶ 7.10

> The students submitted their coursework last week, it is being marked at the moment, the tutors will return the feedback in a few days' time.

This is an example of a *comma splice*, which simply means a comma being used (incorrectly) to join (i.e. splice) two independent clauses together.

Conjunctions

A further correct way of handling these three independent clauses would be to link them together using a *conjunction*. This would also make a compound sentence. Conjunctions are "joining words", for example:

▶ 7.11

- *and*—where the independent clauses express a linked idea or a continuation of a theme;
- *but*—where the independent clauses express opposite or contrasting positions;
- *or*—where the independent clauses are alternatives;
- *so*—where the position in one independent clause leads to the next one.

Which do you think would be appropriate in relation to our three statements? You should spot that these statements are linked and continuing, rather than contrasting or alternatives, so *and* is the appropriate link here (arguably *so* could also be used). However, if we try that, it comes out like this:

> The students submitted their coursework last week and it is being marked at the moment and the tutors will return the feedback in a few days' time.

Although *and* is the right conjunction to use here, using it twice like this sounds childish. When using conjunctions to link clauses into compound sentences you need to take care not to overdo it—the following is better:

> The students submitted their coursework last week; it is being marked at the moment and the tutors will return the feedback in a few days' time.

Where the two clauses express opposing or contrasting positions, then the appropriate conjunction is *but*. For example:

> The Supreme Court can use the Practice Statement 1966 "when it is right to do so",
> but in practice it is used rarely.

Here the two statements are:

1. The Supreme Court *can use* the Practice Statement 1966 "when it is right to do so"
2. in practice it *is* used rarely.

These are both independent clauses (both have a subject and a *finite verb*) but the statements are contrasting: on the one hand the Supreme Court has a free hand to use its Practice Statement power; on the other hand in practice this power is not used very much. Therefore *but* is the right conjunction here.

Could you substitute *however* instead of *but*? The answer here is definitely "no"—although this is a very common mistake. *However* is not a conjunction and therefore *must not* be used to join two independent clauses. It can be used only as *part* of an independent clause—usually at the beginning followed by a comma, but also potentially elsewhere (which sometimes has the unfortunate appearance of being used as a conjunction—we'll show you what we mean by this shortly).

Unfortunately there is no easy trick to help you remember the rule about how to avoid a comma splice. The basic gist is that *however* should only follow a full stop, colon or semicolon, and never a comma, but this is only true where the *however* is at the beginning of its clause. It is fine to re-order the clause so that the "however" comes at the end, in which case it would look like this:

> The Supreme Court can use the Practice Statement 1966 "when it is right to do so".
> In practice, it is used rarely, however.

This means that the above suggestion that "however" mustn't follow a comma is not always true. Hopefully you can see that even with the *however* at the end, the distinction between these two independent clauses has been appropriately marked with a full stop. This is something you will simply have to look out for.

WRONG	RIGHT
The Supreme Court can use the Practice Statement 1966 "when it is right to do so", however in practice it is used rarely.	The Supreme Court can use the Practice Statement 1966 "when it is right to do so", but in practice it is used rarely.
As *however* is not a conjunction but rather, part of an independent clause, this is an example of a comma splice (because the two independent clauses are only separated by the comma). This is a common mistake which might lead to feedback like "you don't always write in complete sentences".	**Why is this right?** Two independent clauses joined with the conjunction *but* is correct.
	The Supreme Court can use the Practice Statement 1966 "when it is right to do so". However, in practice it is used rarely.
	Why is this right? Two simple sentences. *However* is an appropriate beginning for a sentence.

WRONG	RIGHT
	The Supreme Court can use the Practice Statement 1966 "when it is right to do so"; however, in practice it is used rarely.
	Why is this right? The semicolon is an appropriate substitute for the full stop to divide the independent clauses less completely than the full stop would do— and to remind us that the separation is less distinct. The word *however* loses its capital letter as the beginning of the second clause.

Another common mistake is to misuse *this* or *it* in the same way. For example:

> In 1966, the House of Lords issued the Practice Statement, this gave the Lords power to overrule their previous rulings.

The use of *this* makes the second clause here an independent one, because "this" is a subject. Therefore these should be separated with a full stop, linked with a semicolon, or joined with a conjunction.

WRONG	RIGHT
In 1966, the House of Lords issued the Practice Statement, this gave the Lords power to overrule their previous rulings.	In 1966, the House of Lords issued the Practice Statement. This gave the Lords power to overrule their previous rulings.
	In 1966, the House of Lords issued the Practice Statement; this gave the Lords power to overrule their previous rulings.
	In 1966, the House of Lords issued the Practice Statement, and this gave the Lords power to overrule their previous rulings.

Choosing how to join or separate your clauses

It is not always necessary to use conjunctions to join independent clauses. Returning to our previous example of the coursework marking, the original three simple sentences work well, but as a matter of style using simple sentences continually throughout an essay tends to give it rather a simplistic feeling. For example:

▶ 7.12

> Negligence is a tort. It has several elements. The first element is duty of care. The claimant must show they are owed a duty in law and a duty in fact. Duty in law means it falls within the categories of negligence.

Too much of this and your readers will start to feel they are being addressed by a Dalek. It would be better to create more compound sentences, for example:

> Negligence is a tort and it has several elements. The first element is duty of care: the claimant must show they are owed a duty in law and a duty in fact. Duty in law means it falls within the categories of negligence.

On the other hand, it is possible to go too far and leave a reader mentally gasping for breath:

> Negligence is a tort and it has several elements; the first element is duty of care: the claimant must show they are owed a duty in law and a duty in fact; duty in law means it falls within the categories of negligence.

Generally, for the sake of clarity, it is a good rule to limit your sentences to 20–25 words or so. Putting in a full stop gives your reader a bit of breather. Combining the use of simple and compound sentences can be an effective style tool, and we'll consider that later on in the chapter.

One final note about these conjunctions is that technically they should be used *only* to join independent clauses to turn a simple sentence into a compound one. This is the source of the rule that you should not begin a sentence with *and*, *but*, *or* or *so*. However, as already discussed, this is a rule which it is generally seen as acceptable to break occasionally as a matter of style. Nevertheless, you would be wise to adhere to it most of the time: breaking it frequently will tend to make your writing sound too informal (you will note that we've done it quite frequently within our text, because the tone is meant to be less formal). To help you avoid too much use of *but* and *and* at the beginning of your sentences, here are some suggested alternatives to use to begin an independent clause which opens a sentence (you should put a comma after them in this situation):

and	Additionally,
but	However,
or	Instead, Alternatively,
so	In consequence, Therefore,

It is worth noting that the rule in relation to *however* discussed above (i.e. it should be used in place of a conjunction to join two independent clauses) applies equally to the words in the second column.

Dependent or subordinate clauses and complex sentences

7.13 ▶ If the clause does not contain the necessary elements of a subject and a finite verb, then it will be a dependent clause. A dependent clause cannot be a sentence on its own but must be joined appropriately to an independent clause to make a complex sentence.

Have a look at the following example:

> The tort of negligence contains a number of elements which are essential to a successful claim.

The two statements here are:

- The tort of negligence contains a number of elements
- which are essential to a successful claim.

Do you consider these statements to be dependent or independent? If you are unsure, try to identify the subject and the finite verb. If you can spot these then you must be looking at an independent or main clause.

On this basis, you should be able to identify the first statement as an independent clause. It contains a subject (*the tort of negligence*) and a finite verb (*contains*—here in the present tense). You may find, instinctively, that the second statement "doesn't feel like a sentence" rather than being able to immediately identify why. If so, that's fine—you are correct, and the instinct you have about what makes a sentence and what does not will help you punctuate your sentences appropriately. If the second statement does not feel instinctively wrong then try applying the rules instead: does the clause have a finite verb? Yes, it does—*are* (present tense plural form of the verb *to be*). Does it have a subject? No, it doesn't. All it has is *which*, which is not a subject. Therefore this is a dependent (or subordinate) clause. To a be an independent clause, it would have to have been *These elements are essential* rather than *which are essential* ("These elements" would be the subject).

The vital rule to remember with *dependent clauses* is that they *cannot* stand alone as a sentence. Therefore it would be wrong to write:

> The tort of negligence contains a number of elements. Which are essential to a successful claim.

Instead, the dependent clause must be joined to an independent or main clause, using a *subordinate conjunction*. The one in the example is *which*. Other common ones include *when*, *where*, *while*, *until*, *unless*, *although*, *because* (or similar words like *as* or *since*). All of these essentially indicate the 'relationship' between the dependent clause and the independent clause to which it is attached. In legal reasoning, it is important to use these appropriately, and understanding these will also help your reading of texts. There is more on this in Chapter 5.

Making sure your sentence is consistent

Your subject and verb should match each other in terms of being singular or plural. In most cases this is extremely straightforward; you are extremely unlikely to write *The law on this point are discriminatory* instead of *is discriminatory*, or *The Law Lords comes from a narrow social background* instead of *come from*, because both of these examples look and sound so odd.

▶ 7.14

However, the rule about matching the subject and the verb can be more difficult in certain situations, for example with subjects where the line between plural and singular seems blurred (words like Parliament and jury, which can be viewed as a single body or a number of different people). In cases like this, you can treat the body as singular or plural—*it* or *they*—but you do need to be consistent.

A further word which causes difficulty is *none*. Here there is no room for flexibility: although it is common in spoken

TIPS • *The trick to getting this right is to remember that none equals not one—try mentally substituting not one in sentences where you want to use none and you will never make a mistake as to the form of the verb.*

English in particular to regard *none* as a plural (None of us are going) that is wrong, and it must be treated as a singular. Therefore:

WRONG	RIGHT
None of the precedents are binding	None of the precedents is binding

The second is correct because the singular *none* matches the singular form *is*. Here's a quick recap on the terms and rules contained so far:

> Independent clause = simple sentence.
> Independent clause + independent clause = compound sentence (join with a conjunction, a colon or a semi-colon; NOT a comma).
> Independent clause + dependent clause = complex sentence (join with a subordinate conjunction).
> Each sentence needs a capital letter and a full stop (or question/exclamation mark).
> Your subjects and verbs must match each other as to singular and plural forms.

We've touched on common punctuation in discussing sentence structure but we're now going to return to the punctuation mark which seems to cause more problems than all the rest put together: the apostrophe.

WHAT'S ALL THE FUSS ABOUT APOSTROPHES?

7.15 ▶ Misuse of apostrophes (using one when it isn't needed, missing out one when it is needed, using one when needed but putting it in the wrong place) probably accounts for more of the grammatical errors commonly made than any other single mistake. If you can get your use of apostrophes right, then you will be well on the way to making sure your work is of an appropriate standard in grammatical terms.

The most common mistakes to avoid are:

- using apostrophes for plurals;
- mixing up *it's* and *its*;
- mixing up other possessives with omissions;
- putting unnecessary apostrophes in possessive pronouns;
- putting apostrophes in unnecessary places.

Mistake 1: Using apostrophes for plurals
7.16 ▶ No apostrophe is needed for plurals.

WRONG	RIGHT
The court's have indicated that . . .	The courts have indicated that . . .

Mistake 2: Mixing up *it's* **and** *its*

These have different and separate meanings: *It's* means *it is* or *it has*, while *its* means *of it* or *belonging* to it:

▶ 7.17

WRONG	RIGHT
Its important to acknowledge it's influence	It's important to acknowledge its influence

The apostrophe is needed to indicate omission but not (in this case) for possession (because *its* is a possessive pronoun and the possession is therefore already built in to the word).

Mistake 3: Mixing up other possessives with omissions (whose and who's, theirs and there's, your and you're)

▶ 7.18

WRONG	RIGHT
Lord Reid was a very influential judge who's opinions have a very high precedent value	Lord Reid was a very influential judge whose opinions have a very high precedent value

Mistake 4: Putting unnecessary apostrophes in possessive pronouns (his, hers, theirs, ours, yours)

▶ 7.19

WRONG	RIGHT
Her's was the best argument in terms of presentation, but ours' had the legal authority.	Hers was the best argument in terms of presentation, but ours had the legal authority.

Mistake 5: Putting apostrophes in the wrong places

▶ 7.20

WRONG	RIGHT
The judge's opinions were inconsistent (which makes it sound like there was only one judge who was inconsistent with himself or herself—not entirely impossible but the alternative to the right is more likely).	The judges' opinions were inconsistent (this indicates there were several judges whose opinions were inconsistent with each other).

WHEN SHOULD I USE AN APOSTROPHE?

The two most important uses of the apostrophe are the following:

▶ 7.21

1. To indicate a *possessive* (something which "belongs" to something or someone or is "of" someone or something):

> The judge's opinion (one judge)
> The judges' opinion (more than one judge)
> The woman's defence
> The women's defence

2. To indicate *omission* (letters missed out) in a contracted word:

> It's important to note (It is)
> This isn't a valid argument (is not)
> The facts don't raise any issue of negligence (do not)
> There's a problem with this reasoning (There is)
> Who's going to win this case? (Who is)

There are further examples of these on the following pages. In formal academic writing, remember it is best to be sparing with contractions; in other words, use "it is" instead of "isn't". This also has the advantage that if you don't use them, you can't make a mistake with the omission apostrophe.

In contrast, you do NOT use apostrophes for:

1. simple plurals

> The courts are busy.
> These cases can be criticised.

2. possessive pronouns (his, hers, yours, its, ours, theirs) as the "possession" is already built into the word.

There are further examples of when *not* to use an apostrophe later in the chapter.

More on possessive apostrophes

7.22 ▶ Remember possessive apostrophes indicate something which "belongs to" someone or something or is "of" someone or something:

> The barrister's arguments failed to sway the judge

Test whether you need an apostrophe by turning the phrase round into "the arguments of the barrister". This way you can see that the arguments "belong to" the barrister so the apostrophe is needed. On the other hand "The barristers argued before the judge for three hours" would turn round into "The argued of the barristers", which is obviously nonsense. This indicates that barristers in this sense is a simple plural and needs no apostrophe.

Indicating "joint" ownership

7.23 ▶ For example:

> The women's defence

Here, although you are talking about the defence of more than one woman, the plural "women" accounts for this already, so you treat it in exactly the same way as if it were only *one* woman's defence.

On the other hand, if you want to indicate the arguments of more than one barrister, you are talking about the arguments of the barristers, which turns into:

> The barristers' arguments (no extra s is needed after the apostrophe)

This shows that turning the phrase round also helps you work out *where to place* the apostrophe when you are dealing with plurals.

> The judge's reasoning = the reasoning of the judge
> The judges' reasoning = the reasoning of the judges

> **TIPS** • *If you are unsure of whether a possessive apostrophe is needed, or where to put it, always try turning the phrase round like this—but remember the rule doesn't apply to possessive pronouns like his, hers, theirs.*

Singulars which end in s

This can cause confusion, and there are varying opinions. Truss explores these and suggests that the modern approach (which is also the most straightforward, and we'd therefore advise you to follow it) is to treat singulars the same whether or not they end in s. In other words: *Lord Simonds's speech* not *Lord Simonds' speech*. The latter is the more traditional approach, and if that is what you have been taught, have been used to, or simply prefer, then it is perfectly acceptable. ▶ **7.24**

Note: whatever you do, don't remove the s on the end of someone's name just because it seems to resolve the issue more easily: *Lord Simond's speech* is certainly wrong. Lord Simonds would not be impressed! Similarly, a name ending in a *double* s always needs an apostrophe and an s, not just an apostrophe, for example, *Lynne Truss's book*, not *Lynne Truss' book*.

So, in summary:

> Singular, not ending in s—use's: The claimant's action (just one claimant) Singular, ending in s—use's (or'): Lord James's judgment (or Lord James' judgment)
> Singular, ending in ss—use ss's: Lady Justice Windass's
> Plural, not ending in s—use's: The children's wishes and feelings
> Plural, ending in s—use': The defendants' counter-claim (more than one defendant)

In particular in relation to apostrophes we know from experience a lot of students have problems with telling the difference between *it's* and *its*.

The difference between "it's" and "its"

Truss has the following to say (at pp.43–44) about mixing up it's and its: ▶ **7.25**

"The confusion of the possessive 'its' (no apostrophe) with the contractive 'it's' (with apostrophe) is an unequivocal signal of illiteracy and sets off a simple Pavlovian 'kill' response in the average stickler. The rule is: the word 'it's' (with apostrophe) stands for 'it is' or 'it has'. If the word does not stand for 'it is' or 'it has' then what you require is 'its'. This is extremely easy to grasp. Getting your itses mixed up is the greatest solecism in the world of punctuation. No matter that you have a PhD and have read all of Henry James twice. If you still persist in writing 'Good food at it's best', you deserve to be struck by lightning, hacked up on the spot and buried in an unmarked grave."

Admittedly, that particular fate is unlikely to be specified in your institution's assessment regulations, but you can imagine that if that is how such a mistake makes the person marking your work feel, it is not going to have a positive effect on your results.

The good news here is that as Truss says, this is an extremely easy rule to remember and therefore get right. Make it your mission to ensure your work never has this particular mistake in it.

The rule is: *Never use an apostrophe in "it's" unless it makes sense to say "it is" or "it has" instead*.

Let's try this out with an example:

When you write an essay, its not that hard to get its grammar right, and its silly not to check it because its effect on your marks could be important.

Try changing every its to it is:

When you write an essay, *it is* not that hard to get *it is* grammar right, and *it is* silly not to check it because *it is* effect on your marks could be important.

From this, it should be pretty easy to spot that the first and third uses of *its* can be changed to *it is* and the sentence still makes sense. This means that the *it's* needs an apostrophe to demonstrate the omission. On the other hand, the second and fourth uses of *its* make no sense when *it is* substituted—this is *its* in the *of it* sense (get the grammar of it right, the effect of it on your marks), and no apostrophe should be used.

The correct version is therefore:

When you write an essay, it's not that hard to get its grammar right, and it's silly not to check it because its effect on your marks could be important.

However, even better for formal writing would be:

When you write an essay, it's not that hard to get its grammar right, and it is silly not to check it because its effect on your marks could be important.

TIPS • *Generally in writing an academic essay it is usually preferable to say 'it is' rather than 'it's'. You can therefore avoid confusion by resolving always to use 'it is' in full in your essay writing, never 'it's'. This has the simple solution of meaning that your use of 'its' will always be the possession kind and you will never need an apostrophe.*

More omission apostrophes

It's, which we now know without exception to indicate *it is* or *it has,* is the most common use of the omission apostrophe. Other commons ones are: ▶ **7.26**

- isn't = is not
- doesn't = does not
- couldn't = could not
- wouldn't = would not
- shouldn't = should not

These are all pretty straightforward; the only note of caution is that the more you use the shortened versions, the less formal your writing will become, and you do not want to become too informal: use them sparingly, or avoid them altogether.

Some other common ones create more problems because there are other words which sound confusingly similar and can easily be mixed up with them. We've already met some of these earlier in the chapter:

They're = *they are*, not to be confused with *their* (belonging to them or of theirs) nor with *there* (denoting a situation or place):

> They're going there to attend their lecture.

There's = *there is*, not to be confused with *theirs* (a variation on ownership by them):

> There's a handout available at this lecture of theirs.

> **TIPS** • *Both tips for 'it's' and 'its' apply here: try turning the word round, but better still resolve to avoid using the contracted words, and then you know you never need an apostrophe. Then the only problem left is not confusing 'there' and 'their'.*

Who's = *who is*, not to be confused with *whose* (of whom/which):

> Who's going to be the student whose essay is the best?

You're = *you are*, not to be confused with *your* (belonging to you or of you):

> You're probably hoping your essay will be best.

Using an apostrophe to indicate a length of time

This can potentially cause problems. An apostrophe is needed in the following examples: ▶ **7.27**

> In one week's time, the matter will be considered by the Court of Appeal.
> Ten years' adverse possession will enable a squatter to claim legal rights.

The different placement of the apostrophe in the above examples is because one week is singular but ten years is plural (more than one year).

But remember, *no* apostrophe where it is a simple plural:

> The statute was repealed six years ago.

Titles/Names

7.28 ▶ Dealing with names and titles can cause some difficulty as to whether you need an apostrophe. There is no set rule about these—the only rule is that normal rules do not apply. In other words, for names and titles, you have to adopt the "official" version regardless of whether that complies with grammar.

For example, the House of Lords sounds like it might, somehow, need an apostrophe (in the same way that this hat of Jason's would need an apostrophe) but it doesn't (just as Kings of Leon doesn't need one, or indeed Court of Appeal)—this is simply what they are called.

When this does get confusing is if you have to combine such names with possessives. For example:

> In the House of Lords's opinion . . .

In the above examples the trick is to understand that despite the fact that the House of Lords sounds like a plural, it must be treated as singular: it is one court (albeit one made up of a number of judges). When you drop the reference to the court itself, and refer to the judges (the Law Lords or the Lords of Appeal) then of course this is plural:

> In the Law Lords' opinion

> **TIPS** • *If in doubt, try one of the following strategies:*
> 1. *Try and find the phrase in a textbook where it should (hopefully) be punctuated correctly.*
> 2. *Try substituting a similar phrase to help you work out how to treat it: "The Court of Appeal's opinion" doesn't sound so difficult does it? (Then obviously switch back—don't pretend a different court decided the case in the final version!)*
> 3. *If you are really stuck, turn the phrase round and leave it like that—"In the opinion of the House of Lords" is fine!*

Luckily, the Supreme Court is much easier to punctuate than the House of Lords, but since you will still be referring to judgments from the House of Lords in many essays, see the tip box for how to make sure you get it right.

HOW CAN I IMPROVE MY SPELLING?

7.29 ▶ We've already strongly recommended the use of a spell checker to help you improve your spelling if you find that you have trouble. Of course this facility is not usually available to you in an exam, where it is still the norm to expect students to write long-hand, in the absence of extenuating circumstances. However, although we certainly don't want to encourage you to be careless, you are likely to find that the tutors marking your exam work are far more understanding of spelling errors in an exam situation than they would be when marking a coursework assignment where there was substantial opportunity for review and correction.

Further, as we explained, the spell checker is not really checking your spelling but simply looking for the word you have used in its dictionary. If it isn't there, it assumes it is a spelling error and offers you alternatives. Therefore you have to be on the lookout for words which are only mis-spelled because of the context in which they are placed, as a spell checker will not identify these as errors.

Common words which you are likely to use in legal writing and which are open to confusion include:

Principle	Principal
This is the spelling for the noun meaning 'rule' or standard—*the legal principle in this case.*	This is the spelling for the adjective denoting the main or primary item—*the principal argument.* (Confusingly it can also be a noun denoting a headteacher—like Principal Skinner—but you are less likely to use this sense in your legal writing.)
Practise	Practice
Spelt with an *s*, this is the verb form: *I intend to practise as a solicitor* or *I am practising my essay skills.* There is no such word as 'practicing' in British English.	Spelt with a *c*, this is a noun: *In practice, this is not an issue*, or *Legal Practice Course.*
Advise	Advice
Like the previous example, the *s* denotes the verb: *Advise Jim in respect of his criminal liabilities.*	Like the previous example, the *c* indicates the noun: *I received excellent legal advice from this firm.*
Formerly	Formally
Spelt in this way this is synonymous with 'previously'. *The most senior court in England and Wales was formerly the Appellate Committee of the House of lords*	This spelling denotes something done in a formal manner. *When writing formally it is best to avoid contractions such as 'isn't'.*

WHAT OTHER MATTERS DO I NEED TO KNOW?

There are a few other points which may be of use to you in your writing: ▶ 7.30

Referring to judges

Additionally, some law-related plurals (especially those involving legal Latin) are confusingly ▶ 7.31 constructed: the abbreviation for Lord or Lady Justice is L.J. for example, but remember that the plural of this is L.JJ. rather than L.J.s. You can use L.J.s in your own notes if you like but never in formal legal writing, and then only use the abbreviation as part of the name of the judges: *Smith and Jones L.JJ. agreed that . . .* but not *The L.JJ. were unanimous in their verdict*— in that situation, you should write *The Lords Justice were unanimous* or *The Lords and Lady Justice were unanimous* or whatever (although *The appeal judges were unanimous* does the job just as well and avoids the whole tricky problem).

Referring to judgments

In normal English usage, the words *judgement* and *judgment* are interchangeable; inclusion ▶ 7.32 of the middle *e* is simply a matter of preference. However, there is a convention in legal writing that the judgment of a court is always spelt without an *e*. It is therefore common for lawyers to omit the *e* all the time, whatever the context, and it would be a good idea for you to follow this practice so that you never have to think about whether to include the *e*.

Ordering your points

7.33 ▶ When enumerating points, you may wish to denote the order of your arguments by using "First, second, third" and so on (these are called ordinal numerals). If you do so, note that while you can use *second* and *secondly* (and subsequent numbers) interchangeably, you should avoid the use of firstly: simply use first. (It is perfectly correct to use *first*, followed by *secondly* and *thirdly*.)

Citing numbers within your text

7.34 ▶ There is some debate over the correct way to cite numbers in your work. There is general agreement that for lower numbers, the number should be spelt in words rather than given in figures (i.e. you should say 'seven' rather than '7'). An exception to this general rule is where the figures are part of a case citation or other reference where it is correct to use the figures. With higher numbers, it is appropriate to use figures, rather than words ('99' rather than 'ninety-nine'). Again you will have spotted that we have not followed this rule ourselves because we are not aiming for a formal academic style in this text.

The moot point is where the line should be drawn between low numbers which you spell out and high numbers which you don't. Twenty is the conventional place to draw the line, and this is logical because this is the point beyond which the full written forms of the numbers become more unwieldy. However, although this is a useful guide which you may wish to adopt, it is not a universal rule; some suggest ten or twelve.

Citing percentages

7.35 ▶ When referring to percentages in written work, you should avoid the use of the symbol %. Instead, use the full words *per cent* (remember that this is two words, not one).

All right not alright

7.36 ▶ There is no such word as *alright*, despite the fact that it appears to be in common usage. The correct form is *all right*.

Finally, in this chapter on the practical elements of writing, we are going to look briefly at issues around style in formal legal writing.

HOW DO I WRITE IN AN ACADEMIC STYLE?

7.37 ▶ For some reason, it seems to be a common mistake to equate "academic argument" with writing in a pompous tone, or that being "learned" is indicated by the length of the words and sentences used. This is not the case. What you should be aiming for is to write in clear and straightforward sentences and language. We've seen that you should not write in simple sentences all the time but should aim to use a mixture of simple, compound and complex sentences. That said, writing is not a science. We aren't expecting you to think "oh, I've used two simple sentences in a row—I'd better throw a compound one in next". Writing is a more instinctive process than this and you will already have some style in your writing; reflect on whether this style is appropriate to take you through your university studies. Look at feedback on previous work; get someone to read through something written in your normal essay style; ask a tutor to look through something you have written to advise on whether your style is appropriate. It is also a good tip that the more reading you do of academic texts, the more you will get a feeling for an appropriate academic style (although judges, particularly in older cases, will tend to be more verbose than the style you are aiming for—so don't base your style on them).

Writing objectively: avoiding "I think. . ."

There are anecdotal stories—perhaps some of them are true—of students prefacing an answer in a class with "I think" and receiving a reply from their tutor "I don't want you to THINK!". Despite this, it *isn't* that your tutors don't want you to think, but rather that they want you to have thought sufficiently about your sources and arguments to be able to assert with confidence (even if acknowledging, as there frequently will be, that there are counter-arguments).

▶ 7.38

Depending on what you have studied in the past, you may have been used to writing in the first person, which means presenting the work from a personal standpoint—"I think", "in my opinion". Generally this is not seen as appropriate in most legal academic writing, although there may be certain reflective exercises or progress logs you are asked to do which do require you to write in the first person: your tutors should advise you if this is the case. Further, if you progress onto the professional courses for becoming a solicitor or barrister, you will be expected to use appropriate drafting techniques for advice notes and letters to clients, and this will involve use of the first person (because by this time, you are the expert, so your personal opinion is what you are going to be paid for as a professional). At undergraduate or graduate diploma level, however, you will usually be expected to write in the third person. This may be very different from what you have been used to in writing at school or college and it may take you some time to settle into the style of it.

You will note that we've written in the first person throughout this book because we're aiming for a much less formal style than you will need to adopt for your assignments: essentially we're trying to achieve a conversation with you, so that it is easier for you to engage with what we're saying. You are not expected to have a conversation with your tutor in this way: as you know from Chapter 5, you are expected to present conclusions on the basis of evidence.

It may seem odd that while critical evaluation is a key academic skill which involves making judgments about the materials you use, a statement such as "I think" is discouraged. The trick is to realise that phrases like "I think . . ." make your views sounds unsubstantiated, whereas a critical evaluation provides the *evidence* for the conclusion you have drawn. You therefore don't *need* to present this as opinion (even though to some extent it still is).

You may also feel that qualifying your point with "I think" or "in my view" (for example "*I think* Lord Justice Thorpe's dissenting judgment is well-argued" rather than simply "Lord Justice Thorpe's dissenting judgment is well-argued") is *safer*, because you are making it clear you are only presenting your opinion, rather than stating something to be true, which feels riskier if your view might be perceived as wrong (in other words if the marker thinks Lord Justice Thorpe's dissenting judgment was *not* well-argued). However, remember that a vital skill your tutors are looking for is the ability to evaluate the points made by others and draw your own conclusions from them—and to compare differing views and decide which is the better or best. If you are doing this, then you do not need to dilute your points by saying "I think"—it's your essay, so it is taken as read that it contains your thoughts—the vital aspect is that you have formed and are presenting those thoughts on the basis of sufficient evidence to make them valid arguments.

So, whenever you are tempted to write "I think . . .", or when reading through a first draft, you realise you have written it, STOP. Ask yourself: "*why* do I think this?" and you should be able to come up with an answer starting with "because . . .". This "because" statement is the reason for your view, which should include the evidence on which you are basing that view. If that reason/evidence stand up to scrutiny, then the argument is valid: assert it with confidence. If you can't come up with a reason, then you haven't got the right evidence. This means you aren't utilising your sources properly—work through Chapter 5 to help you with this. *Do not include the point in your essay.* We have seen students who seem to feel that writing "I think" or "in my opinion" justifies the inclusion of an un-evidenced point—or alternatively, should be used to distinguish points for which they have no evidence from those for which they do—(it's as if they are saying to the marker "I'm telling you this is just what I *think*, I don't have a reason") but you should never use "I think" or "In my opinion" as a substitute for having evidence. Unsubstantiated opinion has no place in academic writing.

A further difficulty with writing objectively is that it tends to involve writing in a more "passive" style of writing; for example "this argument can be criticised because. . ." rather than "I am criticising this argument because. . ." (the latter is described as "active" rather than passive). Generally, writers are advised that active writing is clearer and more direct than passive writing, but passive writing has been traditional in academic legal writing (although active writing is becoming more preferred). This is likely to be a matter of preference amongst your tutors and therefore we'd advise you to ask for guidance.

Writing formally

7.39 ▶ In academic writing, a certain level of formality is expected. As we've already mentioned, we are not following our own advice because we're deliberately aiming at a less formal style, and therefore we've made more use of informal language and contractions like *don't, shouldn't, can't*. You should avoid these in your writing, and use the full *do not* and so on.

The real mistake to avoid is an assumption that formal writing requires the use of phrases like "it is submitted that" or even "it is respectfully submitted that", both of which will tend to make your writing unnecessarily pompous. Writing in normal, formal English is all you need to do. The style of a quality newspaper or the BBC news website is probably the right kind of tone to aim for.

Writing in a gender neutral style

7.40 ▶ Whilst it is generally accepted that academic writing must be gender neutral (in other words do not write "men" when you mean "people") there are differing views on the best way of achieving this. Particular problems occur when assigning *he* to denote a member of a group who could be male or female. Alternative methods for handling this include:

- using "he or she" and "his or her";
- using "she" and "her" in a straight swap;
- using the artificial creation "s/he";

- using "them/their" instead—i.e. adapting a non-gendered plural, even where a singular is more appropriate.

All of these methods have advantages and disadvantages and different tutors may have different preferences (as do we as authors!); check whether there is a preferred way of handling this in your institution. If there isn't, find your own preferred way and stick to it, rather than switching throughout an essay—in other words, be consistent.

SUMMARY OF CHAPTER 7

- Academic writing requires you to follow normal conventions of grammar and spelling.
- A good standard of English and an appropriate style is part of communicating effectively.
- Spelling and grammar checkers may help you to spot errors but are no substitute for understanding the rules and checking your work.
- Key errors to avoid are misuse of apostrophes, incomplete sentences and spelling mistakes.
- Academic style should be clear and concise.

▶ 7.41

▶ 8
Finishing your work and utilising feedback

WHAT IS THE PURPOSE OF THIS CHAPTER?

8.1 ▶ Once you have completed the writing phase of your assignment it is tempting to think it is ready to print and hand in or submit online. However this is not the case. In this chapter we will explain the additional steps you need to take after finishing writing before submission. You will also, in due course, receive feedback on the piece of work and this can be a valuable source of improvement of the future. Reflecting on feedback should be an important part of your strategy to improve your writing.

By the end of this chapter you will:

- have a better understanding of the elements involved in finishing your work; and
- be able to use your feedback to reflect on your performance and make changes to your future practice.

HOW SHOULD I REVIEW AND EDIT MY WORK?

8.2 ▶ There are different kinds of reviewing/editing:

1. Revision: whether on a large or small scale, this involves examining the entire assignment closely for structure, argument, flow, transition and any weaknesses or gaps or lack of authority that may be apparent.
2. Editing: here we are more concerned with minor problems that can be fixed by deleting or adding a word or two. Put yourself in the reader's position. Will he or she find your writing clear, understandable and easy to follow?
3. Proof-reading: where you are overtly looking for mistakes in your writing, particularly, for example, with punctuation, spelling, sentence structure and apostrophes. This needs to be done carefully—you must consciously slow your reading down to spot mistakes in work which is now very familiar to you.

All writing, whether it is an assignment, a dissertation or even this book chapter, needs to be reviewed. Things may need to be added or deleted, points changed and/or paragraphs reorganised. (We will consider later in the chapter how much review is practical with exam answers.). Doing this task well can turn an average essay into a very good one, so make sure you have left enough time.

The key to doing this well is to adopt another persona—that of your own critical friend.

It's a good idea to leave this until a a few days *after* you have finished your first draft if your timescale allows. (If it doesn't, then make sure you build this in for the next time.) Finish the first draft and put it aside. Do something else. Don't think consciously about your work. Taking a day or two in between finishing your work and reviewing it will give some distance which can help with developing objectivity.

▶ 8.3

Try using this checklist as a guide:

Final checklist

- Go back to your diagnosis of the task and begin by reading the whole assignment again. Have you answered the question? Have you said what you intended to say? What are the strengths and weaknesses of your assignment?

▶ 8.4

- Check the assessment criteria for this piece of work. Have you addressed these? (Do not ignore the very aspects, your markers *told* you they would be looking for.)
- Have you met all the specific requirements (if any) for this assignment in terms of word length, bibliography and so on? (See below for further suggestions on these aspects.)
- Consider your structure. Does it seem clear and logical? Is each point relevant and adequately developed? Does your work flow? Try running the opening sentences of each paragraph together—does that provide a coherent structure which addresses the question?
- Look at your introduction—could someone reading *just* this part of your answer make an educated guess as to what the question you've been asked was?
- Now skip to your conclusion—does it contain an answer to, or your position on, the core question?
- Do your sentences work? Have you written in complete sentences and do they make sense?
- Is every assertion or proposition of law supported by relevant authority or evidence?
- What does your work look like? Is it presented in a typed format in a readable font type and size, with adequate margins and footnotes/endnotes if required?
- Does your use of grammar, including apostrophes and sentence construction comply with the rules in Chapter 7?
- Have you spell-checked? Be aware of your individual pattern of errors. If you are prone to making certain mistakes over and over again, note them down and check for these particularly carefully. If you know there are words that you commonly mistype you could use the find and replace facility in your word processing package to sort these out (see Chapter 7 for more on this).

> **TIPS ●**
> - *Give yourself plenty of time to review.*
> - *Save your work in numbered versions in case you want to return later to something you had previously deleted.*
> - *Use a hard copy of your work to review/ edit as you can miss problems if reading from a computer screen.*
> - *When checking your spelling you may find it helpful to start from the end of the document and work backwards to prevent accidental skim-reading.*
> - *Read your work out loud.*
> - *Ask someone to be your second reader.*
> - *Be someone else's second reader!*

ACTIVITY 8.1

8.5 ▶ You can practise this process using Answer B of the four sample essay questions on the Practice Statement which can be found in Appendix 3. Put yourself in the position of the writer of that answer and use the checklist above to conduct a review of that answer (you may find it easier to imagine yourself as the marker instead of the writer). We think you will find that it is easier to spot the mistakes made by others than the ones you have made yourself. (We will come back to this later on in the chapter.)

Here are some suggestions for making the review process easier:

● Reading your work out loud to see how it sounds can be very helpful. You should be aiming for it to sound like (reasonably formal) speech. Reading aloud is also a good way to tackle the problem of over familiarity we referred to earlier and helps to develop a more objective approach when reviewing/editing (it may also help with spotting punctuation errors). When you take a breath whilst reading out loud consider whether some punctuation is needed at that point.

● Asking a friend or two for help can also be useful. They don't need to be expert writers or even law students (although that can help). Here you are comparing your own subjective assessment with someone else's more objective assessment of the work. You can read your work out loud to them or ask them to read it out loud to you. How does your work sound when being spoken by someone who has never read it before? Do your sentences work when spoken? Does the structure still seem clear and logical? Can it be read fluently and with ease? Does your friend understand the gist of what you are trying to say or are there gaps in your argument which are confusing? Has your friend spotted any typos or grammatical errors that need to be corrected?

DO I NEED TO ADHERE TO THE WORD LIMIT?

8.6 ▶ Yes, you do. You must make sure that your work does not exceed any limit you have been set. Equally it will be important to check it is not significantly *under* the word limit.

It is fairly common to exceed the limit on a first draft.

> **TIPS** • *By keeping the question and your diagnosis of task in front of you, you should be able to check that you have only included relevant material.*

When trimming for word count purposes you must be careful not to cut your core arguments. Instead, look to cut explanation or marginal detail that is just not needed to follow the main lines of argument. For example:

● Have you included a little too much descriptive material (facts of cases, for example)?

● Is there more historical background discussion than is needed?

● Check for repetition—you may have said the same thing in a number of different ways without realising it.

Your goal is to make sure only relevant information has been included. As you read through your work during the reviewing process try to justify your inclusion of all points/sentences/cases, etc.—if you can't then ditch them!

Conversely, you may find your work is short of the word limit. It is not good enough to say to yourself, "Well, I put in everything they wanted and it just didn't take that many words". You need to be more reflective than that. Your tutors have set this word limit for a reason: so if you are well short, it is extremely likely that you have made an error in your diagnosis—either you have missed an issue out, or you have wrongly labelled as a minor point something which needs much more detail as a major point. You need to go back to your diagnosis—and ask yourself again whether you have fully answered the question(s). For example:

- Do you need to include more information or analysis in answering any of the sub-questions?
- Have you used authority to support your argument(s)?
- Have you adopted an academic style?
- Do you need to do some more focused research?

Don't just pad your answer out with more description.

HOW SHOULD I PRESENT MY WORK?

In the context of finishing your work prior to submission, looks do count to some extent. If you were a marker, would you prefer to read a document which is well presented or one which is sloppy with spelling and typing errors and has the pages in the wrong order? Remember that your goal is *clear communication*. Students sometimes confuse the idea of good presentation with the need to provide elaborate title pages, or submit their work in fancy folders. Generally, simplicity is best. If you have been given specific submission guide-lines, then follow them. If not, here are some suggestions for improving the appearance of your work:

▶ 8.7

- Use a standard font-style and size, for example Arial 12 pt.
- Double-space, so the marker can both read and comment on your work easily.
- Leave margins of at least one inch at the top, bottom and sides of the page.
- Page numbers should normally be placed at the bottom of each page. Make sure that all pages are numbered. Title pages (if used) are usually not numbered. Page 1 is the first page of the essay proper, and must be numbered.
- Ensure that the correct means of identifying the work as belonging to you is used on every page, for example your name and/or student registration number. You could use the header facility in your word processing software package for this which will apply these details automatically to each page.

If you have to submit a hard copy:
- Use white paper.
- Do not hand in loose pages; always bind them together. Simply stapling them is best, but alternatively use a folder or plastic wallet.
- Make sure that the whole of the written text is clearly visible. Do not put each individual page into a separate plastic sleeve. This just causes annoyance to a marker as each page must be removed from its sleeve to be marked.

HOW DO I WRITE A BIBLIOGRAPHY?

8.8 ▶ A further aspect of finishing your work is that you will—almost certainly—be expected to submit a correctly formatted bibliography along with your assignment. Your bibliography is a list of sources, i.e. books, articles, reports, cases and statutory provisions which are referred to or cited in the text. To find out how to set out your bibliography, your first step should be to check whether your Law School specifies a format. If there is any guidance available, then of course you should follow it. For example, you may be required to put only secondary sources in a bibliography (although the guidance we've suggested below includes primary sources as well).

If you are not given a specific format to follow, then you may wish to adopt the following practice. First, list legislation referred to in alphabetical order (there is no need to specify particular sections); then list cases referred to with full citations in alphabetical order; and lastly, list secondary sources in one single list in alphabetical order of author. This will look slightly different depending on whether you adopt the Harvard or the Numerical system but should include author, title, date of publication and page references (if relevant) (see Chapter 5 for more on referencing and Appendix 4 for a sample bibliography).

> **TIPS •** *There are examples of how a bibliography might look in Appendix 4 and you will find reference books on this in your library.*

Some Law Schools may expect you to further sub-divide into types of source, e.g. books, journal articles, websites.

HOW MUCH OF THIS IS RELEVANT TO EXAM ANSWERS?

8.9 ▶ Of course you will need to adopt a different strategy in an exam. Here, there will be less emphasis on presentation but you do still need to leave time to check through your answers for any obvious mistakes (like not answering the required number of questions or like forgetting to provide authority) or any other errors (like including irrelevant material or neglecting to deal with a major point in a question) which would make it harder for your marker to understand what you mean. You won't be asked to provide a bibliograhy in an exam.

> **TIPS •** *You may find you need to add clarification, in which case use asterisks and arrows to direct the marker's attention to any additions. However, bear in mind that the need to do this too often is indicative of a lack of planning, so reflect on this for future exams.*

WHEN IS MY WORK READY TO HAND IN?

8.10 ▶ A hard question to answer—this is something which you must decide for yourself, with reference to the advice we've provided in this chapter. You will come to a point when you must decide that the assignment is complete and ready to be handed in. This can be a hard decision. It is tempting to keep writing to improve the piece *ad nauseam*. Resist this temptation. Remember you have already worked hard on this. The potential benefits to be gained from further reworking are not sufficient enough to risk submitting late, or to delay starting your next assignment.

A useful tip is to make some notes for yourself on the process you have just been through. Ask yourself:

- What did I do well in this piece of writing/assignment?
- What would I like to do better next time?

These notes will help you to finish the assignment and also help you to develop an action plan for the next assignment you must complete. In addition to this post-assignment self-reflection you should also, eventually, have access to another source of help, namely feedback on your work.

WHAT CAN I LEARN FROM FEEDBACK ON MY WORK?

You are likely to receive some kind of feedback on your work, whether that work is formative or summative. This may be given verbally or in writing. The feedback you receive may vary but whatever form is takes it has been designed to help you to understand why you were awarded the mark given and also as a tool to improve for the future. So, you can use feedback to improve your performance and can see what you could do differently next time.

▶ **8.11**

It is therefore really important to take time to interpret what the feedback means, and make a plan to act on it.

Whether the mark is as you expected, not as high as you would have liked or indeed exceeds your expectation, learning what you have scored may arouse strong feelings. To get the most out of feedback you need time to let these feelings settle before trying to learn for the future from this piece of writing. So it is really important to learn the skill of dealing *objectively* with feedback. Unless you are exceptionally able, you will from time to time receive marks and feedback which are disappointing to you, especially in the light of the amount of time you spent working on any particular assignment. We've all

> **TIPS** • *With the best will in the world it is sometimes impossible for your tutors to return work as fast as you—and they—would like. If the assignment feels remote by the time you receive the feedback, then get your copy out and read it again so as to make the most of the feedback you get on it. Don't just look at the mark!*

> **TIPS** • *Putting the feedback away for a few days and then coming back to it can help with getting the most out of it.*

been there, and it can be tempting to assume that the marker is at fault rather than your own work. Unfortunately, as we've made clear, the length of time spent on a piece of work does not necessarily equate to the mark awarded. This is frustrating, but it is why we encourage you to focus on all aspects of the writing cycle.

ACTIVITY 8.2

Start by getting out a piece of feedback that you have received before, together with some highlighter pens in different colours. Read the feedback carefully, then re-read the piece of work to see the areas the feedback refers to. Use a highlighter pen to cross-reference the feedback to the work. It is easier to get the specific feedback point being made if the connections are made obvious.

▶ **8.12**

The next step is to break your feedback down into positive and negative comments. Often at first reading feedback will all look negative which makes it tempting to ignore and justify any decision you might already have made not to bother reading it in full. Taking negative points on board is difficult but another reason it is important to read your feedback carefully is to recognise the things you have done well.

● So now with one colour pen highlight the good or positive points that your tutor has made and with another colour the negative comments or areas for improvement. Note down what actions you took in relation to this feedback when you received it. If you did not take any, why was that?

WHAT DOES MY FEEDBACK MEAN?

Understanding my feedback

8.13 ▶ Feedback will vary from tutor to tutor. Naturally, this can make understanding your feedback confusing, particularly when you may be getting feedback from many different tutors and subjects.

> **TIPS** • *Your tutors should always be happy to explain their feedback if you are having trouble "translating" what they mean or even actually reading their comments. Go and see your tutor and ask for their help.*

Translating comments from tutors is a skill. Understanding what has been written is vital for your next piece of work so you will need to spend some time acquiring the necessary skills to do this in order to benefit from any feedback you are given. Tutor comments can address a range of issues, e.g. grammar, structure and layout, referencing, content, errors, and can be positive or be more negative and critical. In order to learn from your feedback, essentially you need to practise the skills in reflection we identified in Chapter 1.

Ask yourself:

● Do I understand the comments?
● Can I identify what they are specifically referring to?
● Do I agree with the comments? If not, why? (Remember "but I worked really hard" is not adequate evidence.)
● What do I need to do to improve my performance?

If you are still unsure of what the feedback you received meant or how to improve then your next step should be to meet with the subject tutor.

Learning from your feedback

8.14 ▶ So, if you are wondering what to do with all those tutor comments on your work, first read them carefully. Then, see if you can determine what kind of comments have been made by the marker and use the following table for suggestions as to what you can do.

If the comments are . . .	Then you should . . .
Positive reinforcement	Feel good and accept any critical comments there are. If this refers to something in particular see if you can incorporate it into your next assignment.
Related to the bibliography	Be sure you are fully aware of any programme, institutional or discipline standard on this and use it!
Related to the range of sources	Try expanding and developing your research strategy. Either you have not read widely enough or you have just

If the comments are . . .	Then you should . . .
	not created a sense of detailed understanding of the topic in your writing.
Related to structure/layout	Follow the comments. If you are not sure what is expected, check your lecture/tutorial notes when information may have been given and look back at Chapter 6 for further guidance.
About grammar/spelling/ sentence structure problems	Read these comments carefully and try to work out where the problems are. Re-read the early part of this chapter and Chapter 7 and leave yourself enough time to proof-read carefully before you submit your next assignment.

Related to errors of law	Learn your material and how to apply it. It is clear that if your work does have a lot of errors on the law, any feedback on content will not be positive
Related to content	See what general lessons can be learnt from it. This is harder to categorise as these comments will be subject specific, but, for example, if the marker suggests that there is something s/he particularly liked in your assignment look at it carefully and try to work out if a similar strategy would work with other assignments.
Related to your referencing	Revisit Chapter 5. This tends to involve a discipline or department specific norm or method and you need to learn what it is in your institution very early on in your legal academic career.
Indicating a lack of analysis	Work on developing the evaluative or analytical parts of your argument. This means you have been too descriptive and have not adopted a style which challenges and evaluates the law on this matter. You need to adopt an improved questioning approach to your next assignment, so look again at Chapter 5.
Related to presentation	Work out what is wrong and fix it—this is easily done and as with referencing there is no excuse for poor presentation.
Related to failing to address the question	Reconsider how you diagnose your task. Read Chapter 3 again to the question get some tips on how to do exactly what it says on the tin!
Related to a lack of authority	Remember every statement or assertion or proposition of law you make needs to be supported by authority or evidence, i.e. primary or secondary sources.

ACTIVITY 8.3

8.15 ▶ Go back to the notes you made earlier when you undertook Activity 8.1. For this activity you are going to extend that exercise by providing feedback on the answer as if you really had marked it. To do this, you will need to consider the matters discussed above. For example:

- Content (to include errors in law and use of authority);
- Structure (to include style);
- Grammar (to include spelling and sentence structure);
- Referencing (to include bibliography and sources); and
- Analysis/evaluation. You are *not* trying to allocate a mark, but considering the comments that might be made by a marker to give advice to the writer of this work that will help them with future assignments.

Activity feedback—here are our thoughts:

- *Content:* Evidence of sound knowledge and arguments show understanding, covers most issues. Tackles important problems connected with the use of the Statement although you could extend this by providing a better insight into the actual *use* of the Statement.
- *Structure:* Logical sequence adopted and your paragraphs are linked. Some of your sentences are confusingly long and tortuous: you need to try and make your good points more accessible in short, succinct paragraphs.
- *Grammar:* Your grammar, spelling and use of apostrophes are poor—e.g. principal, its/it's. This is something you really need to work on. You can seek help from legal writing books in the library and should perhaps consider seeing if your subject tutor or student support tutor can make any suggestions.
- *Referencing:* Secondary sources used (Alan Paterson) and quoted but where are the relevant cases? *Miller v Jackson* is the only case used which was in the Court of Appeal and did not use the Practice Statement.

Analysis/evaluation: Your answer raises the right issues and you have described some arguments including some effort to assess the advantages/disadvantages linked to the Statement. However, you have ignored the instruction to illustrate from case law and you need to offer more judgments and conclusions in relation to the arguments you present in order to improve your critical analysis.

Learning from model answers

8.16 ▶ In our experience, students are often very keen to receive model answers to questions, and while they can be something of a security blanket, there are a number of problems associated with them. The temptation with a model answer is to focus on the content material as opposed to how that content has been used to answer the question. That is: it is not so much what you *know* but what you do with your knowledge and material that impresses the marker. Therefore, a model answer should only ever be indicative of a *process*. Two things which are certain with a model answer is that first, no model essay is perfect, and secondly, the same question will not be coming up in your exam or coursework so the exact circumstances of any answer are valueless. Model answers can lead to blinkered thinking—the more you study the answer for content the more difficult it becomes for you to think and write differently (especially if it is on a subject area which you also have to write an answer on) and the more you run the risk of straying into plagiarism.

The benefit of a model answer is therefore less about the specific content, but more about the clear insight it gives into tutor expectations as far as structure and approach for questions on that particular topic. In other words it is the *technique* used by your tutors in the model answer, to answer this type of question which is more important than the answer itself. There is no rule which says you cannot copy someone else's structure. How to answer a question, in terms of structure, style and approach, in addition to coverage of the material is what needs to be taken from these model answers. These elements are transferable from question to question on the same topic and, in an even more general way, to similar types of questions such as other problem questions.

Learning from exams

The nature and extent of the feedback provided on exam performance varies from institution to institution. You may be provided with individual feedback, generic comments on performance or you may receive your mark and nothing else. It may be that feedback is only provided to those who have failed in order to help them assess where they went wrong and to improve their performance next time. Alternatively feedback may be available on request rather than automatically. You may want to consider asking your tutor for feedback. The scope and depth of any feedback they can provide will usually be up to them but if they have time and are able to, most tutors are willing to help. If you received a surprising examination mark—whether better or worse than you expected—don't go into the next set of exams without understanding why! Find out why by asking your tutor for feedback.

▶ 8.17

Dealing with disappointment

In any area of life you're bound to experience disappointment at some time or other and your legal studies are no different.

Apprehension about writing is a common experience. Because writing is the most common means of sharing our knowledge, we put a lot of pressure on ourselves when we write. This book has given some suggestions for how to help you cope with that pressure. However you may still get an assignment back with a mark on it that you are not happy with. If that happens don't focus wholly on the negative. First look for positive comments. Secondly, jump right back in to an element of the writing process: choose one suggestion the tutor has made and work on it, do some writing or revising as quickly as possible. In this way you can use the feedback to keep developing your writing. Learning often occurs in the wake of a startling event, so use your disappointments positively to keep developing your writing.

▶ 8.18

SUMMARY OF CHAPTER 8

- It is vital to finish your work by reviewing, editing and proof-reading it before submission.

▶ 8.19

- Techniques which may help you finish your work include reading it out loud and asking a friend to look through it.
- You must make sure you comply with any guidance on format and submission.
- When you receive feedback on your work, you should use this to inform your future writing including noting your own strengths.
- Use your feedback to establish which part(s) of the writing cycle you need to work on to improve your performance.

PART 4

Other legal writing

▶ 9
Strategies for other types of writing

WHAT IS THE PURPOSE OF THIS CHAPTER?

The purpose of this chapter is to highlight how you need to adapt the general advice we are ▶ 9.1
giving you on how to improve your writing throughout the rest of this book to particular types
of assignment. We've already discussed what makes a good piece of writing in Chapter 1, and
in Chapter 2 we considered the writing cycle which takes place in successful legal writing, as
follows:

- Step 1: reflection.
- Step 2: diagnosis.
- Step 3: review materials.
- Step 4: research, keeping your diagnosis under review.
- Step 5: planning.
- Step 6: writing.
- Step 7: finishing and polishing.
- Step 8: act on your feedback.

Advice on these steps has been provided throughout the remainder of this book. By the end
of this chapter, you will understand how this cycle can be adapted for other types of writing:

- writing a case note;
- writing a critical analysis of an article;
- reflective writing; and
- writing in an exam.

We deal with writing a dissertation/extended project in Chapter 10.

HOW DO I WRITE A CASE NOTE?

The ability to interpret case law is the cornerstone of legal study. Without being able to under- ▶ 9.2
stand the legal principles from cases, it is impossible to apply those principles to a given situation. It is therefore very likely that you will be asked to demonstrate skills in case analysis in
relation to a given case at an early stage in your studies. The skills you acquire in interpreting
case law will be tested pervasively in numerous other assignments, but in this section we are
going to concentrate on a specific piece of work on a given case, rather than the case analysis
skills you will demonstrate through discussion of essay or problem questions.

Whether this is a formally graded piece of work or a formative piece on which you receive feedback will vary from law school to law school, as may the title of the assignment—case analysis, case note, case task, for example—and the exact elements required may differ. Nevertheless, what all are likely to have in common is the purpose: to show that you can read a primary source of law in the form of a case, and identify and interpret key information from that case—so that you can then use this skill in relation to all the other cases you will encounter and need to apply during your studies and beyond.

A case analysis or case note assignment will commonly ask you to do some or all of the following:

- Identify key factual information from the case, such as the history of the proceedings, the outcome or decision of the case, the court it was decided in, the judge(s) who decided it, and whether their ruling was unanimous.
- Give the material facts of the case.
- Summarise the legal issue(s) which arise.
- Analyse the reasoning the judge(s) have used to reach their conclusions.
- Summarise what use is made of precedent within the judgment.
- Formulate a possible *ratio decidendi*.
- Identify a line of reasoning within the judgment which is *obiter dictum*.
- Discuss the approach to statutory interpretation used by the judge(s).
- Provide critical comment on the case.
- Look up and summarise how the case has itself been used as precedent in later cases.

A more advanced version of this type of assignment might ask you compare and contrast two or more cases in the same area.

Organising the writing of a case note

9.3 ▶ The reading of the case itself is central to the process of writing a case note or case analysis assignment. It is beyond the scope of this text to give a detailed analysis of the principles of legal method, and there are many specific legal method texts which explore the meaning of terms like *ratio* and *obiter*, and approaches to the interpretation of statutes in detail. The following guidance therefore concentrates on key tips to help you complete a case note. We will use the case of *Fisher v Bell* [1961] 1 Q.B. 394 as an example. This is a case which interpreted s.1 of the Offensive Weapons Act 1959, which made it an offence to manufacture, sell, hire or offer for sale or hire certain specified types of knife, including a "flick knife". The defendant had displayed a knife of this prohibited type in his shop window with a price tag on it, and the court had to decide whether he had committed the offence.

1. First of all, be clear about the assignment brief. As already mentioned, the exact format of a case analysis will vary from institution to institution, so make sure you understand exactly what you are being asked to find or interpret from the case. This will help you with the second stage, which is (not surprisingly) to find and read the case or cases which you have been asked to analyse.

2. Start by reading the headnote to get an idea of the main facts and a summary of the reasoning and ruling in the case.

3. Next, if you are required to pick out factual information, such as the court, judges, appeal history, etc., then look for this at the beginning of the case report and make a note of these (if you are required to put these into a short summary of the decision, see below for putting this together). If there is more than one judgment, check whether there is a dissent.

4. Now turn to the judgments for your main reading. Mark up the case (for example, using different coloured highlighter pens) to identify:
   (a) the facts which led to the proceedings and/or proceedings in lower courts;
   (b) statements of law;
   (c) application of law and reasoning;
   (d) any precedents which are referred to in the judgment.

> **TIPS •** *Do not regard the reading of the headnote as a substitute for reading the full judgment carefully—the law is in the judgment(s), not the headnote. However, the headnote gives a useful overview which provides a starting point.*

> **TIPS •** *Further guidance on basic navigation of a case report can be found in a general legal skills text book, for example Anthony Bradney et al, How to Study Law (7th edn, Sweet and Maxwell 2014).*

Then:

(i) Look for the legal issue.

This is the legal question which the judge(s) must answer in order to decide the case. Some judges may give this in a straightforward manner near the beginning of the judgment: Lord Parker does so in *Fisher v Bell*, when he says "the sole question is whether the exhibition of that knife in the window with the ticket constituted an offer for sale within the statute".

However, a note of caution is needed here: you are not simply looking for "magic words" within the judgment: your tutors are testing your ability to *interpret* what the judge has said. What the judge *says* the legal issue is may actually be narrower or broader than what is justified on a close analysis of the case.

For example, suppose that Lord Parker had said "the sole question is whether or not the defendant has committed the offence". In a broad sense, this would be true, but it does not represent the *legal* issue which he has to consider. In such a case, you would need to dig deeper into the judgment to work out what he had to decide in order to conclude whether the defendant had committed the offence.

Alternatively, suppose that Lord Parker had been specific in identifying the *flick knife* (rather than any knife—s.1 also covers other types of offensive knife) within his formulation of the issue. Again, in a narrow sense, this would have been correct, because he is deciding the case in relation to a flick knife. However, the fact that it is a *flick* knife, rather than another form of offensive knife, is only relevant to the legal issue if there had been a genuine question over whether the flick knife itself fell within the statutory definition, rather than, as here, the question being over whether it was "offered for sale". This question is equally applicable whatever the form of knife was involved as there is no suggestion anywhere that the case would have been decided differently if it had been a different type of offensive knife (and the implication of this is particularly important at the later stage of trying to formulate the ratio).

Finally, some judges may not give any statement of the legal issue at the beginning of the judgment, or indeed at all. You will need to do more interpretation of the judgment in order to identify a legal question if you are examining such a case.

(ii) Look for the outcome.

Once you have identified the legal question, then look for the "answer" to that question, in the form of the outcome. At the most basic level, this simply involves looking at which way the case was decided.

In the case of *Fisher v Bell*, the outcome was that no offence had been committed (this can be seen both from the headnote, and from the final sentence of Lord Parker's judgment). We can therefore see that the legal question "does the exhibition of an offensive knife in a shop window with a price ticket constitute an offer for sale contrary to section 1 of the Offensive Weapons Act 1959?" can be answered, in simple terms, as "no". Your assignment brief may ask you to incorporate this into a paragraph including some of the factual information from step 3 (see our "decision" example below).

(iii) Look for the reasoning.

Here, you are trying to identify *why* the court gave the answer it did to the legal question posed, drawing on the sections you have identified as "reasoning" on reading the case. When this is expressed in terms of a legal rule or principle, this is the ratio of the case, but you may also be asked to analyse the process of reasoning which *leads* to the *ratio*—in other words, to show how the judge has justified the conclusion he or she has reached (see our example below). Legal principles or rules which are stated or can be inferred from the judgment but which are not necessary to the outcome of the case are *obiter dicta*. Returning to our example of *Fisher v Bell*, in considering the legal issue and outcome above, we have concluded that this case decided the following:

Exhibiting a knife in a shop window with a price ticket does not constitute an offer for sale contrary to section 1 of the Offensive Weapons Act 1959.

What we now need to do is put "because. . ." on the end of this sentence. What comes after the "because. . ." is the reason for the decision; in other words we will be getting close to a formulation of the *ratio*.

In *Fisher v Bell*, this is reasonably straightforward. Lord Parker gets into his reasoning very early in the judgment, and gives a legal principle in the second paragraph: "It is perfectly clear that according to the ordinary law of contract the display of an article with a price tag on it in a shop window is merely an invitation to treat." He then goes on to apply this to the facts and interpret the statute in the context of this rule, before going on to consider whether there are any precedents which would suggest an alternative approach (and concluding that there aren't). We could therefore finish our "because. . ." statement with something like this:

Exhibiting a knife in a shop window with a price ticket does not constitute an offer for sale contrary to section 1 of the Offensive Weapons Act 1959, because under the ordinary law of contract, putting something in a shop window with a price tag on it is an invitation to treat rather than an offer for sale.

From this we will be able to formulate a possible *ratio*.

However, caution again needs to be taken. Twining and Miers comment:

> "Talk of *finding* the *ratio decidendi* of a case obscures the fact that the process of interpreting cases is not like a hunt for buried treasure, but typically involves an element of choice from a range of possibilities."[1]

This quotation illustrates two important points. First, as with the legal issue, you are not (necessarily) looking for a quotation. Sometimes a possible formulation of ratio may be captured in a single sentence, as it arguably is here, but it is much more likely that you will need to put this into your own words. Secondly, there is no exact "right" answer: there will be legal propositions which are capable of being ratio; in a complex case with multiple judgments, and multiple legal issues, you will have to do some careful reading to work out what represents the majority view on each point. Consult a legal method textbook, or the relevant tutor, for more detailed help with interpreting ratio.

5. Carry out any further research required in the assignment brief (if any)—for example, looking to see if the case has been applied as a precedent later, or whether it has been criticised by academic writers.

You should now be in a position to begin writing your case note.

Process of writing a case note

The process of writing your case note will depend on the specific instructions in your assignment brief. Particular things to check, before you start to write up your answers, are: ▶ 9.4

- that you have identified all the elements which are required by the assignment brief;
- whether you have been instructed to put elements into your own words, or whether a quotation is required—and make sure you comply with any such instructions.

Further general tips:

1. Ensure your case note is *consistent*—the legal issues, material facts and *ratio* are interdependent: if you have identified a particular fact as material, then by implication there must be some reference to that fact within the legal issue and within the *ratio* (the more specific you are in your identification of material facts, the narrower the *ratio* becomes). The scope of the issue you have identified will have implications for the broadness or narrowness of the *ratio* you construe and which of the general facts you consider to be material.

2. Make sure you formulate the *ratio* in abstract terms, in the form of a rule or principle. This is sometimes described as a "principle possessing generality". In other words, it needs to be in this form to be capable of being applied to other cases as a precedent later. Compare the following:

---

[1] William Twining and David Miers, *How to do things with rules* (5th edn, Cambridge University Press 2010) 335.

Under the ordinary law of contract, when Mr Fisher put the flick knife in a shop window with a price tag on it, it was an invitation to treat rather than an offer for sale.	This does contain the right legal principle, but it is specific to the general facts rather than the material facts, because it mentions the name of the shop keeper.
Under the ordinary law of contract, putting a prohibited knife in a shop window with a price tag on it is an invitation to treat rather than an offer for sale.	Here, the name of the shop keeper has been removed (it is not a material fact) and this therefore possesses more generality than the previous version.

Generally a *ratio* expressed as a principle possessing generality will not contain:

- the names of parties (although their position or status may be crucial—think of the case of *Donoghue v Stevenson* for example: it would not be correct to formulate a *ratio* containing the party names, but it would be important to include their positions of ultimate consumer and manufacturer of the product);
- specific days/dates/times (although the sequence in which certain events happened may well be material);
- place names (although a type of place might be material—for example, it might be material in relation to negligence arising from a road traffic accident that a pedestrian was on a zebra crossing);
- specific amounts or an exact product (although it might be material that a large quantity rather than a small quantity was involved, or the general type of product).

Structure of a case note

9.5 ▶ Again, this will depend upon the exact instructions you have been given. Below is an example for the case we are looking at here which covers common elements which you might be asked to deal with in an assignment of this type. Make sure you use the structure required for your own assignment.

1. The legal issues in the case

> The legal issue was whether exhibiting a knife of a form specified in s.1 of the Restriction of Offensive Weapons Act 1959 constituted offering the knife for sale contrary to the same section.

2. The decision

> Lord Parker and Ashworth and Elwes JJ. in the Queen's Bench Division unanimously decided to affirm the decision of the magistrates that the accused was not guilty of offering for sale a knife, contrary to s.1 of the Restriction of Offensive Weapons Act 1959.

3. The material facts

> The material facts were that the defendant had displayed the knife in his shop window with price tag on it implying that it was for sale.

4. The steps in reasoning employed by the judge

Lord Parker reasoned as follows in reaching his conclusion:
1. At first sight, and in ordinary language, displaying an article in a shop window with a price tag on it is offering it for sale.
2. However, an ordinary meaning cannot override the legal meaning of a word.
3. Parliament must be taken to know the general law and therefore must have meant something by using the words "offer for sale" (in contrast to situations where they use the words "expose for sale" which was not the case here).
4. Therefore the law on this is that the action here is an invitation to treat rather than an offer for sale.

5. A formulation of the *ratio* expressed as a general principle

Under the ordinary law of contract, displaying a knife with a price tag on it [in a shop window] is not an offer for sale but merely an invitation to treat (and therefore does not contravene s.1 of the Restriction of Offensive Weapons Act 1959).

6. Example of *obiter*

Lord Parker's reasoning includes reference to statutes where the words "expose for sale" are used, which he contrasts with the statute at issue in the present case. He also cites two statutes where a definition section is included where Parliament's intention is to enlarge the meaning of the words "offer for sale" to include situations of display or exposure.

This is *obiter* in the sense that it is reasoning involving facts which are not applicable to the case (since the statute at issue does not contain the words "expose for sale" or a definition section), although arguably the omission of similar words from the statute is a core step of the reasoning which contributes to the *ratio*.

7. How precedents and authorities are handled in the judgment

If there were no precedents, Lord Parker says he would have found it impossible to say that the knife was offered for sale. However, he does then consider two cases which the prosecution have offered in support of their contention that this is an offer for sale.

He distinguishes *Keating v Horwood* (1926) 28 Cox C.C. 198 on the grounds that it was decided on the basis of "exposure for sale" rather than offering for sale; any comments on offer for sale are therefore *obiter* and not binding. He also identifies a lack of clarity in the reasoning by the judges and points out that the case wasn't fully argued as the rules of contract were not discussed and the defendant was not represented.

Lord Parker also distinguishes *Wiles v Maddison* [1943] 1 All E.R. 315 because it was about "exposure for sale" and "was a very different case". He states that he cannot find anything of assistance in the reasoning of the judge.

Lord Parker adopts the approach to statutory interpretation used by Lord Simonds in *Magor and St Mellons Rural District Council v Newport Corp*, by rejecting the possibility of "filling in the gaps" between what Parliament said in the statute and what they might have meant.

He refers to two statutes, the Prices of Goods Act 1939, and the Goods and Services (Price Control) Act 1941, which provide a definition section, where it is Parliament's intention to give "offer for sale" a meaning which would cover display in a shop window.

8. The approach to statutory interpretation used

Lord Parker adopts the literal approach to statutory interpretation, in the form of interpreting the words according to what they say (incorporating the technical legal meaning of the words "invitation to treat", which falls within the scope of the literal rule). He acknowledges that this may, "at first sight", produce an absurdity but adopts the approach of Lord Simonds in *Magor and St Mellons Rural District Council v Newport Corp*: if Parliament has made an error in omitting the words "expose for sale" then it is not for the court to correct the error, but for Parliament to do.

9. Subsequent history of the case

The case of *Fisher v Bell* was applied in the following subsequent cases.
● *British Car Auctions v Wright* [1972] 1 W.L.R. 1519;
● *Partridge v Crittenden* [1968] 1 W.L.R. 1204.
It was followed in *Mella v Monahan* [1961] Crim. L.R. 175 DC.
It is still good law in that it has not been overruled by a subsequent case. However, the Restriction of Offensive Weapons Act 1961 (c.22), s.1 inserts the words "or exposes or has in his possession for the purpose of sale or hire" into s.1 of the 1959 Act, which extends the meaning of the section to cover the circumstances which occurred in the case.

HOW DO I WRITE A CRITICAL REVIEW?

Critical reviews/article analysis

9.6 ▶ As part of the assessment on your degree, you may be asked to demonstrate the skill of analysis in the form of a critical review. A review of this type is not to be mistaken for a critical review of literature which you might do as part of a larger type of text, e.g. a chapter of your dissertation. A critical review is an evaluation of an academic text: for example an article, report, essay or book. Basically you are asked to make judgments, positive or negative, about the text using various criteria. The information and knowledge in the text needs to be evaluated, and the criteria that should be used in this task can vary depending on your tutor or module. Analysing the text will help you focus on how and why the author makes certain points and prevent you from merely summarising what the author says. Assuming the role of an analytical reader will also help you to determine whether or not the writer fulfils the stated purpose of the book or article and enhances your understanding or knowledge of a particular topic.

Organising the writing of a critical review

All critical reviews involve two main tasks: summary and evaluation.　　▶9.7

Summary

You first need to summarise or describe the text that you have read. In your summary you will ▶9.8
focus on points within the article that you think are interesting. You will need to summarise the
main ideas or argument of the author(s). You also need to explain how these ideas/argument
have been constructed. For example, is the author basing his or her arguments on data that
they have collected? Are the main ideas/argument purely theoretical? Try looking in the
Abstract, Introduction and Conclusion for the main ideas/argument.

In your summary you might answer the following questions:

● Why does the author think this topic or question(s) is important?
● What are the arguments made?
● What structure or method to answer the questions has been used?
● What evidence has been used?
● What conclusions are reached?
● Are there any further questions raised but not answered?

Be careful not to give too much detail, especially in a short review.

Evaluation

Evaluation is the most important part in writing a critical review and will involve stating ▶9.9
whether you agree or disagree with what the author says or has done. This is where you critically evaluate or give your judgment (using the criteria set out in the module) about the quality
or value of the text (for other researchers, or to practitioners in the field, or to students). (There
is more on developing your critical skills in Chapter 5.)

When evaluating the text you could answer some of the following questions:

● Is the question the text tries to answer relevant, interesting, new, useful?
● Who will find the text useful?
● Does the text give new answers to an old question?
● Is the text detailed, or brief? Simple or complex?
● Is the evidence presented to support the answer extensive? Strong? Weak?
  Contradictory?
● Are the conclusions reached final, or preliminary?

Process of writing a critical review

Start by skim reading the text noting the main question or questions the text tries to answer ▶9.10
and the main answers it gives. Think about the criteria you need to use to review the text. Read
the text again and note the important points in detail such as the subject, question, arguments
and/or evidence, and conclusions made, and your evaluation using your criteria. You might
also find it useful to read related texts to note similarities and differences. Start writing an
outline trying to relate points made in summary to points you wish to make in your evaluation
of the text. Start to write the review.

Structure of a critical review

9.11 ▶ The *title* usually looks like an entry in a bibliography:

> Example: Matthews, P 'Registered land, fraud, and human rights' L.Q.R. 2008, 124(Jul), 351–255.

The *introduction* should contain an overview of the subject under discussion, your evaluation of the importance of this and a brief explanation of how you will organise your review.

> Example: The existing arrangements for registration of title allow for individuals to fraudulently register themselves as owners of land and then apply for a loan before absconding without repaying it. This article examines the solutions offered by the government and argues they are problematic.

The *body* of the review should contain a *summary/description* of the text followed by an *evaluation*. You may not always feel you are able to judge whether the argument in a text is correct or not. Perhaps you could first explain how the arguments given in the text are the same, or different from arguments given in other texts on the same topic. Then, if they are different, explain which argument you find more convincing and why.

> Example (summary): Matthews examines how the intended rule change involving verifying the identity of the transferor will work in practice and intimates that whilst this all sounds good in theory, making the relevant forms available to the public online negates any benefit. He suggests alternative possibilities for dealing with the problem recognises that all have issues of one kind or another but argues that any new system of certificates (even when given statutory sanction) will simply not prevent Land Registry fraud and we will see an increase.

> Example (evaluation): Matthews makes good use of the ideas of others. His insights and ideas for action are relevant but the need for further analysis is apparent. [You should explain why in more detail.]

Critical reviews don't always need a *conclusion* so you must decide whether to include one or not. If you think a conclusion is necessary it should obviously reiterate your overall view of the text.

> This is a useful comment on a controversial problem. Matthews presents a critique of the options suggested by the Law Commission and the government and highlights some additional possibilities to resolve the problem which remain in need of exploration.

HOW DO I WRITE A REFLECTIVE ASSIGNMENT?

9.12 ▶ We have stressed the importance of reflection in the writing cycle in preparation of your assignments, and in particular in Chapter 8 we have discussed the importance of reflecting on the feedback you receive on your assignments in order to improve.

In some cases you may be asked to demonstrate your ability to reflect by the submission of a specific piece of work, such as a reflective statement, commentary or report. Different examples might include:

- Reflection on the whole of a year of study, perhaps as part of personal/professional development planning (PDP), including your progress and acquisition of knowledge and skills required;
- Reflection on a particular experience, for example involvement in a pro bono scheme or clinic work or a legal placement;
- Reflection on the preparation of a specific other assignment, for example a commentary accompanying a research-based assignment such as a dissertation, critically analysing and justifying the decisions taken as an indication of such skills as independent learning.

Why are you asked to reflect?

The purpose of reflective writing is to encourage you to engage in the development of your learning and to show that you can articulate your development in the light of experience.

▶ **9.13**

Gibbs argues: "It is not sufficient simply to have an experience in order to learn. Without reflecting upon this experience it may quickly be forgotten, or its learning potential lost. It is from the feelings and thoughts emerging from this reflection that generalisations or concepts can be generated. And it is generalisations that allow new situations to be tackled effectively."[2] As noted above even if you aren't formally required to reflect it's nevertheless an excellent habit to get into and will help the development of your legal writing generally.

What is effective reflective writing?

The key to good reflective writing is to provide an honest account of your progress which identifies your strengths, as evidenced by your feedback, any challenges you have faced (for example, part of the course you have found difficult or for which you have received feedback that you need to improve, or external factors, substitute work or family commitments which have affected your progress), actions you have taken in relation to these challenges and any further actions which you aim to take. You should consider the implications of your first year experience for your future studies.

▶ **9.14**

Reflective writing will differ from traditional legal assignments because it is about your experience and progress and therefore you will be expected to write in the first person (using "I"). However, what reflective writing has in common with other legal assignments is that first you must use evidence to support your reflection, and secondly you will be required to write a narrative in formal, correct English—your work must not be in note form.

A number of different authors have provided models for reflection. Below you will find one adapted from the work of Price & Maier which captures the process required.[3]

---

2   Graham Gibbs, *Learning by Doing: A Guide to Teaching and Learning Methods* (Further Education Unit 1988)
3   Geraldine Price and Pat Maier, *Effective Study Skills* (Pearson 2007) 9–13.

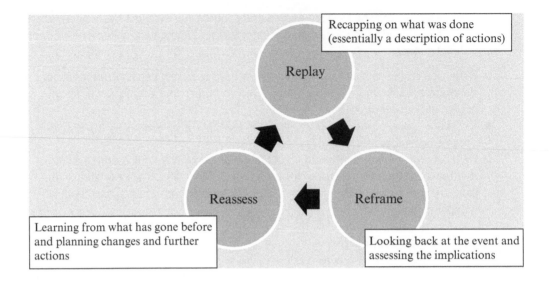

What issues could I reflect on?

9.15 You will no doubt be given guidance on what mattes to include and it will depend on the nature of the reflective activity.

When reflecting on your personal development over the course of a year the matters you may be asked to consider may include:

1. **Management of your time and learning**

Some indicative questions which may help you reflect: How have you found the experience of studying? Have you received any tips to aid your study, for example from a tutor, or a fellow student, and if so have you acted on these and did they work? What did you learn from any formative assessments and the feedback received—did this help you to improve? How have you kept motivated through the year? Have there been any low points or "light bulb" moments and if so what did you learn from these? What aspects of the course did you enjoy/ do well in, and which did you find more challenging and why? What have you learned from this?

2. **Problem analysis and provision of advice**

Some indicative questions which may help you reflect: how have you found using recommended techniques for problem-analysis (e.g. IRAC)? What feedback have you received on this? Were suggestions made for improvement and if so, have you acted on these? Have you discussed your approach to problem-solving with a tutor, and if so, what advice did you receive and have you acted on it?

3. **Legal writing skills, including referencing**

Some indicative questions which may help you reflect: How confident are you about your skills in the following areas: identifying the issues/themes in a question, structuring an answer logically including writing an introduction and conclusion, providing evidence to support the points you make and referencing these appropriately, structuring a bibliography? What feedback have you received related to these areas and have you identified any areas for improvement from this? If so, what action have you taken to improve? Again, have you discussed these matters with a tutor, and were there any actions you took following this?

4. **Research and reading skills**

Some indicative questions which may help you reflect: are you confident you can find primary and secondary sources to support your work? If you are unsure, what steps can you take? Have you discussed strategies with a tutor or with the Law Librarian? Have you reviewed any guidance provided to help you? What strategies have you developed to cope with reading materials effectively?

What to avoid in reflective writing

The commonest mistake to avoid is to confuse reflective writing with writing a diary. They key thing with reflective writing is that you are not just describing what you did but why you did it, what the result was and how things may need to change for the future.

▶ 9.16

For example, in the context of a reflective commentary on carrying out a research project such as a dissertation:

Descriptive	Issues to consider to make it more reflective . . .
"I thought of this topic . . ."	How? Why? What influenced you?
"Then I talked to the Law Librarian . . ."	What did you learn from this? Did it help you?
"Then I had a chat with a tutor . . ."	How did this influence you? Did you act on suggestions made by the tutor?
"Then I revised my topic . . ."	Why? How does this link to previous actions? Did you discover your topic was to broad/too narrow/not suitable?

Finally, don't confuse reflection with giving feedback on the course, your experience and so on. The reflection is about you and your responses. There will be other opportunities to feed in your views on the course.

HOW DO I TACKLE EXAMS?

Exams are still the most popular form of assessment in the study of law. Over the course of your legal studies you may encounter different types of exam to test your writing skills. Common examples include:

▶ 9.17

Unseen—this is the "traditional" form of exam in which you do not see the exam questions in advance.

Seen—this means that the questions will be made available to you before the exam, giving you some opportunity to prepare your answers.

Closed book—this means that you are not allowed to take in materials (although you may be allowed a statute book).

Open book—this means that you can take materials in to the exam (there may be limits on the quantity and type of material which you can take in).

Takeaway—this is a variation on seen and open book exams where the exam paper is collected and a short period is given to students to takeaway, complete and return it.

Despite the increasing use of a range of assessment methods, the most popular assessment for law degrees remains the unseen, closed book exam, which is likely to consist partly of essay questions and partly of problem questions in most subjects. Much of what we have said about approaching essay questions and problem questions throughout the rest of this book also applies to answering these questions in exam situations, but in this section we are going to explore the aspects of writing in exams which differ from the general advice provided elsewhere.

Coursework criteria, as discussed in Chapter 1, are unlikely to apply formally to traditional closed book exams, but nevertheless these criteria (other than matters of presentation, which are less significant in an exam) represent what your tutors think makes a good piece of writing; this, after all, is what you are aiming for. So assessment criteria are likely to have some relevance to your exam work as well. Keep focused on the purpose of your writing while you revise and don't make the mistake of overestimating the differences between exams and coursework: although we explore some differences below, good writing is required in an exam situation in the same way as it is for coursework.

TIPS • *There are many books on the market which cover exam preparation, skills and techniques. If, having reflected on your exam performance in the past, you feel you need some extra help on this, go to the library and see what books are available. Your university may also run workshops or drop-in sessions to help students deal with exam fears, or you may wish to discuss the situation with your personal tutor.*

Many students find sitting exams very stressful, and this can make it more difficult to carry out the techniques which, outside pressured exam situations, you know perfectly well you should be applying to the writing in question. You may find it helpful to reflect on your recent experience of exams. Try to identify in specific terms exactly what you found problematic so that you can take steps to counter this in your next exam by picking out the parts of this chapter which are most useful to you.

How to adapt the writing cycle for exams

9.18 ▶ In relation to an unseen exam, the most important way in which the process differs from the writing cycle we have discussed in Chapter 2 is that in an exam situation you do not have the opportunity to carry out the research phase after your diagnosis. In essence, you have to anticipate the research which is going to be needed, and carry this out as part of the revision process. The other vital difference—in a closed book exam at least—is that you will not be able to refer to your research during the exam but must rely on having it in your head. This can cause two possible problems which you must avoid:

1. You may be tempted to prepare a generic answer on each topic prior to the exam and then use that generic answer regardless of the exact question which is asked.
2. You may tend to focus on information rather than technique or process. In other words, the danger is that your revision is geared towards learning facts and principles rather than practising what to do with them, i.e. actually answering exam questions. This mass of knowledge or information becomes a security blanket because you feel that you have learnt the topic when in fact what you have actually done is *memorised* the topic—which is not the same thing at all.

> **TIPS** • *Think of your revision as being flexible—it can "stretch" in different directions to suit the exact wording of a question, but you want your final answer to be a good fit.*

Both of these problems will lead to exam answers which fall into the common faults we identified in Chapter 1: "does not answer the question" or "discusses irrelevant issues". To avoid this, adapt the cycle accordingly. Break up the diagnosis phase: before the exam, carry out a general diagnosis in which you identify a technique for tackling questions on particular topics, and carry out your research and revision accordingly (and practise that technique). However, what is absolutely vital is that in the exam itself, when you see the questions, you still carry out a (quick) *specific* diagnosis on the question you have been asked.

Before the exam: your general diagnosis

Here are some suggestions for the general diagnosis which should form a vital part of your revision:

▶ 9.19

- Make sure you are familiar with instructions as to how many questions you have to answer in the exam, and any official guidance about what topics will be on the paper.
- Make sure your revision is focused on techniques for tackling questions, not simply memorising cases and facts. Remember you are making a general diagnosis about what is likely to be needed to answer a question effectively on the topics you've chosen, so look at past papers and notes from tutorials or seminars and any guidance you have been given about how to tackle a particular topic or question, so as to be able to come up with a general plan for tackling that type of question.
- During your revision, practise relevant questions: make the most of the opportunity you have to do as much as possible to prepare in advance. In practising, you are doing two things: first you are giving yourself the opportunity to write for the relevant amount of time and in similar conditions. This may sound pointless but these days we tend to be much more used to writing with a word processor than with pen and paper, so if the only time you write for an hour on a regular basis is making lecture notes then this is inadequate preparation for writing continually for an hour (or even two or three hours) in an exam. Secondly, by practising answers you are testing out your technique in adapting your general pre-prepared diagnosis to the specific diagnosis needed for this particular question. Remember your general

advance plan will not be enough in itself (that is the mistake poorer students make) but will need to be fine-tuned on the spot. The snag is that you are doing this without your notes and in a time-pressured environment. So you must practise how to do this.

In the exam: your specific diagnosis

9.20 ▶ As we said above, diagnosis in an exam requires the same skills as for coursework, but what is different is:

- You have to carry it out quickly and under pressure.
- You have to rely on what you have in your head—there is no opportunity to carry out a materials review to identify any shortfalls in your understanding, for example.

Before you start writing, identify the topics being assessed by the various questions and then select which ones you are going to answer. Use the same techniques of looking for key words, instruction words and so on to make sure you are really focused on the question. This is where you move from the general to the specific, so you need to make decisions about what to keep and what to ditch from the general plans you have devised during revision. For example, in planning a general answer on negligence you will probably have anticipated being asked to deal with situations like a claimant with an egg-shell skull or a rescuer who suffers damage. But when you move to the specific (i.e. when you come to answer a question on negligence *in an exam*) you must forget the aspects of that general plan that are not relevant to the actual question on negligence that you have been set. If there isn't a rescuer then do not talk about the law on that aspect. This is where your imaginary bin is needed. Don't forget to take it in to your exams with you (mentally!) and use it to dump the material from your general plan that is not needed for the specific question you have been asked.

From experience of marking exam papers, we know it is especially hard in an exam situation for students to risk discarding material which isn't needed for a particular question. However, in an exam just as with coursework, your diagnosis will involve making decisions about what to include and what not to include. It can feel like a waste to simply abandon work you have spent time on; you might feel you know everything there is to know about (and have read three erudite academic journal articles on) professional rescuers, but if there is no profes-sional rescuer in your negligence question, there cannot be any marks for discussing it, so you would be wasting time writing on it.

If it helps, think about it this way: Imagine going on holiday to somewhere where you aren't quite sure what the weather will be like—you'd take a variety of clothes to cover the possibilities. Would you get dressed on the first day without checking what the weather is actually like? Or, having checked the weather and found out it is sweltering hot would you wear your thick sweater on the beach on the basis that you went to the trouble of packing it, so you are going to wear it? It is unlikely, but this is essentially what you would be doing if you wrote a pre-prepared answer without reference

> **TIPS •** *Practice making a quick diagnosis— get hold of as many old exam questions as you can and give it a go. See if you can read the question and identify what the subject area is and make a rough note of the areas it is asking you to consider. This is a good revision activity and your tutor may be happy to look over your results—if not, then trade ideas with a fellow student instead.*

to exactly what you've been asked, or put irrelevant material in an answer just because you spent time revising it.

Is it better to answer a problem question than an essay in an exam?

Many of our students tell us that they find the prospect of answering essay questions more daunting than problem questions in an exam situation. If this strikes a chord with you, consider the following advantages to answering an essay question. It is especially important, if you do not know in advance which topics are going to be examined with a problem question and which with an essay, that you do not narrow your choice of questions by trying to avoid writing an essay.

▶ 9.21

Here are some suggestions about the advantages of essays:

- Flexibility in terms of devising a structure for your answer (this is often pre-determined by the actual question with a problem question).
- The ability to adopt a more expansive reflective approach to your writing.
- The opportunity to explore theoretical aspects in more detail.

By being positive and considering the benefits inherent in answering essay questions we are demonstrating that essay questions actually give you more freedom. This is because, whilst you are given a framework shaped in general terms by the question, it is up to you how you answer it. Some of the reasons that our students give us for why they prefer to tackle problem questions in exams are as follows:

- "I don't have enough time to answer essay questions—there is too much to say". This is a reasonable fear but remember everyone else is in the same position, and the question has been set to be answered in the time allocated. Plan very carefully and focus on exploring in depth a limited number of points rather than many points at a basic level.
- "Essay questions ask me to 'critically assess' the topic. I don't know how to do this." This is essentially a matter of confidence. If you follow the advice we provide on how to critically evaluate materials, and how to utilise this to form your own arguments, then your revision should place you in a position to tackle an analytical essay.
- "I don't understand what the question is getting at. What if I get it wrong and everything I write is irrelevant and off the point?" The fear here is that it is harder to make a diagnosis on an essay question than on a problem, especially under stress. However, if you follow the advice in Chapter 3 and have revised the topic well, you should not have anything to fear. Use the introduction to set out what you think the question is asking and why.

However, don't do an essay question just because:

- you have revised the topic (unless of course your revision has been too narrow and you don't have a choice—if that is the case, reflect on this when revising for your next exam);
- you think it gives more scope for generalities—you must focus on the question.

The point is that essay questions are not any easier or harder than problem questions—they are just different. As you found out in Chapter 1 they assess different skills and so will naturally require a different approach when answering them. It is important to remember that each type of question offers its own challenges, so your revision should be geared to preparing you for both.

The writing phase in an exam

9.22 ❯ Some students find that the time constraint imposed by an exam helps them to write more concisely; others find this problematic. Here are some tips to help you improve your writing in an exam:

1. Managing your time

9.23 ❯ This is a fundamental aspect of good examination technique and requires some simple mathematics before you go into the exam: how long is the exam and how many questions do you have to answer? Assuming the questions are equally weighted in terms of marks available, divide the writing time by the number of questions you have to complete to work out the time you have available for each question. Have this fixed in your mind before you go in to the exam; jot down the timetable for when you move on to each question on your paper as soon as you are allowed to start writing. Stick to these timings. Five minutes before the end of each time slot begin to draw your answer to that question to a close and be ready to move on to the next question as soon as your allocated time is up. If you cannot do this simply stop and move on when your time is up leaving space for you to come back and finish your answer if you have time at the end. You must be ruthless with yourself—resist the temptation to spend a few extra minutes winding up your answer as every extra second you spend on that question is one less second to spend on the next. Tutors hate to mark a paper with two good and well-prepared answers and a final short one with the words "ran out of time" scribbled hastily at the end—resolve now that you will never need to do this.

> **TIPS** • *Remember, the first 40 marks (i.e. the pass mark) out of 100 are easier to gain than the last 40 marks, so training yourself to move on when the time is up is vital so as not to penalise yourself from the start.*

2. Dealing with a mental block

9.24 ❯ If you get stuck while preparing a piece of coursework then you can use various strategies to get over this, such as taking a break, having a cup of tea, or whatever. As long as you haven't left it to the last minute, you can come back to it the next day. In an exam situation you don't have this luxury, so you must devise different strategies for coping with a mental block.

To start with, a mental block is much less likely to occur if you have revised and practised techniques and principles, as we've suggested above, rather than just lists of information. However, inevitably there will be some things you can't remember, a common example being case names (of course some rote learning is required to try and commit the case names to memory). Students often ask: does it matter if I forget the case names in an exam? This is a tricky question and you are likely to find tutors differ slightly on it. Our answer is as follows: essentially, what we are testing in an exam is your understanding and your technique rather than your ability to remember information, so forgetting the odd case name is not going to ruin an answer which displays a sound understanding of the relevant principles. However, you are writing a legal assessment, and although case names are essentially information they are important information because they provide the legal authority for the principles you are applying. Hence an answer with no cases in it will score poorly for lack of authority. Nevertheless fixating on whether you will struggle to remember the case names tends to indicate that you haven't yet got the right emphasis on technique in your revision, so reflect on this if you are concerned about remembering the cases.

If you find yourself really struggling in an exam then:

- try giving yourself a five-minute break from writing—think about something else entirely;
- try reproducing diagrams or flowcharts from your revision notes to get your mind going again;
- cut your losses and start a different question (this is one of several reasons why it is advisable to make sure you revise sufficient topics, and resist the temptation to revise only the exact number of topics that you have to answer questions on).

> **TIPS** • *If you do forget a case name or section number from a statute, leave a space or draw a line in your work and fill in the blank if and when it comes back to you. If you have time you could also outline a few of the important facts thereby demonstrating that it really is a memory lapse rather than that you never learnt the relevant authority in the first place!*

However, we would emphasise again that if you concentrate on practising your approach to answering questions in your revision, rather than trying to memorise your textbook, then this sort of thing is much less likely to happen at all.

3. Your handwriting must be legible

Remember an examination is an important form of communication from you to the marker (your final award may be at stake!) and this will obviously be much more effective if the communication is easily readable. If you know that your handwriting is hard to read you will be doing yourself a great disservice in all your examinations if you don't do something about it. Practice is the key here; don't leave this until the week of the exams to sort out.

❱ 9.25

> **TIPS** • *Consider writing on every other line of the answer booklet. If you find that your writing becomes more and more illegible the more you write in an exam then this can help a reader to separate words out from others and generally help their understanding of what has been written.*

The finishing phase in an exam

The advice given in Chapter 8 on finishing your work is designed for coursework situations. In an exam you will not have the opportunity to polish your work in this way, and it is unlikely you be specifically marked on your presentation. Nevertheless, it is wise to leave five minutes at the end for a quick read through so that you can correct any obvious mistakes.

❱ 9.26

Reflecting on your exam

Don't conduct a post-mortem with your mates, as this tends to lead to confusion and anxiety. This exam is finished and there is nothing that can be done now about improving what you have just written. Besides, immediately after a stressful situation is usually not the best time to think about how you have done. It is likely that you will need to prepare for another exam the next day or soon after so your time is best spent looking ahead to that

❱ 9.27

> **TIPS** • *Remember, although exams can be a stressful experience they are not meant to be full of tricks and traps, and the legal writing techniques you have practised throughout the year with your other assessments will stand you in good stead. Contrary to popular belief, exams are designed to allow you to shine, not to catch you out.*

exam rather than dwelling on the past one. However, once your exams are over, take a few minutes to reflect on how your planning, preparation, timing and writing actually went for each exam. Don't think about what you wrote but rather how you wrote. Were you happy with how these aspects went or do you need to consider making adjustments to these for your next exams? Ask for feedback on your exams and if necessary seek extra help.

SUMMARY OF CHAPTER 9

9.28 ▶
- Some types of legal assessment require modification of the general process of writing identified in Chapter 2.
- Certain assignments such as case notes and critical reviews require specific comprehension and analysis skills.
- Reflective writing requires you to take a step back from your learning which will help you improve.
- In exams, you carry out your general diagnosis and research through your revision prior to a more specific diagnosis in the exam itself.

▶ 10
Writing at the next level: dissertations/projects

WHAT IS THE PURPOSE OF THIS CHAPTER?

In your final year at university you may be required or you may be able to choose to write a ▶ 10.1
dissertation.

This is an in-depth project in which you are required to research and write about an aspect of the law that you are particularly interested in, in the context of a hypothesis (which means a working theory in the format of a statement, the truth and validity of which you test through your argument). This will almost certainly be the most ambitious (and longest) piece of writing you will undertake during your undergraduate studies. You may also find it is the most rewarding.

Dissertations have much in common with essays, but there are some key ways in which they differ from other legal writing. The purpose of this chapter is therefore to explain how the writing cycle we have explored in previous chapters can be adapted to the process of writing a dissertation. Completing a dissertation gives you the opportunity to explore something that you are really interested in to a greater depth, which presents an exciting challenge, but sometimes the comparative enormity of this writing task can be overwhelming. Following the advice here about the writing cycle, and how to adapt it appropriately, should help make the process more manageable. Similarly, if completing a dissertation is an optional part of your course, we hope that the advice in this chapter will help you choose whether to take this option.

> **TIPS** • *The best way to get an idea of what a dissertation looks like is to look at examples. Check your law library for dissertations which have been submitted in the past.*

By the end of this chapter you will:

● understand how to apply your writing skills to your dissertation;
● understand issues particular to the writing of dissertations;
● have a better idea of what to consider when deciding whether to choose a dissertation as an option;
● understand the process of putting together a research proposal, if one is required.

HOW DO DISSERTATIONS COMPARE WITH OTHER LEGAL WRITING?

10.2 ❯ The factors in common include:

- The same writing processes are used (see Chapters 2, 3 and 6).
- The need to plan and conduct effective research and make your materials work for you (see Chapters 4 and 5).
- The need for analysis and evaluation in your writing (see Chapter 5).
- The same ability to write in good English is required (see Chapter 7).

The key ways dissertations differ from any other legal writing include:

- You will have chosen your own topic and therefore essentially set your own question rather than responding to a question set by a tutor, which has significant implications for the diagnosis phase of the dissertation.
- You will work independently on it rather than attending lectures and seminars/ tutorials, although you will be able to get guidance from one of your tutors, and you will therefore need to pay particular attention to issues of time management and motivation.
- You will usually have a member of staff with expertise in the area in which you are pursuing your dissertation to act as your *supervisor*. Essentially your supervisor is a guide who can provide advice on the scope of your dissertation and will work with you one-to-one to help you develop your ideas. They will almost certainly comment on draft chapters and give you feedback as you go along to improve your work. Your supervisor is also likely to be one of the final markers of your dissertation.
- Your dissertation will be longer than other work you write (length will vary from institution to institution, but is likely to be somewhere between 8,000 and 15,000 words). It is common to feel at the outset that you'll "never get that much written", but actually it is far more common to have too much to say than too little by the time you have finished. This will have an impact on the writing phase, which will be a longer process than with other assignments, and also on the research phase, which will need to be more extensive than for any other legal writing. This is why we suggest tackling your dissertation in chunks and we explain this further later in the chapter.
- You will also need to be particularly fastidious at keeping clear, full and accurate records of what you read in order to make sure you can reference your dissertation appropriately.

A final difference with dissertations is that the process involves use of terminology and techniques which are conventional in academic research but with which you may be unfamiliar in the context of your legal studies: terms like *supervisor*, *hypothesis*, *abstract*. We will explore the meaning of these terms in this chapter. First we will consider why you might choose to write a dissertation.

WHY CHOOSE A DISSERTATION AS AN OPTION?

Your choice of options or electives in your final year is likely to be influenced by a number of factors, for example: interest in the subject area, the assessment regime or even previous positive experience of the teaching staff. These are all likely to contribute to your wider motivation of wanting to get good marks in your final year and overall degree. The same holds true of choosing whether to do a dissertation as an option. Ultimately this therefore requires you to reflect on your existing skills. Generally a student who does well in their dissertation is one who:

● 10.3

- has already received good marks in coursework;
- is able to motivate themselves for independent working;
- likes to research;
- likes writing;
- is able to respond to feedback (because this plays a greater role in the writing of a dissertation).

Students sometimes perceive the value of choosing a dissertation as being one less subject to cope with and one less exam to do. There is some, but only some, merit in this pragmatic approach. Yes, a dissertation avoids an exam. However it is a mistake to assume therefore that it is less demanding than an examination-based subject—in many ways you may find it more demanding. If exam avoidance is your primary motivation think carefully about whether you exhibit the necessary skills, not least time management of your writing, to justify this strategy. However much you like to feel you produce coursework well under this pressure this will simply not work for producing a dissertation of a good standard. It may be better to tackle your exam technique.

Common format

There is no single model for a dissertation but a common format is as follows:

- Title page.
- Abstract (condensed factual summary of the dissertation including its conclusion—always written last).
- Contents page.
- Introductory chapter (introduces the themes and research questions usually with reference to the theoretical perspective being adopted in the work—may also, depending on the nature of the dissertation contain an outline of the methodology adopted).
- Content chapters (where you explore your research questions—there is no magic number of content chapters and it will to some extent depend on the word limit for your dissertation—three to six is usual).
- Concluding chapter (where you draw together the threads of the work and take a final position in relation to your hypothesis).
- Bibliography.
- Appendices (if appropriate).

WHAT IS A RESEARCH PROPOSAL?

10.4▶ Some institutions require submission of a research proposal as a pre-requisite to a dissertation, and in some cases a particular standard must be reached in this in order to proceed to the dissertation itself. Other institutions may require submission of a proposal as an informal means of first contact between you and your supervisor. The research proposal brief will vary between institutions (so if you are asked to write one, check the brief carefully), but it is likely to consist of some or all of the following:

- Indication of topic and/or perspective.
- A draft title.
- Your hypothesis.
- Your key research questions and/or research strategy.
- A draft plan showing outline contents for each chapter.
- A preliminary literature review and/or initial bibliography.

Even if you do not have to complete a research proposal, it would be a good idea to think in terms of one as part of your planning, and discuss it with your supervisor.

Whether or not you are writing a proposal, the sample research proposals given in the appendices are relevant examples of many of the terms we are going to discuss in the remainder of this chapter. They will give you a good idea of the sort of preliminary work which needs to go into the planning of your dissertation.

IS THE WRITING CYCLE DIFFERENT FOR A DISSERTATION?

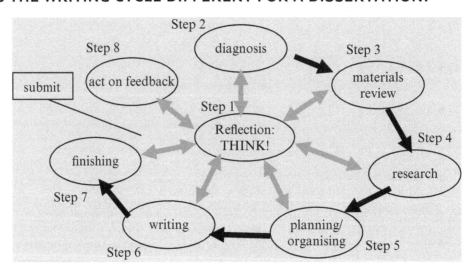

10.5▶ Yes. In Chapter 2, we suggested carrying out your research (keeping your diagnosis under review) and then writing up. Because of the length of your dissertation, you cannot adopt this approach by carrying out **all** your research before writing **any** of it up. Instead, use the cycle on a chapter by chapter basis. Don't delay writing until you have finished your research because:

- You will be doing much more research for your dissertation than for other pieces of legal writing and it is much easier to manage this by working on particular sections at a time.
- You'll get bogged down in your research and lose your focus.
- If you don't get something written early on you'll lose the benefit of the advice your supervisor can provide about your writing.
- You'll end up having to rush the writing, and trying to write a whole dissertation in a short space of time is incredibly daunting.

Therefore a better approach would be as follows:

1. Carry out the diagnosis phase in broad terms in relation to the whole of your dissertation and make a plan of what is going to go in each chapter.
2. Then carry out Steps 2–6 of the writing cycle in relation to each chapter in turn—in other words, a more specific diagnosis, then carry out your research, plan your chapter, and write it.
3. Then hand your chapter in to your supervisor so that you can use their comments and advice as part of the reflection stage on that chapter, before making any adjustments which are needed.
4. Finally, once you have carried out this process in relation to each chapter, you carry out the finishing and polishing stage of the cycle in relation to the whole dissertation.

> **TIPS** • *To write a successful dissertation, work steadily throughout the year. Writing on computer means you can revise your work easily when you get feedback, so research a chapter, write it up, hand it in, get feedback from your supervisor, utilise those comments and use them to improve (a) that particular chapter and (b) your approach to writing a dissertation generally—remember that this is going to be the most complex piece of writing you undertake.*

So, there are aspects of the cycle which will require particular attention:

- Diagnosing your task, which will include posing a *hypothesis* and *research questions*, and choosing your own *title*.
- Structuring your dissertation, since it is a more ambitious piece of work in both length and scope.
- The writing phase, which will require strong skills in time management, and working effectively with your supervisor.
- Fulfilling the particular requirements of dissertation submission in the finishing stage, since there are particular requirements to fulfil specific to a dissertation.

We consider these in the rest of the chapter, beginning with diagnosing your task.

HOW DO I DIAGNOSE THE TASK FOR A DISSERTATION?

You are now very experienced at diagnosing a task which has been set for you by somebody else. The diagnosis phase is very different in relation to a dissertation because instead of working from a question you have been set, you have decided on your own area of interest, and then within that area of interest, identified your particular focus. This has its benefits and drawbacks.

▶ 10.6

In Chapter 1, we stressed that the purpose of asking you to write a dissertation is to test that you can do the following:

1. Propose a suitable research hypothesis, and pose research questions.
2. Sustain a detailed and in-depth investigation into a particular topic of your choice.
3. Plan and carry out a more ambitious piece of work with only limited supervision.

Keep this in mind when you are thinking about the diagnostic phase of your dissertation. A common mistake to make is to think you are simply being tested on your ability to write "on" the topic you've chosen: this shows confusion about the purpose of a dissertation, and will result in the work being descriptive. Just as we would never set you an essay title called "write everything you know about divorce reform" we don't want you to set yourself what would amount to such a title for your dissertation. Instead what you need to do, to make sure you adopt the right approach, is to work from a hypothesis and pose research questions. You will then be in a position to choose an appropriate title.

HOW DO I CHOOSE AN APPROPRIATE DISSERTATION TOPIC?

10.7 ▶ The first step is to think about the general subject area you want to investigate. You will then need to refine this into a more specific topic, then go on to consider your hypothesis and research questions which we consider further later. So here are our top tips for choosing a suitable topic area:

Tip 1: Make sure it is something you are interested in

10.8 ▶ You will already be aware how much easier something is to do if you are interested in it, so you should pick a topic which interests you for your dissertation. This is especially true given that your dissertation is going to involve more independent working than any other piece of writing you have tackled and therefore your motivation is going to be especially important. If you start out with only lukewarm enthusiasm for your subject-matter then you will find it very tough to work on it through to the finish.

If you haven't yet thought of a topic area consider these questions to see if they help you brainstorm an idea for a topic:

● Which have been your favourite subjects so far on the course? Have they been mainly case-based subjects or theoretical subjects? Can you isolate anything more specific about your preferences which might guide you towards a topic?

● Which assessments have you most enjoyed working towards on the degree so far? Can you draw on any topic you've done as a past coursework or project and "work it up" into a research topic? This can provide a useful starting point but is something which sometimes causes confusion. In many cases, your interest in a topic may well be sparked by an area of previous study. So, are you allowed to do the same area for your dissertation? Answer: yes, your institution will probably allow you to do something on the same topic but they are unlikely to allow you to replicate work which you have previously submitted. So, choose a new angle for your area, investigate a different aspect, or look at the area from a fresh perspective. You will of course in any case be looking in much greater depth for your dissertation than for any other assessment. Institutional approaches may vary on this so it's vital to check this out with a tutor at your own Law School to make sure whatever you are planning is allowed.

● What legal issues have been coming up in the news lately? Is there anything there which grabs your interest? Do bear in mind that your topic needs to be sufficiently legal, and also that just because you've taken an item from the news, you mustn't take a journalistic approach to your writing (we'll be looking more at what's appropriate later in the chapter).

● Do you have practical experience of, or professional interest in, a particular area of law? This can provide a good source of material but it is important to make sure your approach is legal enough, and also scholarly rather than anecdotal (see below).

● Have you been to the library and looked at past dissertations? Of course, you won't want to just copy someone else's idea, but looking at the range of topics and approaches may well spark something else off if your mind is a blank.

Tip 2: But remember that interest is only a starting point
Just because you are interested in a particular issue, it doesn't automatically mean that it is therefore a good research topic.

▶ **10.9**

George Watson comments:

> "It is always hard to realise that intensity of conviction, of itself, validates nothing. It can all too easily be seen as worthless: worthless not because it is false . . . but because it is trite. That realisation may be called the hard landing of the apprentice scholar: to be told that his view, though earnestly and even passionately held, is of no interest to others. . . ."[1]

In other words, it is important to make sure that your proposed research area is a good choice in terms of its potential to produce a scholarly work. The following tips should help you do this.

Tip 3: If possible, try to make sure your research topic offers some opportunity for new ground
Returning once more to Watson, he points out:

▶ **10.10**

> "There is little point in writing a thesis about what everybody already knows and already believes. Research is supposed to make a difference, after all, to what everyone knows or believes, even if only a tiny difference. It is pointless to plant a flag with an air of discovery at the end of Brighton Pier."[2]

In other words, it is best to try and avoid very well-trodden ground, unless you can put some kind of new slant on your work; for example in terms of the perspective which you intend to

---

[1] Greg Watson, *Writing a Thesis* (Longman 1987) 5.
[2] Greg Watson, *Writing a Thesis* (Longman 1987) 13.

pursue, perhaps looking at a traditionally "black letter" area from a more socio-legal stand-point, or considering the impact of human rights legislation on the area. Also bear in mind that if you got interested in the topic through completing previous coursework on it, you will find there are many other students with the same interest—you may wish to rethink and come up with something more unusual as your topic.

Some suggestions for finding new ground include topics in which:

● there has been a recent new case, which is likely to have an impact on the future direction of the law (check the Supreme Court's judgments page for ideas *http://supremecourt.uk/* which you could analyse whether it is a welcome development.

● there is or likely to be forthcoming legislation—you could examine the rationale for the reform and look for evidence as to its anticipated effectiveness in meeting its aims (see the current List of Bills before Parliament and Acts of the UK Parliament *http://services.parliament.uk/bills/*).

● there has been a recent report proposing reform which you could evaluate in comparison to the existing law. The Law Commission's A–Z of existing projects may give you ideas (*www.lawcom.gov.uk/projects.htm*).

Tip 4: But remember that you are not expected to be completely original at this level

10.11 ▶ Although it's best to avoid very well-worn topics you aren't expected to produce a major piece of original research for an undergraduate dissertation.

In particular, unless you have gained permission from your supervisor:

● don't carry out a survey (most undergraduate law dissertation students have neither the time nor the resources to design and pilot a survey, nor to ensure that this is representative enough to be of value either as qualitative or quantitative data).

● don't carry out interviews (this requires particular skills as well as resources, additionally the ethics involved in interviewing means that it is usually reserved for postgraduate research in the legal discipline).

Instead your dissertation should consist of your own analysis of other people's research. This is sometimes referred to as desk-based research rather than field-based research; in other words you are essentially carrying out a form of extensive literature review. The originality comes from the research area itself (i.e. it's an unusual topic, or a topic where there is some external new development, like a new case, statute or report) or from the approach you take to exploring the material, rather than original data.

Tip 5: Check the amount of quality source material available about the topic

10.12 ▶ Bearing in mind that the bulk of your dissertation will take the form of analysis of existing literature, rather than original data, it will be hard going if there isn't much literature out there.

Before you settle on a final research area, then you should carry out preliminary searches on the legal databases (we don't just mean a Google search) to ensure that there is enough information, in the form of texts, analytical articles, review papers and so on. Your university may ask you to include this information in the form of a research proposal.

Remember to record these searches because you will want to return to the material later.

Tip 6: But make sure your focus is sufficiently narrow

The reason this is important is that better dissertations are those which are focused and ana- ▶ **10.13**
lytical. If you choose a very wide area for your dissertation, then so much of your word count will
be needed for descriptive explanations that the whole structure of the work will be weakened.

Therefore it is now time to stop thinking about, for example, "children and the law" which
is too broad and which will throw up too many aspects which require investigation and think
instead about "contact applications in the case of domestic violence" or "the voice of the child
in court proceedings" instead.

Tip 7: Talk to a member of staff

Check out your ideas with a subject tutor with expertise in the area you are thinking of. They are ▶ **10.14**
likely to have supervised dissertations in this area before and will have useful advice.

Finally . . . If a dissertation is a compulsory part of the course there comes a point when
you do actually have to decide on a topic. No-one else can make this decision for you and you
can't delay too long because it is eating into the time you have to research and write your dissertation. If writing a dissertation is an optional part of your course and you really can't think of
an area to investigate then this may indicate that the dissertation option is not the one for you.

HOW DO I CHOOSE A CRITICAL PERSPECTIVE FOR MY DISSERTATION?

As well as choosing the subject matter of your dissertation, you will also need to decide the ▶ **10.15**
approach that you are going to take to the investigation of that topic. The concept of critical
perspectives is a complex one and we give only an outline here. You will want to speak with
your supervisor in more detail or your institution may provide introductory lectures outlining
the different approaches which can be taken. If they do, make sure you attend them as understanding the different perspectives is challenging. Broadly you are likely to choose to write
either what is referred to as a "black letter" or doctrinal style dissertation or alternatively adopt
a more socio-legal approach.

What do these terms mean? Salter and Mason[3] describe a "black letter" approach as
being one which provides "a detailed and highly technical commentary upon, and system-
atic exposition of, the content of legal doctrine". In other words, in a black letter dissertation you would expect to focus on the law as it is; to undertake a detailed examination of
primary legal source materials (statutes and cases but with more emphasis on the latter).
In contrast, a socio-legal approach aims to set the law in context by looking more critically
at the *effects* of the law in reality (for example in order to conclude that it is discriminatory).
This can encompass adopting a particular emphasis, for example a feminist or Marxist
interpretation.

Your choice of perspective doesn't just affect your conclusions but the whole way the
research is conducted and the materials you look at.

For example, a dissertation on the topic area of abortion would consider different questions, depending on the perspective:

---

3   Michael Salter and Julie Mason, *Writing law dissertations* (Pearson 2007) 49.

Black letter	Socio-legal
• a detailed examination of the rules on abortion, case law on actions for wrongful birth, etc.	• does the Abortion Act 1967 represent medicalisation rather than liberalisation? • consideration of whether the state is trying to regulate within the "private sphere"

The following table further contrasts black letter with socio-legal:

Black letter	Socio-legal:
You are essentially answering the question "what is the law on X", by looking at what issues/problems arise and how these have been dealt with by the courts in order to draw underlying conclusions about what the law is.	You are essentially answering the question "what is the effect of law in society" or "how does this work in practice", perhaps in order to conclude that reform is needed.
You will ask questions like: Was this case rightly decided? Do the cases in this area fit into a coherent whole? Are there gaps or situations not accounted for in the law in its current state?	You will ask questions like: What's the reality? How does the law work in practice? What theories about how the law works can we draw on? Does the law affect particular people differently—is there discrimination in the way the systems operate?
You are conducting a textual analysis.	You are conducting a textual analysis (at undergraduate level).
You will be looking at primary legal sources—a detailed examination of case law is needed.	You will look at legal sources, but also at a wider range of materials—for example: statistics and empirical research (done by others).
You will be trying to make sense of the law.	You will look at policy and reform in a broader sense.
You will use articles which have adopted a black letter approach as your secondary sources.	You will use articles which have adopted a socio-legal or law in context approach as your secondary sources.
You may look at the historical development of the law.	You may look at the historical development of the law.
You may look at comparative sources.	You may look at comparative sources.
You will not look at the social or policy implications of the law.	You will look at the social or policy implications of the law.

10.16 ▶ Generally which perspective you choose will depend on your view of the law; it is sometimes said that it is harder to write a good "pure" black letter dissertation but this obviously depends very much on the individual. Similarly there are some topics which lend themselves more readily to one approach or the other—or alternatively you may already have settled on your approach without necessarily realising it whilst choosing your topic area. If you need further help with choosing your perspective, seek advice from your supervisor who will be happy to explore the different approaches and their implications for your own work with you.

WHAT IS MEANT BY "HYPOTHESIS" AND "RESEARCH QUESTIONS"?

These are both tools to help you develop your research as a course of critical inquiry. A hypothesis is a *statement of position* which gives a view or theory on the topic at hand, the truth or otherwise of which can be tested. It therefore forms the frame of the investigation you are going to carry out. The hypothesis is tested by posing research questions: critical questions which need to be answered in order to establish whether and/or to what extent the hypothesis is true. Without critical questions there will be no line of argument: the dissertation will simply be a collection of information.

▶ **10.17**

In bald form therefore, a hypothesis is an *initial position*: think "what I am trying to prove or disprove in this work?" For example:

> "The current legal framework on adverse possession unduly favours the paper-owner as opposed to the occupier."
> "The electoral system in the UK should adopt proportional representation in order to become truly democratic."

In our experience there are two things which students find difficult about framing a hypothesis:

1. Feeling that they do not know enough yet to take an initial position.
2. Being concerned that the initial position might turn out to be wrong.

You should not allow either of these concerns to hold you back from trying to form a hypothesis. If you know enough about the subject to pick it as your topic, then (if you've carried out the process of choosing your research area with the right critical approach) you will know enough to highlight the key issue, and you can therefore articulate this into your hypothesis. Similarly, do not worry about being "wrong": the whole point of your hypothesis is that it forms the framework for your dissertation. It is not supposed to represent the final conclusion. If you were able to conclude with certainty before doing your research, then there would be little point carrying it out.

Some students find it easier to turn the hypothesis round into a question as this makes it clearer that they do not yet have a view on what the answer is. It can also make it easier to remember that your dissertation is about exploring both sides of the argument, although with the aim of reaching an overall conclusion. (One note of caution here: if you are asked to frame a hypothesis as part of an assessed research proposal, then do make sure you frame it as a statement rather than a question, if the assignment brief requires you to do so).

The following example demonstrates the relationship between the hypothesis, as an initial position, and the research questions which test its truth. Imagine three students are writing a dissertation on the same topic. Student 1 has framed a hypothesis suggesting that reform is needed, whereas the working theory of Student 2 is the opposite: that reform of the same area is *not* needed. Student 3 has adopted the approach of turning the hypothesis into a question rather than a statement. It is logical for all three to pursue the same research questions to carry out their investigation:

	Student 1	Student 2	Student 3
	We need statutory reform of this area of the law of X.	We do *not* need statutory reform of the law of X.	Is reform of the law of X needed?
Research question 1	What context is there to this issue? (This would depend on the perspective the student was planning to take, for example theoretical context for a socio-legal project, or historical background for a black letter project.)		
Research question 2	What is the current law? (This would be essentially descriptive; you'd be "fact finding" here.)		
Research question 3	What are its strengths and weaknesses? (This would be essentially evaluative.)		
Research question 4	What options are there for reform? (Again, this may well be essentially descriptive.)		
Research question 5	What would be the pros and cons of introducing reform? (Back to evaluation here: this would include looking at the strengths and weaknesses of the alternatives, perhaps by looking at other jurisdictions; maybe also taking into account the practicalities of introducing reform; all this still in the light of the theoretical context identified.)		
Conclusion	This would draw on the research questions to decide whether reform is needed or not—in other words establish whether the hypothesis was true (or in the case of Student 3, to establish the answer to the question).		

This illustration makes it clear that your initial position merely provides the context for inquiry via your research questions; you are not setting out to prove that your hypothesis *is* true; you are setting out to prove *whether and/or to what extent* it is true.

It should be clear from this that an essential requirement is that your hypothesis is researchable. We have stated above that a hypothesis must be a statement but not all statements are hypotheses: a statement of fact is not a hypothesis. A hypothesis must be a statement of *position*.

For example:

● *Only one judge out of 12 in the Supreme Court is a woman*.

This is a statement of fact, but beyond the 10 seconds required to check that it is true, it is not researchable. However:

● *The appointment process for senior judicial positions discriminates against women*

is a statement of position: by researching further into the judicial appointments system, you would be able to discuss whether and/or to what extent it is true.

See the sample research proposals for further examples of hypotheses and research questions. Once you have developed a framework for your dissertation, you are ready to select an appropriate title.

HOW DO I CHOOSE AN APPROPRIATE TITLE?

We have already identified that one of the main distinctions between a dissertation and a coursework assignment is that you are not going to be given the title to your dissertation—you need to choose the title for yourself.

▶ 10.18

However, this does not mean choosing coursework style title. The wording used in coursework questions is not always appropriate for a dissertation title—for example a quotation, followed by the word "discuss" is a common format for a coursework title but is not a suitable title for your dissertation. You are carrying out an investigation of an area of law and the title must reflect that investigation by indicating the subject matter and scope of the work. It is best to do this in a simple and straightforward manner. Over-elaborate or pun-laden titles should be avoided. There is some debate about whether a question is a good format for a dissertation title and you should seek the advice of your supervisor about this.

Example title	Comments	Improved title
The age of criminal responsibility in England and Wales should be raised. Discuss.	The problem with this is that it is framed as an essay discussion question, which is not suitable as a dissertation title.	"An examination of whether the age of criminal responsibility in England and Wales should be raised." Or if your institution allows dissertation titles to be framed as a question then "Should the age of criminal responsibility in England and Wales should be raised?"
Suffer the children? An analysis of the law aimed at preventing child abuse in England and Wales. Is reform required?	The problem here is that the initial question is emotive and unnecessary—try to avoid this in your dissertation title.	"An analysis of the law aimed at preventing child abuse in England and Wales. Is reform required?" (if your institution allows questions) or "An analysis of whether the law aimed at protecting children from abuse in England and Wales is in need of reform."
Whither the squatter?	This is vague and gives neither the scope nor the topic of the dissertation: a good title will indicate to the reader what the dissertation is about.	"A critical study of the rights of the squatter following the Land Registration Act 2002."

There are some further illustrative examples in the research proposals in Appendix 5.

HOW DO I PLAN AND STRUCTURE MY DISSERTATION?

10.19 ▶ The structure of your dissertation is particularly important for two reasons: first, it is a longer piece, and therefore needs to be well-organised so that the reader can understand it, and secondly, because it is an investigation, the development of the argument needs to be clear and logical. Therefore it is essential to spend time in the development of a coherent plan.

In order to make the process of writing your dissertation more manageable you need to set out a broad overall plan before you can move into the researching and planning phase for each chapter (although you'll also need to plan each chapter individually in more detail once you've carried out the research into that chapter and understand the issues more clearly). The ordinary rules of using a good structure apply equally to the writing of a dissertation as to the writing of any piece of legal writing. Any differences arise from length and coverage, so to be readable and understandable a dissertation must be broken up into more manageable chunks by the use of chapters. Chapters are particularly useful for breaking up your writing and to delineate the different ideas and themes you want to explore.

Luckily, your research questions are likely to provide the basis for your broad content chapters. Begin by looking at your research questions and seeing whether you wish to consider one per chapter or whether some can be logically grouped together within one chapter. We are going to return to the example of the students who were framing their research questions and hypothesis. Here are the research questions we considered above:

- What context is there to this issue?
- What is the current law?
- What are its strengths and weaknesses?
- What options are there for reform?
- What would be the pros and cons of introducing reform?

Example: Drafting a plan

This example shows the notes a student might make for their draft plan which takes these generic research questions and applies them to the topic of property rights and cohabitants. The plan shows how each chapter deals with each research question. We will assume for the purpose of this example that the student is adopting a socio-legal perspective, and their hypothesis is that the property rights of cohabitants on relationship breakdown requires statutory reform.

Title: A critical examination of the property rights of co-habitants on relationship breakdown.

Chapter 1: Introduction

(a) What is the context of cohabitation in relation to relationship breakdown (with reference to statistics)?
(b) What theoretical issues does the topic raise?
— questions over whether "special" rules are needed for family situations (and if so, how should "the family" be defined)?
— feminist arguments about discrimination;

- questions over autonomy versus regulation (and also debate over models of regulation such as whether this should be formula-based);
- whether providing protection for cohabitants undermines the institution of marriage.
(c) What is the historical background to the current state of the law? A brief outline of:
- trust-based approach subject to criticism;
- Law Commission papers;
- Draft legislation (Private Members' Bills).

Chapter 2: The current law?
Outline of the existing legal positions, to cover:

(a) What is the current legal position on cohabitation? Look at land law principles, including:
- resulting trusts-case law;
- constructive trusts-case law.
(b) How does this contrast with the position if the couple is married or in a civil partnership?
- brief outline of the "needs-based approach" s.25 MCA 1973 provisions, yardstick of equality, *White v White*, fairness.

Chapter 3: What are its strengths and weaknesses?
Critical examination of the current law (relate this to theories outlined in introduction) including:

- Case law framework confusing;
- Financial contribution emphasis tends to discriminate against women.

Chapter 4: What options are there for reform?

(a) Outline possible options:
- Self regulation (cohabitation agreements);
- Apply s.25 style principles to cohabitants;
- Introduce a separate statutory scheme.
(b) Discuss strengths and weaknesses of these options, including link back to introduction:
- are claims that it undermines marriage to regulate those who have chosen not to get married justified?
- is it unfair to impose regulation on those who have chosen to live outside it?
(c) Analyse the Law Commissiosn proposals in the light of the above (could also include some comparative material, e.g. law in Scotland?)

Chapter 5: Conclusion
Draws together conclusions from each chapter and takes a final position on the hypothesis in light of these.

A plan like this would form a useful starting point for the first meeting with the supervisor. Once you have completed a working draft and discussed this with your supervisor, you are ready to move to the research and writing phases.

HOW DO I RESEARCH AND WRITE UP MY DISSERTATION?

10.20 ▶ Use the advice in Chapters 4–8 to help you carry out this phase, bearing in mind what we've suggested earlier about working on a chapter at a time, rather than trying to do all your research and then all your writing. In taking this chapter by chapter approach, it is important to keep a sense of how each chapter fits in to the rest of your dissertation. Plagiarism can be a particular issue with dissertations, so it is especially important to consider the advice on how to record your sources in Chapter 4, and how to acknowledge where you got your ideas from and how to utilise them to help form your own arguments in Chapter 5. However, if you've developed good habits in relation to your coursework then you won't find this an issue. During the process of research and writing, you'll need to work effectively with the supervisor you have been allocated and also take particular care to manage your time effectively.

Managing your dissertation writing

10.21 ▶ Because of the amount of work involved and the degree of independent working needed for a dissertation, managing your time effectively on a dissertation is a greater challenge than for any other piece of work you will undertake. Keeping on top of this is crucial if you want to get a good mark.

The first step is to make yourself a timetable. Working backwards from the hand-in date, list in a column all the things you can think of that you will need to do to complete your dissertation before you can hand it in, making sure you include all of the following:

- Time for binding.
- Final checks and amendments.
- Last advice from supervisor on final chapters (check whether your institution sets a "last chance" deadline for this—even if they do not, be sure to factor in university holidays when your supervisor may not be available to look at your work).
- Writing up.
- Research work (we suggest you do this on a chapter by chapter basis).
- Planning—including selection of your topic.

Now work out how many weeks there are between the date you complete the timetable and the hand-in date. Against each task you've listed in your first column, allocate an estimate of the amount of time you'll need in order to do that task effectively. This activity can be quite sobering when you realise you probably have a maximum of around six or seven months to plan, research and write up to 15,000 words as well as preparing for all your other classes, coursework and exams (and presumably wanting to have a life during this period).

Remember the hand-in requirements for your dissertation, in terms of presentation and style, are likely to be more formal than for your coursework and so will take more time. You will also probably want to make sure you consider other time constraints that may crop up like illness, breaks in the holidays, availability of your supervisor and other coursework preparation.

Be pragmatic throughout the year in terms of how much time you allocate to your dissertation. If it is worth one taught subject, then you need to spend as much as time on it as you would spend on that taught subject: count up the number of hours you spend preparing for and attending classes in a subject each week, plus the time you'd spend preparing the coursework and/or preparing and revising for the exam. If your dissertation is "double-weighted" (i.e. takes the place of *two* taught subjects) then accordingly you need to spend twice as much time on your dissertation as on any other subject.

Carry out this calculation and you are likely to realise that you should be spending the equivalent of a day a week on your dissertation in order to do it justice. If your timetable permits, you may find it helpful to set aside a particular day for your dissertation preparation to make sure you work at it regularly and don't let things slide.

> **TIPS** • *Some institutions may require you to submit a formal proposal before you begin your dissertation; in some cases reaching a satisfactory standard in this may be a pre-requisite for the dissertation option, which will give you a headstart with some tasks on your "to do" list. Others may expect a proposal or progress summary/ draft chapter at a midway point. Check your own institution's requirements carefully and adjust your timeline accordingly.*

Working with your supervisor

To get the most out of this relationship you will need to revisit your draft timetable and build in time to meet with your allocated tutor and get their advice at regular intervals. It is up to you to arrange these meetings and get the most out of them—don't expect your supervisor to "chase" you and don't expect them to drop all their other work to deal with you at short notice either. Use your supervisor to:

> **TIPS** • *It is never too early to start planning and researching your dissertation. The summer holidays prior to the year when you must complete your dissertation are a good long break when you can get started. If you are doing some legal work experience over the holidays why not see if there is anything you can be doing on your dissertation at the same time?*

1. Check that you are on the right track at the earliest opportunity. At your first ▶ **10.22** meeting take along any guidance you've been given about your dissertation, your initial timetable plan, your topic ideas and a suggested hypothesis and/or research questions, so that you can find out their view on your plans, in terms of whether it is a suitable area and whether your hypothesis/research question are sufficiently focused.
2. Discuss your research and the ideas you are forming from it. Your supervisor may also be able to suggest further reading. Remember that this is your work, so your supervisor can't do it for you but often he or she will be able to point you in useful directions for research.
3. Get feedback on draft chapters, although bear in mind:

   ● There may be a limit to the amount of drafts your supervisor is able to look at (check this at your first meeting).
   ● There is no point in handing in something which is only a collection of notes: although a draft, it should be sufficiently finished to make it worth your supervisor's time in reading and commenting on it.
   ● Your supervisor's role is not to correct your work but to provide feedback to enable you to improve it yourself. It is also unlikely that your supervisor will agree

to give an estimated mark for your work, because this can only be judged in relation to the whole, finished work.

● When you get comments from your supervisor, remember to revise the relevant section or chapter straight away when the feedback is fresh in your mind.

One note of caution: Your supervisor is likely to be supervising a number of other dissertations as well (and conducting their own work). The earlier you hand work in for consideration, the more of your supervisor's attention you will get. Inevitably, if five students each hand in three or four new chapters to the same supervisor close to the deadline, the amount of time the supervisor can spend looking at each piece will be correspondingly limited.

WHAT PARTICULAR REQUIREMENTS ARE THERE FOR THE FINISHING STAGE?

10.23 ▶ Once you have completed your chapters and acted on the advice of your supervisor to improve them, then you will need to draw the dissertation to a coherent whole. The advice contained in Chapter 8 on polishing your work is equally applicable to dissertations, but there are some additional factors involved, as the formal requirements for the presentation of your dissertation are likely to be more complex than in relation to other written work. Ensure that you comply with any rules on how you present your chapters, referencing, double spacing of text and so on. Additionally, it is likely that you will have to write an abstract and it may be appropriate to include appendices. Check your institution's requirements for submission, e.g. double copies, binding, etc.

What is an abstract and how do I write one?

10.24 ▶ An abstract is a short factual statement which appears at the beginning of your dissertation, summarising your aims, your research hypothesis, the evidence on which you rely and your conclusions, usually on a chapter by chapter basis. It gives the reader information about what to expect in the dissertation and it should be concise (about 150–300 words, but check whether your institution specifies a word limit for it). Although it is presented at the beginning you should leave it until the end to write because it must be an accurate reflection of what is actually in your dissertation, not a woolly statement of what you were hoping to achieve when you started.

It is important not to confuse an *abstract* with an *introduction*. An abstract is a summary. It does not raise issues or pose questions. The purpose of the abstract is so that the reader can see how your investigation proceeded, what evidence you have looked at and what conclusions you have reached.

Do I need to use appendices?

10.25 ▶ It is a mistake to assume that the use of voluminous appendices makes the dissertation seem more weighty and intellectual. This is certainly not true. Further, appendices should not be used as a means of providing additional material over the word limit. Generally, use of an appendix is appropriate where there is source material to which you have referred which is otherwise inaccessible for the reader (raw data, for example, or unpublished or obscure material). As noted above, at the level of an undergraduate dissertation you are not expected to carry out empirical research in the form of questionnaires or interviews so unless you are relying on someone else's unpublished data you would not need to use an appendix for this. If you have relied on a comparatively obscure source extensively then you might want to provide a copy in your appendix—perhaps a print out of a website which you have cited but which has since been changed or removed from the internet—but easily available material such as statutes or cases is unnecessary in an appendix.

SUMMARY OF CHAPTER 10

- Dissertations require many of the same writing skills as other legal assignments but particular attention is needed to certain phases of the writing cycle.   ▶ 10.26
- To write a successful dissertation you must choose a suitable researchable topic and adopt a critical framework by posing a hypothesis and research questions.
- Write a plan for your whole dissertation at the outset, and then carry out the research and writing chapter by chapter.
- Manage your time carefully and make the most of the opportunity to gain feedback from your supervisor.

APPENDICES

APPENDICES

APPENDIX 1—SAMPLE ASSESSMENT GRADE DESCRIPTORS

These grade descriptors provide an example of different levels of attainment in respect of some typical assessment criteria for a legal assignment. Criteria vary from institution to institution. Make sure you are familiar with whatever criteria apply to your assignment.

	100 – 80 per cent	79 – 70 per cent	69 – 60 per cent	59 – 50 per cent	49 – 40 per cent	39 – 35 per cent	34 – 21 per cent	20 – 0 per cent
Question diagnosis **10 Marks**	Identifies major and minor points and shows outstanding perception in identification of hidden issues. Includes no irrelevant material.	Identifies major and minor points and shows excellent perception in identification of hidden issues. Includes little or no irrelevant material.	Identifies major points and most minor points and shows some perception in identification of hidden issues. Includes little irrelevant material.	Identifies most major points and some minor points. Unlikely to identify hidden issues. May include some irrelevant material.	Identifies many major points but lacks attention to minor points. Some mistakes in weight attached to points and/or includes some irrelevant material.	Fails to identify some major points. Weight attached to points is inappropriate and/or includes irrelevant material.	Fails to identify many major points. A significant proportion of the work addresses irrelevant or wrong issues.	Fails to identify most or all major points. Most of the work addresses entirely or almost entirely irrelevant or wrong issues.
Knowledge & understanding **20 Marks**	Displays complete and detailed knowledge of relevant law (and/or other required material) with full, balanced and accurate explanations.	Displays comprehensive and detailed knowledge of relevant law (and/or other required material) with full, balanced and almost entirely accurate explanations.	Displays broad and mainly detailed knowledge of relevant law (and/or other relevant material) with balanced and generally accurate explanations.	Displays good knowledge of the relevant law (and/or other relevant material) but explanations need more detail / balance or contain some mistakes.	Displays basic knowledge of relevant law (and/or other relevant material) but explanations lack detail / balance and there are a number of mistakes.	Fails to show satisfactory knowledge of much of the relevant law (and/or other relevant material). Lacks sufficient explanation and/or explanations contain significant flaws.	Fails to show knowledge of most of the relevant law (and/or other material). Offers little explanation and/or explanations are irrelevant or significantly inaccurate.	Fails to show any real knowledge of relevant law (and/or other material). Offers no explanations or those which are offered are irrelevant or wholly inaccurate.

Application & argument **20 Marks**							
Shows outstanding ability in problem-solving and/or interpretation of knowledge, offering entirely sustained, evidenced and logical conclusions and exploring alternative arguments.	Shows excellent ability in problem-solving and/or interpretation of knowledge, offering sustained, evidenced and logical conclusions and exploring some alternative arguments.	Shows very good ability in problem-solving and/or interpretation of knowledge, offering mainly sustained, evidenced and logical conclusions, and considers some alternative arguments.	Shows some ability in problem-solving and/or interpretation of knowledge but conclusions drawn are not completely sustained by the supporting argument. More attention needed to alternative arguments.	Shows competence in problem-solving and/or interpretation of knowledge but with some flaws in the conclusions drawn. Some supporting argument is made, but little attention given to alternative arguments.	Fails to show competence in problem-solving and/or interpretation of knowledge. Insufficient application; conclusions are limited or flawed. Little supporting argument is made and gives no attention to alternative arguments.	Fails to show more than sketchy ability in problem-solvingand/or interpretation of knowledge. Has little application; conclusions are few or significantly flawed. Gives little or no supporting argument.	Fails to show any ability in problem-solving and/or interpretation of knowledge. Has little or no application; draws no conclusions or those which are drawn are completely flawed. Gives little or no argument.
Research and evidence **10 Marks**							
Utilises a comprehensive range of quality sources showing independent research. Sources are appropriately acknowledged and fully integrated into arguments made.	Utilises a wide range of quality sources showing excellent independent research. Sources are appropriately acknowledged and fully integrated into arguments made.	Utilises a good range of quality sources showing independent research. Sources are appropriately acknowledged and mainly integrated into arguments made.	Utilises a basic range of sources showing some independent research. Sources are appropriately acknowledged and partly integrated into arguments made.	Utilises a basic range of sources showing little independent research. Sources are appropriately acknowledged but not sufficiently integrated into arguments made. Some assertions lack evidence.	Fails to utilise a sufficient range of quality sources. No evidence of independent research. May fail to acknowledge sources appropriately. Assertions are made with limited supporting evidence.	Fails to utilise more than a very limited range of source and shows little evidence of research or reading. Fails to acknowledge sources appropriately. Assertions are made with little supporting evidence.	Fails to utilise sources and shows little or no evidence of research or reading. Fails to acknowledge sources. Assertions are made with no supporting evidence.

	100 – 80 per cent	79 – 70 per cent	69 – 60 per cent	59 – 50 per cent	49 – 40 per cent	39 – 35 per cent	34 – 21 per cent	20 – 0 per cent
Evaluation **20 Marks**	Makes impressive judgments by identifying fully gaps/flaws/inconsistencies in the material discussed. Reaches a fully reasoned position. Offers an outstanding critique.	Makes excellent judgments by identifying all or almost all gaps/flaws/inconsistencies in the material discussed. Reaches a fully reasoned position. Offers a full critique.	Makes very good judgments by identifying main gaps/flaws/inconsistencies in the material discussed. Reaches a well-reasoned position. Offers a sound critique.	Makes some judgments but identifies only some gaps/flaws/inconsistencies in the material discussed. Position is not sufficiently reasoned but offers some limited critique.	Makes limited judgments and identifies few gaps/flaws/inconsistencies in the material discussed. Offers more description than critique.	Fails to make sufficient reasoned judgments and those which are made are weak or unsubstantiated. Offers mainly description and little critique.	Few if any judgements are made. No or almost no critique of the material is offered. Commentary is essentially descriptive.	No judgments are made. No critique of the material is offered. Any commentary is entirely descriptive.
Structure **10 Marks**	Effective, thorough introduction and conclusion. Explicit and logical links between discussion points. Clear signposting of argument.	Effective introduction and conclusion. Explicit and logical links between discussion points. Clear signposting of argument.	Good introduction and conclusion. Logical ordering of content. Appropriate links between discussion points. Clear signposting of argument.	Good introduction and conclusion. The content is presented in a generally logical order. Some links between points. Some signposting of argument.	Basic introduction and conclusion. Some attempt to present content in a logical order. Limited signposting of argument but work is coherent.	Fails to give sufficient introduction or conclusion. Disorganised content. Weak signposting of points. Work is sometimes incoherent.	Fails to give any introduction of conclusion. Disorganised content. Little signposting of points. Work is frequently incoherent.	Fails to give any introduction or conclusion. Completely disorganised content. No signposting of points. Work is incoherent.

Presentation 10 Marks							
Outstanding use of English and sophisticated writing style. Accurate spelling, grammar and referencing/ bibliography.	Excellent use of English and sound writing style. Accurate spelling, grammar and referencing/ bibliography.	Very good use of English and good writing style. Mainly accurate spelling, grammar and referencing / bibliography.	Good use of English and competent writing style. A few spelling or grammar errors. May be mistakes or inconsistencies in referencing / bibliography.	Generally competent use of English but writing style is basic. Some spelling or grammar errors. Mistakes or inconsistencies in referencing / bibliography.	Fails to reach a competent level of English. A number of spelling and grammar errors. Serious mistakes / inconsistencies in referencing / bibliography.	Poor use of English. Serious spelling and grammar errors. Referencing and bibliography are seriously flawed or may be missing.	Use of English raises serious concerns. Numerous spelling and grammar errors. Referencing and bibliography are seriously flawed or may be missing.

APPENDIX 2—PLANNING LOG

In this appendix there is a pro forma which you may want to use to help you diagnose your task and plan your research with ideas for how you would complete each section.

Planning Log with guidance

Assignment title	Insert the title given.
Diagnose your task *See Chapter 3 for further advice*	Write what you think the question is asking for, i.e. identify the topic under consideration and specific angles or elements required by the question. It may help to try the following: • Imagine why the marker set this particular question in this particular way. • Put the question round another way: if it's a statement, put it as a question; then break it into further questions.
Key words	Identify the key words—i.e. the words which define the subject and scope of your assignment.
Instruction words	Identify the instruction words—the words which tell you what to do with your material.
Materials review *See Chapter 4 for further advice*	Note down what materials you already have on this topic, for example lecture notes, tutorial preparation notes, notes from your textbook(s), suggested reading lists, etc.
Search for relevant primary materials *See Chapter 4 for further advice*	Remember that by primary sources, we mean cases and statutes. Note down: (a) which database(s) you searched and why you chose this database; (b) the search terms you used; and (c) with reference to the results generated evaluate whether the search was effective in helping you address the question set (did it generate too few results? Too many results? Results which were not relevant to the question?). (d) if your initial search was not effective, describe what changes/refinements you made for your next search (did you change your search terms? Search within results? Narrow your search to only particular sources? Narrow your search by date? Use a different database altogether?)
Search for relevant secondary materials *See Chapter 4 for further advice*	Remember that by secondary sources we mean commentary on the law rather than the law itself (e.g. books, articles, etc.) Note down: (a) which database(s) you searched and why you chose this database; (b) the search terms you used, and (c) with reference to the results generated evaluate whether the search was effective in helping you address the question set (did it generate too few results? Too many results? Results which were not relevant to the question?). (d) if your initial search was not effective, describe what changes/refinements you made for your next search (did you change your search terms/search within results/narrow your search to only particular sources/narrow your search by date/use a different database altogether?)

APPENDIX 3—SAMPLE ANSWERS ON THE PRACTICE STATEMENT QUESTION

Answer A: Critically assess the effect of the Practice Statement 1966 on the doctrine of precedent, illustrating your answer with case examples.

The Practice Statement 1966 was passed in 1966 by the House of Lords and had a big impact on the way the doctrine of precedent operates. The doctrine of precedent or stare decisis as it is more properly known is the system that is used in English law to determine how cases in the legal system are influenced by previous cases, this will depend on three important elements, a system of law reporting, a hierarchy of courts and a concept of ratio. Ratio is the principle of law which decides the case in the context of or in the light of the material facts.

The purpose of the doctrine of precedent is to create certainty, this is essential for us to have confidence in the idea of justice. There is an argument that we need flexibility to make sure each case can be decided fairly, but I think that it is more important for people to be certain about what the law is. Otherwise solicitors and barristers will not be able to advise their clients properly, this will increase costs and cause unfairness.

An example of a case where the House of Lords used the Practice Statement is the case of *Miliangos v George Frank Textiles*. This was a case about whether judgment could be made in sterling or not. Lord Denning in the court of appeal had stated that it could be made in any currency, which was contrary to the position in the case of Havana Railways, this had said that judgment must be given in sterling. Bristow J said that it had to be given in sterling in the High Court. When the case got to the House of Lords, their lordships decided that Lord Denning had been wrong to disobey the previous case of Havana because it should have been binding (this was in another case called *Schorsh Meier v Hennin*). However, the House of Lords also decided that Lord Denning had been right about whether to give judgment in sterling. This meant they used the Practice Statement to depart from their own previous decision and changed the law. Havana Railways was no longer "good law" after this.

Another case where the House of Lords used the Practice Statement was in *R v Shivpuri*, the issue they had to decide was whether it is possible to be convicted of a criminal attempt if it was impossible to do the crime. Mr Shivpuri had handled a suitcase full of harmless powder thinking it was drugs. This was the same as the previous case of *Anderton v Ryan*, the defend- ant in this case had handled a video recorder which she must of known was stolen, because it was suspiciously cheap. She admitted to the police officers that she had suspected that it was stolen because of the cheap price she paid for it however the police did not prove that it was actually stolen. This meant that she could only be convicted of attempting the impossible, but the House of Lords interpreted the Criminal Attempts Act 1981 to decide that she was not guilty. Lots of legal academics decided that this was plainly wrong, so the House of Lords used the Practice Statement to overrule *Anderton v Ryan* in the case of *Shivpuri*. This was the first time the House of Lords had decided to use the Practice Statement in a criminal case, which shows how serious it was. Previously they had said it would be better to keep hanging people than create uncertainty.

Another case where the House of Lords used the Practice Statement was *Murphy v Brentwood*, this was to overrule the case of *Anns v Merton Borough Council*. The reason they did this was because interpretation of the case of *Donoghue v Stevenson* was getting out of hand.

Donoghue v Stevenson was the famous case about the snail in the ginger beer bottle (although actually it was never proved whether there was a snail in the bottle because Mr Stevenson died and his executors settled the case out of court). In *Grant v Australian Knitting Mills* they widened this ratio to include any product which might injure your neighbour (in this case, the goods in question were long underpants which had given him dermatitis). By the time of the *Anns* case, this had been extended to include pure economic loss. The House of Lords used the Practice Statement to depart from this decision because they felt that the law would be unworkable otherwise because the "floodgates would open".

This shows that whenever the House of Lords decided to use the Practice Statement 1966 to depart from their own previous decisions, it had serious implications for the doctrine of precedent because it creates uncertainty. However, we must always remember that the House of Lords only used this power rarely. The Supreme Court will probably do the same.

Answer B: Critically assess the effect of the Practice Statement 1966 on the doctrine of precedent, illustrating your answer with case examples.

The Practice Statement 1966 was a Practice Direction issued by the House of Lords in which they indicated that they would no longer consider themselves bound by their own previous decisions but would be free to depart under certain circumstances. This was in itself a departure from the pervious position which had stated that the House of Lords would be bound by it's own previous decisions, in the interests of certainty, because if the House of Lords was free to depart from it's own previous precedents then no legal issue would ever be decided finally, which would create serious issues for precedent and the legal system. The House of Lords was replaced by the Supreme Court in 2009 and the Supreme Court kept the same powers as under the Practice Statement. The Practice Statement did not specify what circumstances would need to apply in order to justify departure, but stated that the House of Lords could do so when they thought it was right to do so, so this therefore had the potential to return the legal system to the position of no case ever being decided finally and whether or not this actually happened was to be in the hands of the Law Lords, and now the Justices of the Supreme Court. In this essay I shall examine whether this happened or not.

There are a number of reasons why certainty is thought to be beneficial for the legal system. First of all, the idea of certainty corresponds with usual notions of justice and fairness, which state it should be possible for people to be able to predict whether or not it is worth pursuing a case by reference to previous cases which have been decided as this is the whole point of the principal of stare decisis, which literally means "stand by what has been decided", which is the central feature of our common law legal system in contrast to the alternative European 'Code' system. A further point in relation to this is that it would not seem very fair if someone could pursue a case and get a particular result, and then another person pursuing a very similar case later should get a different result, as this would result in a lack of confidence in the legal system in the eyes of the general public, because the legal system would appear to be subjective rather than objective. An example of this is the case of *Miller v Jackson*, where Lord Denning's judgment appeared to indicate that he was deciding the case contrary to precedents which should have been binding on him on the basis that he liked cricket! Certainty is also important because legal relationships are formed on the basis of the law existing at the time they are made, so if the Supreme Court was prepared to overrule it's previous decisions frequently, and those of the House of Lords, this would have implications for contracts which might have been formed which could potentially be worth millions of pounds, so the Supreme Court must always bear this in mind. A final benefit of certainty within legal system is that it provides a basis upon which lawyers can advise their client's, and thus reduce litigation, because if the Supreme Court was prepared to reopen areas of settled law frequently it would always be worth pushing a case to the Supreme Court, even if the authority's suggest the con- trary, on the basis that previous precedents could be overruled, and this would increase the costs involved and lead to more cases than the legal system could cope with.

It is therefore reassuring to note that the House of Lords only exercised their discretion to overturn existing precedents by using the Practice Statement 1966 on rare occasions. However there are certain circumstances under which the House of Lords felt that it was necessary to use the Practice Statement, and the power that it has to do so can be used to combat some of the problems which exist within the doctrine of stare decisis. The first of these is that the doctrine of precedent is rigid. From the point of view of certainty, this is a good thing because it leads to the benefits I have discussed earlier in this essay, but it also has its drawbacks, for example the fact the law is prevented from developing to meet a modern societies needs, and that bad decisions are perpetuated. Therefore circumstances in which according to Alan Paterson in The Law Lords (1982) the House of Lords might be prepared to use the Practice Statement include to modernise old legal decisions, and to correct serious errors of law, although the House of Lords indicated that it would not use the Practice Statement to overrule a previous decision on the grounds that it was 'merely wrong' but only where both the reasoning and the decision were wrong and there is a public interest in correcting the law.

In conclusion therefore it seems that the House of Lords got the balance right in choosing whether to exercise it's discretion to use the Practice Statement. They did so in order modern- ise the law and prevent the legal system becoming stifled, but generally paid heed to the vital need for certainty in the legal system and so used the power only rarely. It seems likely that the Supreme Court will adopt the same approach although we will have to wait for more cases to see how that pans out.

Answer C: Critically assess the effect of the Practice Statement 1966 on the doctrine of precedent, illustrating your answer with case examples.

The Practice Statement 1966 indicated a radical departure from the traditionally con- serva- tive position adopted by the most senior judges in the kingdom, namely the Lords of Appeal in Ordinary, that the needs of certainty within our legal system outweigh other considerations and indeed their own desire for judicial creativity. The classic embodiment of this conservative position was the statement in the *London Tramways* case in 1898, in which the (then) Lord Chancellor, declared that it would be a "disastrous inconvenience" if the House of Lords could review each previous decisions because it would mean ". . . having each question subject to being re-argued and the dealings of mankind rendered doubtful by reason of different deci- sions, so that in truth and in fact there would be no final court of appeal." In this essay the writer proposes to consider the effect on the doctrine of precedent of this "disastrous inconven- ience" which was rendered possible by the Practice Statement. The writer will then identify the impact of the new Supreme Court on this aspect of the legal conundrum.

The Practice Statement opened the doors on the potential to revisit and rejudge each legal issue afresh; nevertheless their lordships house has demonstrated their unwillingness to walk through these doors on more than a handful of occasions. A notable early exception to this unwillingness is the case of *British Railways Board v Herrington* in which the court reconsidered the rules on liability to child trespassers in the light of modern attitudes to the issue. This, then, is a typical example of why the House of Lords was prepared to offer itself the very freedom afforded by the Practice Statement, namely that "too rigid adherence to precedent may lead to injustice in a particular case and also unduly restrict the proper development of the law. . ." as the wording of the Practice Statement itself states. A further example is the case of *Miliangos v George Frank Textiles* where the House were prepared to extinguish from the precedent books a ruling that sterling should be the only currency in which judgment can be awarded, a position which, as Lord Denning asserted in the court of appeal was appropriate to the days of the empire than to modern global economies.

If it were only in the interests of modernising and developing the law and the need for a legal system to maintain its grip on current affairs that the law lords were prepared to use the practice statement then we might justifiably conclude that the small loss to certainty would be a worthwhile price to pay in order to maintain a modern and vibrant legal system. However this writer submits that the House of Lords created confusion by its attempts to impose rules upon its own use of the Practice Statement, and its subsequent departure from these rules in arbitrary cases. The epitome of the House's confusion over appropriate use of the practice statement is the case of R v Shippuri, in which the House took the opportunity to overrule its own very recent decision in Anderton v Ryan. In doing so, they appeared to show a reckless disregard for principles which previous incarnations of the House had declared to be applicable in deciding whether use of the Practice Statement would be appropriate. The first of these considerations was that the House should be especially cautious in using the Practice Statement in criminal cases, because of the "especial need for certainty" in criminal cases (as stated within the text of the Practice Statement itself). The second was that they should not use the Practice Statement to overrule a decision relating to statutory interpretation since this would constitute an infringement of the fundamental constitutional cornerstone that it is for Parliament to amend its statutes not the judiciary. Finally the house appeared to succumb to pressure to change a decision because it was 'merely wrong'. The academic furore which had resulted from the *Anderton* case had proved embarrassing and the House of Lords felt compelled to admit that they had got it wrong.

Thus we can conclude that for the main part, the House of Lords maintained a conservative position to the use of the practice statement and has shunned the radical opportunities it offers. Nevertheless we cannot state this with absolute certainty because of the examples which conflict with this position. The response of the supreme court justices to a case in which they might themselves consider exercising the very freedom with which their predecessor court had bestowed upon them was anticipated with much debate in the circles of the law. In *Austin v London Borough of Southwark* the supreme court resisted the temptation to turn the tide on a decision of its own previous self, for reasons which resonated similarly to the caution of the house of lords.

Hence it seems that the ultimate effect of the Practice Statement has been to create uncertainty and thus attack the notions of justice upon which our legal system is based. Yet although we cannot predict when the supreme court will use the Practice Statement this writer submits that there use of it is likely to be as rare as the house of lords; too rare for the contention that there is now a lack of certainty in the legal system to realistically be sustained.

Answer D: Critically assess the effect of the Practice Statement 1966 on the doctrine of precedent, illustrating your answer with case examples.

The Practise Statement 1966 gave the House of Lords the opportunity to depart from there own previous decisions. Previously these had been binding on them under the principle of the *London Tramways* case decided in 1898. The justification for the old position was that it would cause uncertainty if the House of Lords changed it's mind all the time, and certainty is often equated with notions of justice, fairness and equality, as Holland and Webb point out in Learning Legal Rules, page 122. By 1966 the House of Lords had realised that if they always adhered rigidly to precedent they would be stuck with decisions which might be out of date and inappropriate for modern circumstances. So the Practise Statement gave the House of Lords a certain amount of freedom. In order to assess the affect of the Practise Statement, it is necessary to look at examples of how they used this freedom, to conclude whether this has been at the expense of certainty. A further question is whether the Supreme Court, which assumed the powers of the House of Lords as the most senior court, will adopt the same approach to using the Practise Statement as the House of Lords did.

It was impossible to draw firm conclusions about when the House of Lords would or would not use the Practise Statement, because it was a matter for there discretion in each case. Alan Paterson in The Law Lords in 1982 suggested that the House would consider use of the Practise Statement in order to modernise the law. Two examples of this are the cases of British Railways Bord v Herrington and Miliangos v George Frank Textiles. The former changed the law on liability to children who trespass and harm themselves which previously had been based on Victorian liassez faire morality. In Miliangos, the question was over whether judgement should be given in sterling or in any currency. The more modern view was that sterling was no longer the gold standard it was in the previous case of Havana Railways, and that therefore the House of Lords should overrule its previous decision.

However, the House of Lords also used the Practise Statement to restrict the law, as well as develop it. An example of this is Murphy v Brentwood where limitations were imposed on the liability for pure economic loss by overruling the case of Anns v London Borough of Merton. Here, the House of Lords appeared to realise that liability for negligence under Donoghue v Stevenson had been taken too far and therefore narrowed it down again.

The House of Lords gave guidence in some cases about when they might use the Practise Statement, for example the statement itself says they would be more cautious in criminal cases because of the "especially need for certainty", and this is shown by their refusal to overrule the criticised decision of DPP v Shaw in R v Knuller. They also stated in Jones v DHSS that they would not use it in cases of statutory interpretation because this was a constitutional issue for Parliament rather than the judges to correct. They also stated that they would not use it simply to correct errors (although it might be argued they did this in Murphy v Brentwood). A case which seems to break all these rules is R v Shivpuri. This overruled Anderton v Ryan on the interpretation of the Criminal Attempts Act 1981. The issue was whether someone could be convicted of attempting to do something which was actually impossible, and there had been widespread critisism of the ruling. So the House of Lords ignored all their own guidelines and overruled it.

By looking at the way in which the House of Lords used the Practise Statement, it seems that they paid a lot of attention to the fact that the more they used it the less certain the law will be. If the highest court changes it's mind often, then there will be more litigation because people will not have confidence in the system of precedent and lawyers will not be able to advice there clients. It will also be difficult for people to form contracts with confidence based on the existing state of the law. The House of Lords had to remember that people rely on the certainly of the law. So they only used it rarely.

Will the Supreme Court will use the Practise Statement in the same cautious way as the House of Lords did? One argument was that they would be likely to do so, because most of the judges are the same. The opposite argument was that a new court might be more radical in its approach to reforming the law. This was tested in the case of Austin v Southwark Borough Council, where the Supreme Court decided not to use the Practise Statement to overrule a House of Lords case because of the relianse which had been placed on the previous decision.

Although it is wrong to draw firm conclusions from one example this supports the argument that the Supreme Court will adopt a similar approach to the House of Lords. It seems that the most likely case where they would use it is to modernise the law, if they thought this would not have too many ramifications on people who had relied on the old law, and according to the terms of the statement itself, this is probably the most appropriate circumstance for them to use it, as long as this is done sparingly. This would result in a positive effect on precedent without too much disruption.

APPENDIX 4—SAMPLE BIBLIOGRAPHY

The following shows a sample bibliography using the OSCOLA format. Use this format only if your institution does not provide a specified layout for bibliographies.

Note that primary sources are given first, and OSCOLA states that case names are not italicised in the bibliography. Secondary sources may be classified into different types of source (as in the example below) or given in one list of secondary sources in alphabetical order by author name. OSCOLA requires author names to be given differently in the bibliography than in the footnotes (Family name followed by initial, as below).

Statutes
Children Act 1989
Environmental Protection Act 1990
Landlord and Tenant Act 1985
Protection from Eviction Act 1977

Cases
Bishop Auckland Local Board v Bishop Auckland Iron and Steel Co (1882) 10 QBD 138
Lee v Leeds C; Ratcliffe v Sandwell MBC [2002] 1 WLR 1488
R (on the application of Vella) v Lambeth LBC [2005] EWHC 2473
Summers v Salford Corporation [1943] 1 All ER 68

Secondary sources
Books
Black J and others, *A Practical Approach to Family Law* (8th edn, OUP 2007)
Cowan D and A Marsh, *Two Steps Forward: Housing Policy Into the New Millennium* (Policy Press 2001)
Stewart A, *Rethinking Housing Law* (Sweet & Maxwell 1996)

Articles
Jennings W, 'Courts and Administrative Law – the Experience of English Housing Legislation' (1936) 49 HLR 426
Luba J, 'Landlords' Obligations for the Condition of Residential Premises – A Law Full of Holes' (2002) 6 L&T Rev 49

Official Published Sources
Burridge R, Ormandy D and Battersby, R, *Monitoring the New Housing Fitness Standards* (HMSO, London 1993)
DoE, Circular 6/90, *Area Renewal, Unfitness, Slum Clearance and Enforcement Action* (DoE, London 1990)
Law Commission, *Renting Homes: Status and Security* (Law Commission Consultation Paper No.162 HMSO, London 2002)

Electronic Sources

Hart D, 'Environmental Rights and the Public Interest': *Hatton* v *United Kingdom/Dennis* v *Ministry of Defence* <http://www.1cor.com/1158/?form_1155.replyids=20> accessed 28 November 2014

Radley-Gardner O, 'Chargees and Family Property' [2001] <http://www.bailii.org/uk/other/journals/WebJCLI/2001/issue1/gardner1.html> accessed 28 November 2014

Wolverhampton City Council, 'CCTV Images and You' <http://www.wolverhampton.gov.uk/legal_services/advice/cctv.htm> accessed 10 June 2008

APPENDIX 5—SAMPLE RESEARCH PROPOSALS

Here are two sample research proposals with comments to illustrate what might be expected when preparing a dissertation.

SAMPLE 1: *FAMILY LAW* RESEARCH PROPOSAL WITH SUPERVISOR COMMENTS

A. Draft Title
"The law relating to division of property on relationship breakdown for couples who cohabit outside of marriage or civil partnership is inequitable and requires urgent reform." Discuss.

You've chosen an interesting area to research, and this has the potential to be a good piece of research. However, the problem here is that you've formulated your dissertation title like an essay title. Avoid using the word 'Discuss' like this—instead try to make your title into a critical statement.

B. Hypothesis
Cohabitants are discriminated against when it comes to division of property on relationship breakdown because land law principles are used which make no recognition of non-financial contributions like child-rearing.

You've understood the purpose of a hypothesis and have thought out a sensible 'working theory' for your research investigation.

C. Proposed research strategy
The research questions I intend to investigate are:

This is mainly good. You have set out clear research questions, the investigation of which will enable you to take a concluding position in relation to your hypothesis, although your hypothesis makes specific mention of non-financial contributions like child-rearing, which isn't mirrored in any of your research questions—presumably you would address this aspect when examining the current law? You might want to consider including reference to human rights issues under question 3.

1. How are cohabitants dealt with currently in relation to property disputes? (This will involve looking at the land law principles and the case law on establishing a trust.)
2. How does this compare to the position for married couples and civil partners? (This will require an examination of the statutory framework under s.25 of the Matrimonial Causes Act 1973 in order to contrast the "needs" based approach used with the property based approach used for cohabiting couples).
3. Can the discrepancy be justified and is it discriminatory? This will include examining the arguments of opponents of reform so further sub-questions here include:
   (a) Are claims that it undermines marriage to regulate those who have chosen not to get married justified?
   (b) Is it unfair to impose regulation on those who have chosen to live outside it?
4. What alternatives might there be, e.g. giving cohabitants the same rights as married people or a different set of rights?
5. What would be the strengths and weaknesses of any new proposed system? What would be the impact of introducing reform in this area?

Overall this should enable me to conclude whether or not reform of this area is required, in accordance with my hypothesis.

I intend to use a socio-legal approach. This is appropriate for my investigation because although I will be looking in some detail at the current law, I will be looking at the effect of the law in practice and how this relates to changing notions of the family, in particular the increase in the number of. I will also be looking in detail at the relevant case law, particularly in relation to questions 1 and 2 () but not in the context of a purely black-letter analysis as I intend to investigate whether the case law is discriminatory.

I intend to answer these questions by carrying out an extended literature review, including

The big problem here is your plan to conduct interviews in support of your research. You haven't presented a rationale for this, or set out your proposed method, and therefore it isn't clear what purpose this would serve or how it would be managed (or indeed how it links in with any of your research questions). In relation to this area of the law, I would suggest that a literature review in itself is more than sufficient without any empirical research of your own. Can you use the empirical research of others, e.g. British Social Attitudes Surveys perhaps?

reviewing cases, articles and relevant texts. I will also be conducting interviews with a number of friends and work colleagues who are cohabitants.

D. Literature review

Because of the nature of my dissertation, much of the review I will carry out will be of the relevant cases, for example:

> Midland Bank v Cooke[1]
> Lloyd's Bank v Rosset[2]
> Cooke v Head[3]
> Burns v Burns[4]
> Grant v Edwards[5]
> Eves v Eves[6]
> Hammond v Mitchell[7]
> Wayling v Jones[8]

The beginning part of your review reads rather more like a list than a review; where you have not yet looked at a source, include it in your sources list rather than in your literature review. This has reduced the number of words actually spent reviewing the literature but once you get into discussion of the secondary sources, you are showing the right skills. You've picked some good quality sources here, and you've shown you can begin to evaluate them. The major limitation of your literature review so far is that you need reference to more recent materials. For example, the Law Commission has issued two major reports on this in the last few years&this will need to be a major source for your research, and should have been referenced in your literature review. Look back at your notes on how to source up-to-date material.

In terms of secondary sources, an overview of the current law on cohabitant's property is provided in the following textbooks:

Herring J. *Family Law* (6th edn, Pearson 2013). Herring explores some of the theoretical issues in contrasting cohabitation and marriage as well as looking at criticisms of the law and possible reform options.

Masson J, Bailey-Harris R & Probert R. *Cretney's Principles of Family Law* (8th edn, Sweet and Maxwell 2008). Cretney goes into depth on the cases and provides some critical analysis of the problems in the current law.

Lowe N. and Douglas G. *Bromley's Family Law* (10th edn, OUP 2006).

Remember to give the pages when citing a book chapter&and who is the author or editor of the whole book?

More detailed critical analysis is provided by the following authors: Bailey-Harris[9] gives a detailed critique of the strengths and weaknesses of the existing system. Although she does find some positives, for example, that the property law based system currently in use is gender neutral, and allows for development by judges (for example, Lord Denning extend- ing rights to the "wives" in cases like *Eves v Eves*) she has a number of criticisms of the law, which she proves be reference to relevant case examples as evidence. For example, the fac that it causes unfairness in failing to reward equally different types of contribution to the welfare of the family, by favouring monetary contributions over non-monetary contributions such as child-rearing. In practice this would therefore tend to favour men over women as, in the majority of the cases (with one or two exceptions), the man is the legal owner who has made the most

---

[1] [1995] 2 F.L.R. 915.
[2] [1990] 2 F.L.R. 155.
[3] [1972] 2 All E.R. 38.
[4] [1984] 1 All E.R. 244.
[5] [1987] 1 F.L.R. 87; [1986] 2 All E.R. 426.
[6] [1975] 3 All E.R. 768.
[7] [1992] 2 All E.R. 109.
[8] [1995] 2 F.L.R. 1029.
[9] Rebecca Bailey-Harris. Dividing the Assets on Breakdown of Relationships outside Marriage: Challengers for Reformers in: *Dividing the Assets on Family Breakdown* (Family Law 1998).

financial contributions to the property and the woman is trying to demon- strate a trust on the basis of smaller financial contributions.

Placing greater emphasis on financial contributions to the family is in contrast to the position taken on divorce under the statutory regime in the Matrimonial Causes Act. The simplicity of the latter in contrast to the system for cohabitants is praised by Taylor.[10] However, despite the criticisms made of the current law, Bailey-Harris does not consider that extending s.25 to cohabitants is necessarily the answer, and recognises that there are a number of issues to be weighed up before proposing reform. She sets out a "blueprint" which reform should measure up to.

You aren't using the correct form for citing these three articles in the footnotes. Remember to give the full name of the author when citing these articles in the footnotes

Lawson enlarges on the theme of how different forms of contribution can be valued, and points out that there may well be a gender bias in operation in that the courts seem to place more value on a contribution which does not conform to usual gender stereotypes (for example, a woman who does heavy renovations, or a man who undertakes carer responsibilities).[11]

Glover and Todd[12] provide a more "black letter" style critique of the law. Their main theme is not the injustice caused by treating cohabitants differently from married couples, but that the line of case law which has developed in respect of cohabitants does not conform fully with the requirements of trusts law. They criticise the fluidity which the common law has occasionally shown in order to justify making an award to a "deserving" party, and in particular the willingness of the judges to find that there is express common intention arising out of a statement apparently intended to "mislead" instead of using the doctrine of estoppel.

E. Draft plan

Chapter 1—introduction

This will set the social context, for example statistics showing the rise in cohabitation and introduce the theoretical theme for the dissertation, namely whether those in family rela- tionships require special legal protection and if so, how should the family be defined? This *an* will be set in the context of recent changes in how the family has been defined. Alternative 'models' for regulation such as formulas versus discretion.

This draft plan is a sensible outline for how your dissertation could proceed A good work. It demonstrates a logical approach to the topic, and shows understanding of the importance of linking your chapters together, and drawing on the theoretical context to evaluate both the current law and possible reforms. You may want to refine the chapter titles as your research proceeds. As noted above, I would strongly recommend ditching your proposed empirical research, in which case Chapter 3 will need adjustment. I think you'll find plenty on the strengths and weaknesses from the literature to fill this chapter in any case.

Chapter 2—the current law

This will look in detail at the relevant case law on cohabitants' property, in order to demonstrate how the law currently operates, and then set out the contrasting position (in rather less detail) which applies under s.25 of the Matrimonial Causes Act for married couples/civil partners.

Chapter 3—critical analysis of the current law

This chapter will provide a detailed critique of the strengths and weaknesses of the current law, with particular reference to the concept of discrimination and gender bias. This will also look at the criticisms made by the Law Commission in their report.

---

[10] Taylor, 'Section 25 – Quick, cheap and conciliatory' [1999] *Fam Law* 403.
[11] Lawson, 'The things we do for love: Detrimental Reliance in the Family Home' (1996) 16 *Legal Studies* 218.
[12] Glover and Todd, 'The Myth of Common Intention' (1996) 18 *Legal Studies* 325.

I note that you've included areas here which are not actually listed in your research questions (for example the theoretical matters in Chapter 1). You may wish to revisit your research questions and break them down into more detailed questions and then frame your plan with reference to these questions before tackling the rest of the research, in order to make sure you stick the right questioning, critical approach as you investigate these areas. Secondly, you will need to revisit Chapter 4 in particular (but also potentially Chapter 3, and there'll be a knock-on effect on Chapter 5) in the light of the recent Law Commission papers on reform (see comments above).

Use OSCOLA for your referencing. You have referred above to the Law Commission report so this should have been cited in your Sources List.. I would have expected rather more sources than this at this stage, given the nature of your topic which has been written about widely.

Chapter 4—reform alternatives

This will look in more detail at the possible ways forward for the law by looking at different models for financial regulation (drawing on material from Chapter 1), what happens in other jurisdictions, whether a s.25 approach should be applied for cohabitants or whether some other form of regulation would be more appropriate.

Chapter 5—conclusions

This will draw together the framework of the dissertation by comparing the reform propos- als, given the difficulties which might result from introducing them (for example, the dif- ficulties of categorising cohabitants and regulating those who have chosen to live outside regulation) with the current regime in order to make an overall judgment about whether reform should take place and if so what form it should take.

F. Sources

HERRING, J. *Family Law*, 2nd ed. Harlow: Longman/Pearson Education, 2004.

CRETNEY, S.M et al. *Principles of Family Law*, 7th ed. London: Sweet and Maxwell, 2003. Cretney goes into depth on the cases and provide some critical analysis of the problems in the current law.

HAYES, M. and WILLIAMS, C. *Family Law: Principles Policy and Practice*, 2nd ed. London: Butterworths, 1999.

LOWE, N. and DOUGLAS, G. *Bromley's Family Law*, 10th ed. Oxford: OUP, 2006.

Lawson, 'The things we do for love: Detrimental Reliance in the Family Home' (1996) 16 *Legal Studies* 218

Wragg, 'Constructive Trusts and the Unmarried Couple' [1996] *Fam Law* 298.

Glover and Todd, 'The Myth of Common Intention' (1996) 18 *Legal Studies* 325.

Palowski, 'Midland Bank v Cooke – A New Heresy?' [1996] *Fam Law* 484.

Taylor, 'Section 25 – Quick, cheap and conciliatory' [1999] *Fam Law* 403.

Probert, 'Homesharing – Widening the Debate' [1999] *Fam Law* 153.

SAMPLE 2: *LAND LAW* RESEARCH PROPOSAL WITH SUPERVISOR COMMENTS

A. Draft title

You've chosen a good area to research although you may discover it to be a little narrow (see further comments below in relation to your literature review). Your title gives the reader a good idea of where you are going BUT remember that some supervisors are not keen on 'questions' as titles, and you may wish to discuss rephrasing it. Can you think how to turn this round into a statement?

This is not phrased as a hypothesis (and actually doesn't quite make sense). Remember the purpose of the hypothesis is to state a position, which is capable of forming a working theory for you to research into or test. So, something like 'Contractual licenses are not a proprietary interest in land and therefore not capable of binding third party purchasers'.

"Contractual licences—an interest in land?"

B. Hypothesis

Discussion of whether contractual licenses are proprietary interests in land and therefore will not bind third party purchasers?

C. Proposed research strategy

The research questions I intend to investigate are:

1. What are licenses? I will examine nature and characteristics of licenses—including bare and contractual licenses—and the case law on the various types.
2. Why was it suggested that contractual licenses were special and should be treated differently? (This will require an examination of the license as a personal right in contrast to the argument that a licence is a proprietary right)
3. Can the position of Lord Denning in *Errington v Errington* be supported?

You jump from questions 2n3 with an apparent gap. It is not clear how the 3rd question connects with the 2nd question. Your research questions should form a logical sequence which then enables you to make a conclusion in relation to your hypothesis—it is not clear that this is the case here. The first two sub-questions appear fairly descriptive. Whilst some of your research questions should by necessity be descriptive, Two out of three is not the right balance between descriptive and evaluative questions. You need to flesh this out with further evaluative questions.

Where is your discussion of the binding nature of the right if it is regarded as proprietary? Your hypothesis suggests you will be exploring this.

Overall this should enable me to conclude whether or not contractual licences are a proprietary interest in land or not.

Case law analysis, coupled with academic commentators' work will be key to my research as there is no relevant legislation in this field at all.

You have not articulated your perspective: if you are looking mainly at cases this would indicate a black letter approach.

I intend to answer these questions by carrying out an extended literature review, including reviewing cases, articles and relevant texts.

Is this not an area of settled law with cases and comment available from the late 80s/ early 90s but not much since? If you had consulted a tutor about this area, they would have been able to give you guidance on this.

D. Literature review

Because of the nature of my dissertation, much of the review I will carry out will be of the relevant cases, for example:

Tanner v Tanner, Hardwick v Johnson, Hurst Pictures Theatres Ltd, Winter Garden Theatre (London) Ltd v Millennium Productions Ltd, Hounslow LBC v Twickenham Garden Developments Ltd, Errington v Errington, National Provincial Bank Ltd v Ainsworth, Ashburn Anstalt v Arnold, Prudential Assurance Co Ltd v LRB, etc.

In terms of secondary sources, an overview of the current law on contractual licences is provided in the usual textbooks on Land Law.

What happens in these cases? You are expected to review these, don't just list them! How do they help you investigate your research questions?

Mackenzie J-A & Phillips M, *Textbook on Land Law* (14th edn, OUP 2012)
Smith, R.J. *Property Law* (8th edn, Longman Law Series 2014)
Burn, E.H. & Cartwright J. *Maudsley & Burns Land Law Cases and Materials* (9th edn, OUP 2009)

Smith, R.J. *Property Law – Cases and Materials* (5th edn, Longman Law Series 2012). Lots of detail provided here with relevant analysis of pertinent cases. Queries consensus position because some recent cases have adopted the *Ashburn* position, e.g. *IDC Group Ltd v Clark* (1992) and *Nationwide Anglia BS v Ahmed & Balakrishnan* (1995).

Chappelle D, *Land Law* (8th edn, Pearson Longman 2007) The author is adamant that although Lord Denning did cause an upset in *Errington* with his revolutionary decision the matter was more or less resolved by a *per curiam* statement by the CA in *Ashburn Anstalt* that a contractual licence does not create a property interest. In addition Millett (obiter) in *Camden LBC v Shortlife Community Housing* said that "the CA had finally repudiated the heretical view that a contractual licence creates an interest in land capable of binding third parties". See also *Habermann v Kochler* (1996) which stated that *Ashburn* NOW governed contractual licenses

Academic commentators did make some useful comments around the time of *Ashburn* indicating a shift in thinking—see below.

Graham Battersby 'Contractual and estoppel licences as proprietary interests in land' (1991) Conv Jan/Feb 36
Mark Thompson 'Leases, licences and the demise of Errington' (1998) Conv May-Jun 201
Peter Sparkes 'Leasehold terms and contractual licences' (1988) LQR. 104(Apr) 175

E. Draft plan

Chapter 1—introduction

This will describe and define the various types of licenses including the *of this* contractual licence. *area in terms*

Chapter 2—the current law

This will look in detail at the relevant case law on contractual licenses in order to demonstrate how the law has developed in relation to moving from the license as a purely personal right to the license as a proprietary right capable of binding third parties such as purchasers

Chapter 3—critical analysis of the current law

This chapter will provide a detailed critique of the current law, and in particular the cases of *Errington v Errington* and *Ashburn Anstalt*. In addition more recent first instance case law will be examined in order to see which way the wind is blowing!

Chapter 4—conclusion

This will draw together the framework of the dissertation by comparing the two main positions and commenting on them. I will conclude with the current prevailing opinions.

F. Sources

Mackenzie J-A & Phillips M, *Textbook on Land Law* (14th edn, OUP 2012)
Smith, R.J. *Property Law* (8th edn, Longman Law Series 2014)

Burn, E.H. & Cartwright J. *Maudsley & Burns Land Law Cases and Materials* (9th edn, OUP 2009)

Smith, R.J. *Property Law – Cases and Materials* (5th edn, Longman Law Series 2012)

Graham Battersby 'Contractual and estoppel licences as proprietary interests in land' (1991) Conv Jan/Feb 36

Mark Thompson 'Leases, licences and the demise of Errington' (1998) Conv May-Jun 201

Peter Sparkes 'Leasehold terms and contractual licences' (1988) LQR. 104(Apr) 175

If you feel that this topic is too narrow but you still want to concentrate on licenses you may want to consider addressing the position of licenses and proprietary estoppel as well as contractual licenses. This is a natural extension and it was an element also looked at in Ashburn and commented on by Battersby in his article on informally created interests of land.

Index

LEGAL TAXONOMY
FROM SWEET & MAXWELL

This index has been prepared using Sweet and Maxwell's Legal Taxonomy. Main index entries conform to keywords provided by the Legal Taxonomy except where references to specific documents or non-standard terms (denoted by quotation marks) have been included. These keywords provide a means of identifying similar concepts in other Sweet & Maxwell publications and online services to which keywords from the Legal Taxonomy have been applied. Readers may find some minor differences between terms used in the text and those which appear in the index. Suggestions to sweetandmaxwell.taxonomy@thomson.com.